Success

in Reading and Writing

Second Edition

Grade 5

Jean F. Bernholz
Patricia Horne Sumner

Helen G. Cappleman, Series Editor
With grateful acknowledgment to the late Anne H. Adams,
the originator of *SUCCESS in Reading and Writing*.

GoodYearBooks

An Imprint of ScottForesman
A Division of HarperCollinsPublishers

Cover illustration by Jennifer Meadows.
Cover design by Amy O'Brien Krupp.
Book design by Carolyn McHenry.

Good Year Books

are available for preschool through grade 6 and for every basic curriculum subject plus many enrichment areas. For more Good Year Books, contact your local bookseller or educational dealer. For a complete catalog with information about other Good Year Books, please write:

Good Year Books
Scott, Foresman and Company
1900 East Lake Avenue
Glenview, Illinois 60025

▶ Preface

Jean F. Bernholz and Patricia Horne Sumner, authors

SUCCESS in Reading and Writing invites teachers to use their professional knowledge and creativity to help students become thinking communicators. SUCCESS classrooms are characterized by heterogeneous, whole-group instruction. Each student reads and discusses books of his or her choice. Students read a wide range of materials to locate information. They write every day, expressing their own ideas. Students work with their peers, organizing, discussing, and sharing knowledge.

As students and teachers become co-investigators in each day's four thirty-minute reading and writing lessons, they expect that they will learn something new. SUCCESS gives everyone a chance to be surprised. The common goal of the class becomes not just to cover, but to discover and uncover the curriculum. SUCCESS is based on a philosophy that respects teachers and learners and proclaims that learning from and with others is exciting.

This revision of SUCCESS provides a clear explanation of an integrated language arts philosophy, a rationale for why this approach is appropriate, a guide for practical application, and a framework for 180 lessons. The revision comes in response to the educational research supporting a more natural way of teaching reading and writing and to the discoveries of teachers who have been using SUCCESS during the last twelve years. More attention is given to the writing process, to integration of the lessons with content-area subjects, and to the use of literature throughout the program. These changes reflect the positive experiences of teachers who have become decision makers and curriculum designers. Based on this input, the authors have attempted to preserve what works with SUCCESS and to make changes for clarity and consistency.

The basic procedures for each module have remained the same. The names of three modules have been changed to identify more clearly what takes place during each thirty-minute period. The Spelling/Phonics module has been renamed Word Study. The focus of this module is on the joy and delight of learning new words and how to use them. Composition has been renamed Writing. The writing process is presented in the lessons so that students think and behave as writers. Study Skills is now called Research. In this module, students develop the skills of researchers as they expand their knowledge. Recreational Reading retains its original name, and its emphasis remains on reading books of choice every day while the teacher has conversations with the students. There is more flexibility in the methods of conferencing, as well as more opportunities for sharing reading experiences. The value of daily reading aloud is emphasized, and suggested books are listed in each lesson.

The authors hope that these modifications will be helpful and appropriate for today's teachers and students. However, it should never be forgotten that the process of revision is ongoing. Teachers will revise from year to year what is presented today in this book. Learning about learning does not stop.

▶ Acknowledgments

SUCCESS in Reading and Writing workshop leaders, who have helped shape SUCCESS as it has developed in classrooms across the country:

Mary Armstrong	Becky Haseltine	Cam Newman
Peggy Bahr	Debby Head	Kathy Newport
Jean Becker	Paula Hertel	Ola Pickels
Patti Bell	Bridget Hill	Libby Pollett
Jean Bernholz	Tina Hinchliff	Karen Powell
Barbara Blackford	Robbie Ivers	Susan Quick
Jill Board	Connie John	Donna Rea
Elaine Bowie	Shae Johnson	Cathy Reasor
Ann Bryan	Delores P. Jones	Patty Redland
Jacqueline Buckmaster	Joanne Jumper	Mary B. Reeves
Helen Cappleman	Janice Keegan	Carole Reindl
Stacey Carmichael	Nancy Kerr	Pat Reinheimer
Kathi Caulley	Dana Kersey	Marilyn Renfro
Betty Cramer	Annie Kinegak	Janice Reynolds
Donna Croft	Barbara Krieger	Marlene Rotter
Suzie Desilet	Esther Lee	Pat Scherler
Bobbi Donnell	Sue Lippincott	Janet Schneider
Marilyn Enger	Lisa Lord	Shirley T. Scruggs
Betty S. English	Kathy Malick	Celeste Singletary
Sandra Fain	Judy Mansfield	Kathleen Smith
Debra Fetner	Howard Martin	Patty B. Smith
Neita Frank	Judy Martin	Pat Sumner
Carol George	Lila Martin	Pam Tate
Randy Gill	Nancy J. Mayhall	Donnye Theerman
Lynn Gori-Bjerkness	Becky Miller	Shirley A. Thompson
Letha Gressley	Debbie I. Miller	Jean Weaver
Andra Gwydir	Debby Miller	Beth Whitford
Carol Hall	Paul Moller	Pat Wong
Mary Harris	Cinda Lee Moon	Michael Wong
Roberta Harrison	Avril Moore	Kristin Zeaser-Sydow

For their loving support and understanding, we thank our families, friends, and colleagues, especially Blake Bernholz, Dustin Sumner, and Michael Bernholz. We also want to thank SUCCESS teachers who sent artwork and ideas from their classrooms. Our thanks to each other for the special friendship that has allowed us to examine and challenge our personal beliefs as educators. And finally, we thank our students who pushed us to find a better way.

▶ Art Acknowledgments

The following young artists have contributed to this edition of *SUCCESS in Reading and Writing*, Grade 5:

Demetrius Duncan, Inman, South Carolina
Matthew Fowler, Spartanburg, South Carolina
Kelly Spencer, Quitman, Georgia
Linda Williams, Quitman, Georgia
David Key, Spartanburg, South Carolina
Jeff Ley, Quitman, Georgia
Mary Beth Burns, Spartanburg, South Carolina
Catherine Kizer, Hillsborough, North Carolina
Casey Premo, Spartanburg, South Carolina
Jeremy Knight, Spartanburg, South Carolina
Dustin Spencer, Quitman, Georgia
Joel Townsend, Hillsborough, North Carolina
Jaime Smithie, Quitman, Georgia
Jennifer Meadows, Hillsborough, North Carolina
Christine Eldridge, Quitman, Georgia
Jeremy Gossett, Spartanburg, South Carolina
John Thomas, Hillsborough, North Carolina
Toby Edwards, Quitman, Georgia
Ben Bridwell, Spartanburg, South Carolina
Kristy Kay Cheatwood, Spartanburg, South Carolina
Brian Hauser, Carrboro, North Carolina

Contents

SuccesS

in Reading and Writing

Second Edition

Grade 5

Chapter 1 SUCCESS: The Basic Assumption

What is *SUCCESS in Reading and Writing?* SUCCESS is a student-centered instructional design based on the belief in the expertise of professional teachers to guide the development of readers, writers, and thinkers. The SUCCESS philosophy scraps jargon, eliminates stereotyping of students, and removes obstacles to the growth of communication skills and knowledge. It signals a new day of respect for what happens in classrooms.

▶ SUCCESS in Action

How does SUCCESS look in action? Open the door to a SUCCESS classroom, and you will see pairs or groups of students reading and writing, sharing and reacting. All is not quiet. The unobtrusive noise signals that students are involved and excited about what they are learning. Students are using a variety of materials to learn about specific topics. Students are making decisions about what is important to include as they collect information and organize it to share with others. The body of information keeps changing, and what they learn is spontaneous. An authentic learning community exists. Examples of students' work are displayed throughout the room. A print-rich environment is evident from shelves full of books, reference materials, magazines, newspapers, and other resources. Where is the teacher? The teacher is among the students observing, encouraging, and instructing. The classroom has a real worked-in, learned-in look.

SUCCESS promotes student interaction with print materials and with other learners. Students are actively involved in their learning. They are learning that reading, writing, and thinking are inseparable aspects of the process of becoming a literate person. Students make choices about how and what to learn. They accept the responsibility for their own learning.

The teacher is not viewed as the single provider of information. Two of the greatest teachers, Socrates and Plato, taught that the answers did not lie within the teacher. They suggested that true learning took place through discussion and clarification of ideas. Students learn from each other; they learn through exposure to many different materials and resources; they learn through questioning.

SUCCESS offers many opportunities for

1. improving the learner's self-image and confidence as a learner;
2. valuing the opinions and contributions of others;
3. broadening knowledge and concepts;
4. clarifying thoughts and ideas;
5. making direct and indirect association of information;
6. applying skills to make relevant connections to life;
7. strengthening communication skills;
8. discerning and organizing important information;
9. developing group and individual presentation techniques for sharing information;

Demetrius Duncan

10. evaluating resources, information, products, and presentation techniques;

11. establishing lifelong learning skills and goals.

▶ Basic Structure of SUCCESS

Four modules provide the basic structure for SUCCESS. Each module has 180 daily lessons corresponding to the length of the current school year in most school districts. Each module provides a different, yet complementary, approach to teaching reading and writing.

THE MODULES

In the fifth grade the modules are Research, Recreational Reading, Writing, and Word Study. Each lesson within these modules allows for the development of readers and writers with attention to the processes necessary to this development.

Research In the Research module students practice the processes of locating, organizing, and sharing information from a wide range of resources. It enables them to expand their knowledge base as well as their creative and critical thinking skills.

Recreational Reading Students read books of their choice and have conversations with the teacher and other students to share their growth as readers and their joy of reading.

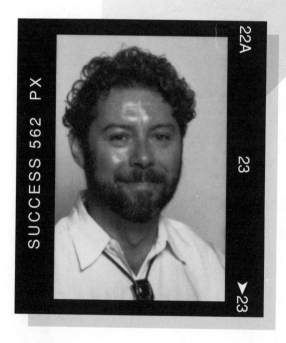

SUCCESS has given me the opportunity to offer knowledge to my students in a relevant and meaningful manner. Its whole-language approach to learning allows me to integrate all subjects of learning rather than teach in isolated segments. The students are allowed to be creative and move at their own pace and ability.

Paul G. Chaplin, teacher

Writing Students write creative and/or factual material each day making choices about topics and practicing the steps of the writing process to complete and share published work.

Word Study Students expand their vocabulary and thinking as they select words they associate with a topic. They also learn to recognize spelling patterns and develop strategies.

DAILY SCHEDULES

With the daily SUCCESS schedules, students can always count on a time during the day to read, write, think, and share. A regular and consistent schedule helps students know what to expect. A predictable schedule helps eliminate confusion and allows students to plan and think ahead about what they will be doing.

The schedule allows thirty minutes for each module. The four modules may be taught in any order and at any time of the day. The decision about when to teach the SUCCESS modules rests with the teacher, who must take into consideration the needs of the students and other daily schedule demands.

The following two examples show that the order and time of day are flexible. Some SUCCESS teachers prefer devoting an uninterrupted time block of two hours to the modules:

RECREATIONAL READING	8:30–9:00
WRITING	9:00–9:30
RESEARCH	9:30–10:00
WORD STUDY	10:00–10:30

Others prefer teaching other subjects in between modules. Often students are scheduled for special classes outside the classroom, and teachers must arrange the SUCCESS schedule to accommodate these students.

WORD STUDY	8:45–9:15
WRITING	10:00–10:30
RESEARCH	1:00–1:30
RECREATIONAL READING	2:15–2:45

When teachers determine the time for each module, they post the schedule with the name of each module and the time it is taught outside the classroom door. Posting the schedule informs visitors of the time for specific modules that they may want to observe. The posting of a schedule is also an excellent way to help students learn to budget their time. Once it is posted, the teacher should adhere as closely as possible to the module schedule each day, although it may be impossible to stay exactly on the thirty-minute target.

At the beginning of the year, students may need more than thirty minutes per module (except for the Recreational Reading module) until they learn the format and procedure for each. Thirty minutes may be too long at the beginning of the year for some students to read library books silently during Recreational Reading. Teachers may wish to start with fifteen minutes for this module and gradually build to thirty minutes.

Teachers who do all four modules daily have a balanced and complete language arts program. When modules are omitted, important segments of SUCCESS are lost to the students. SUCCESS lessons are designed to help students move forward each day. In all fairness to the teacher, to SUCCESS, and especially to the students, all four modules should be taught each day. Chapters Two through Five explain how to teach each module.

▶ The History of SUCCESS

A NEED FOR CHANGE

SUCCESS in Reading and Writing was born from the need for change. The late Dr. Anne H. Adams describes the beginning of the program in the original edition of *SUCCESS in Beginning Reading and Writing (1978)*

Although I did not realize it at the time, research for this book began in 1964 when I found myself under contract to teach 36 first graders, none of whom could read. It was one of the most frustrating years of my professional life; however, through those experiences I began to identify some of the major problems and concerns expressed orally or in the literature with specific reference to beginning reading instruction. My approach was direct. I tried to analyze each problem as a springboard for an exploration of alternatives that might eliminate or alleviate the problem. Part of the analysis was my doctoral dissertation, in which I researched the concept of correlated language arts in the first grade without use of basal readers.

Until 1976, the contents of this book were in the form of a rough draft and had become one of those things "I would finish one day soon." Matters were expedited that year when I was asked to work with 17 first-grade classes in the Durham (North Carolina) City Schools. . . .

The reader should be aware that the program described in this book was not initiated under ideal conditions. It should have been difficult enough to ask teachers of 17 classes to stop doing what they had been doing and start a different program the next day. Most of the teachers, however, were willing to give it an honest try because they were neither satisfied with the way things had gone nor content with the reading/writing abilities of many of their students in the past. One teacher said she "boxed up things I'd been using for 20 years" and started this program the day after our first meeting. It took a few of the other teachers longer to break the traditional spells; however, as the program gradually unfolded, they, too, discarded some methods and materials in favor of this approach, and each added her own expertise to its dimensions.

Durham City Schools is an inner-city school district, supposedly populated with scores of youngsters destined for, if not already in, remedial classes. According to the proposal submitted by the Durham City Schools for the Right-to-Read grant, approximately 50 percent of all the stu-

Matthew Fowler

de..ts in grades 3 to 11 were below the 23rd percentile achievement level on the Science Research Associates reading test. Because such large numbers of black and white parents had put their children in private schools or had moved to other school districts, the Durham City Schools' 1969 enrollment of 14,101 had dropped to 9,389 in 1975. Of those who remained, approximately 80 percent were on government-subsidized lunches. Under these conditions, the program was begun in mid-October 1976, in approximately half of the first-grade classes. . . . At the end of the year, the teachers reported the total absence of nonreaders in their classes. No longer could the blame be placed completely on variables such as the students' homes, parents, vocabularies, and/or socioeconomic conditions.

IMPLEMENTING CHANGE

Many teachers quickly embraced the ideology of Dr. Adams. They were trained, caring, and dedicated professionals who believed they could make a difference in the learning of their students. They believed their students could learn to read and write, but with a different approach from what had proven in too many cases to be unsuccessful.

When the authors of this text first learned of the SUCCESS program, Dr. Adams had only written the first-grade manual, *SUCCESS in Beginning Reading and Writing*. We were team-teaching a fifth-grade class and were frustrated because many of our students did not enjoy reading and writing. Like many teachers, we were searching for a better way.

By chance, we discovered Dr. Adams and sought to learn of the new ways she advocated for teaching. She responded immediately to our needs. She believed that the same basic principles outlined for first-graders could apply to our students in fifth grade. We worked with Dr. Adams to develop lessons for our class during the 1977–78 school year and were invited to be co-authors of the fourth- and fifth-grade editions in the spring of 1978.

▶ SUCCESS Today

*W*ith SUCCESS, children seem to be more eager to check books out from the library. The "Classroom Libraries," which are library books, stimulate a variety of reading interest.

Anna Edgerton, teacher

The reasons that SUCCESS has survived and is constantly being embraced by more and more teachers are the same as the reasons that led us to try this new promising approach. The keys to teaching reading and writing have always been and will always be (1) the teacher and (2) what is taught.

At first, teachers were attracted to SUCCESS because what they were using was not working; both they and their students were bored with more traditional methods.

Research now exists to support the principles of SUCCESS: Students should be taught to read and write using materials, such as newspapers and real books that are now available to them and will be in the future. Students should have choices about their reading and writing. They should have the opportunity to write every day and develop the ability to think and make associations and connections to real life through their reading and writing. Research has further helped us to identify the steps in the writing process and to expect that there is a natural development of this process when students are given opportunities to use these steps. The growing body of research also supports cooperative learning and the noncompetitive support of peers as meaningful ways to facilitate learning.

Everything that we have learned from research and from teachers has strengthened our basic belief in the foundations of SUCCESS.

Most SUCCESS teachers are receptive to new ideas and philosophies that offer better learning and teaching opportunities. They are, however, not willing to change from one way of teaching to another if they do not think this will lead to improved learning. They also want learning to be fun and enjoyable. They are interested in educating, not schooling, their students.

WILLINGNESS TO CHANGE

SUCCESS offers hope for those who are ready for change. It offers a more natural, spontaneous, and supportive structure for teaching language arts. It provides an alternative. The number of teaching hours and days could possibly change in the future, but the most important change must be what happens in classrooms during those hours and days.

What will it take to make the change? People must recognize the need for change and must want to make a change. Teachers must believe that a change will be in the best interest of their students. Teachers who decide to change should not be overwhelmed by the process. Dare to take the risk and accept the challenge.

PROMISES OF CHANGE

What is different in a SUCCESS classroom? What will change? Many SUCCESS teachers have shared the following observations with us:

Group learning activities are based on student interest, student needs, and student choice. These choices include topics, partners, directions for exploration, and methods of sharing.

Teaching students in three to six ability groups is eliminated with the SUCCESS program. Students are not to be grouped for reading instruction according to their standardized tests scores. Trying to identify artificial "reading levels" is of little importance. Labels such as *high, medium,* and *low* are eliminated.

Materials and resources are as open and varied as the imagination allows. Academic textbooks are only one type of reference material. Creating and using a print-rich environment becomes a major goal and focus of the SUCCESS teacher.

Clerical chores, such as checking boxes on student skill sheets; parroting questions and other ideas from "canned" teacher's guides; or any other robotlike activities are eliminated. Instead, the teacher becomes the facilitator of myriad learning activities.

The students' writing, thinking, and reading about anything in print and their opportunities to discuss and validate their thoughts are the foci of learning.

For some teachers and students, change is embraced with enthusiasm and energy. For others, change is an evolutionary process. Both need support and encouragement.

Whether teachers decide to read further and use SUCCESS, they are still faced with a decision. What will they do with their students this year to best facilitate their learning?

> In the long run, if we dare to take risks, we will find that we have achieved excellence. Instead of being defeated by the massive size and overwhelming ethnic diversity of our public school systems, we will have turned those systems into generators of economic productivity and social creativity. The question is, do we dare try?[1]

---

[1]The National Governors' Association *Time for Results: The Governors' Report on Education*

Chapter 2 The Research Module

A North Carolina teacher was asked to develop a tornado drill plan for her elementary school. After making a plan of the drill, she turned to her students with this challenge: "What might be a good way to share this drill with all the classes?"

Groups quickly listed possible ways to share information and made a plan as a Research Project. First, they collected information about tornadoes, how they form, and their dangers. Then they made charts and pictures to explain what a tornado was to the students. They wrote and acted out short skits about how to seek a safe place during a tornado drill at home, outside, and at school. Students practiced and evaluated each other on their effectiveness as teachers sharing the seriousness of a tornado but not frightening the students. Groups then presented their information in classrooms throughout the school. The problem had been solved. The group presentations were extremely successful.

Recent research findings indicate that some problems of student motivation and achievement are related to the lack of relevance of classroom instruction and activities to real life. Often students ask, "Why do I need to know this?" Too often comes the reply, "It will be on the test." Educators must ask themselves, "What is important for students to learn: facts for a test or how to learn and process new information?"

▶ The Rationale

In our current age of rapidly changing information and knowledge, students, to be successful, must know how to process information and make meaningful connections. It is learning how to learn that will produce and sustain lifelong learners. Lifelong learners are always questioning and seeking new knowledge. Even trying a new recipe can engage a person in the pursuit of knowledge, not because it is necessary for the Bouillabaisse to taste good, but because the desire to learn has been stimulated. Learning is fun! Satisfying a desire to know something is a pleasurable experience.

The Research module gives students the opportunity to ask questions, find answers, and work together as a learning community to share knowledge. For thirty minutes each day, students read, write, and share information about a selected topic. They practice the research process and become familiar with many resources. Through small group and class research projects, students discover new information, decide how to share the information, and learn valuable group interaction skills.

▶ Becoming Lifelong Learners

The Research module is designed to help students develop and use skills for forming questions and finding the answers to what they want to know, when they want to know it. This module establishes the practice of personal inquiry as the foundation for the lifelong learner. Students learning

Kelly Spencer

with and from each other, expanding their knowledge, and discovering how to learn are the building blocks of this foundation.

STUDENTS LEARN WITH AND FROM EACH OTHER

Students work with a partner, a small group, or with the whole class during the Research module. Because there is always a shared purpose or goal (Research Project), it is important for students to value the opinions and contributions of others. Often the group must choose a topic, subtopics, resources, what facts to include in the final presentation, and how to organize and share their information. This requires the students to be active listeners, as well as participants, in the decisions that must be made in order to reach the goals of the group. Each student becomes a valued member in a community of learners.

STUDENTS LEARN NEW INFORMATION

During each Research lesson students are engaged in activities that allow them to expand their knowledge in several different directions. They may gain a new understanding of group processes as they plan a report. The new knowledge may be something they learn and share about the research topic. It may be finding out how to use a new resource. Students are free to explore a topic in depth by using a wide range of materials. This freedom encourages discovery of new information.

The integration of the Research module with content areas reinforces and expands the curriculum. Most fifth-graders study Native Americans. Lessons 26 through 35 are designed to broaden the base of students' knowledge beyond what may be found in their social studies textbook. Teams

SUCCESS is an active, creative, and positive program. I have more interaction with my students. My teaching is more dynamic! The students experience the pleasure of empowerment! Choice! Cooperation!

Denise Baxter-Yoder, teacher

of students each select a tribe of Native Americans for special in-depth research and study. After locating and organizing the information they discover, they plan how they will share this information with the rest of the class. Through the use of resources other than a textbook, students might find that this study is not limited to the past, but that Native American populations face important issues today. Students become aware of a world of information through their unlimited use of resources.

STUDENTS LEARN HOW TO LEARN

When students attach meaning to a learning task, they apply the skills and strategies needed to accomplish the task. Students must decide where to look for information, which resources are most appropriate, and how to use those resources. When a research team selects a topic, such as the Iroquois, they discuss what subtopics (homes, weapons, way of life, etc.) to investigate and where they will look for the information. The team might choose encyclopedias, social studies textbooks, maps, books about Native Americans, and fiction books. As they look for information, they become adept at using glossaries, indexes, tables of contents, chapter outlines, headings, and subheadings. The connections between their need to know and how to find out become apparent. Students learn through repeated practice that they can make decisions about what is important to learn and how to best learn it.

RESEARCH AND REALITIES

If this sounds idealistic, teachers should consider what research has demonstrated. Students learn best when the following takes place.

- interaction with print materials and other learners
- reading, speaking and writing are accepted as inseparable aspects of the process
- students are actively involved in their learning
- students are given choices for how and what to learn
- the responsibility for learning belongs to the student

A consideration of realities leads to this question: What specific changes will promote these learning conditions in the classroom? The following alternatives should be examined:

- Instead of students working independently and silently, pairs or groups of students read and write, share and react to information they discover through their research. The activity and talking mean real learning is taking place.
- Instead of copying facts word for word from reference materials or from teacher's notes on a chalkboard, students figure out for themselves what information is important to collect and how to organize it to share with others.
- Instead of the teacher lecturing at the front of the classroom, he or she moves among the students, from one group to another, questioning, guiding, assisting, and learning with them.

- Instead of the teacher relying on textbooks as the primary source of one set of facts to be learned by the students, the students use a variety of materials to learn about specific topics. They are not limited in their learning but encouraged to explore topics as they choose.
- Instead of the teacher working diligently to cover a mandated curriculum, the curriculum becomes a guide but does not dictate or limit how and what the students will learn. What to learn keeps changing.
- Instead of fill-in-the-blank questions as the source of the teacher's assessment of students' knowledge, teachers are observers of the total learning process. This enables them to evaluate their students' abilities to ask questions and select appropriate materials for answers, make connections to real life, and share the information.

Probably nowhere is it more necessary for teachers to be flexible and open to different approaches than in the Research module. Teachers must recognize that students learn by discussing and clarifying their ideas with others; that they learn through exposure to many different materials and resources; that they learn through questioning themselves, their peers, and the information found in the resources they select.

▶ Prepare for the Research Module

Creating an environment conducive to research and preparing oneself and the students to become active researchers is important.

GATHERING THE MATERIALS

Here are the basic things teachers will need to do to assemble the materials for the Research module.

1. Provide a file folder for each student to be stored in a permanent file drawer or box somewhere in the classroom.

2. Gather the basic resource materials: a variety of textbooks, fiction books, nonfiction books, maps, newspapers, magazines. Other materials needed for lessons include such things as pamphlets, schedules, contest forms, sweepstakes forms, tax forms, product labels, catalogues, and telephone books.

3. Discuss arrangements with other teachers and media specialists/ librarians for using and sharing encyclopedias, atlases, subject/content area media kits, videos, records/tapes, etc.

4. Ask parents, doctors, lawyers, and others to donate magazines.

5. Arrange for students to be instructed in using video and other audiovisual equipment.

6. Form close ties with the public library. If possible, arrange for regular Bookmobile stops at the school.

7. Obtain a schedule of educational TV programming and plan lessons that use TV as a learning resource rather than entertainment.

8. Become familiar with the growing resources for Research in technology products—from telecommunications-based software to laser videodisc (see Chapter 6).

CLASS MANAGEMENT

Once the materials are assembled, teachers must establish ground rules with the students for group activity. Working in groups and sharing resources and information might require thinking about different classroom arrangements. Desks, tables, and chairs should be arranged to allow for easy movement into small- and large-group configurations. Resource materials are more readily accessible to students if they are labeled and kept visible.

▶ How to Teach the Research Module

The three sections of the Research module are the Lead-in, Research Project, and Sharing.

LEAD-IN: INTRODUCING THE RESEARCH PROJECT (5–10 MINUTES)

During the Lead-in, the teacher introduces the topic and focus and the resource(s) to be used. The class shares ideas or directions for beginning the research project. The directions to the class should be very short and very specific. Many students will understand the assignment and will be ready to begin work immediately; others will need additional explanation and some assistance.

As the students begin their work, the teacher should move immediately from student to student, helping as many as possible on an individual basis.

In many of the lessons, suggestions are made for class structure. If students are working in groups, the teacher may decide how the groups are to be structured, or students may select their partners and/or group members. Students should always understand the ground rules under which the groups operate. The Lead-in might go like this:

> **Teacher:** Today you will be working with a <u>partner</u> to locate <u>different kinds of information</u> in your <u>social studies textbook</u>. (The teacher writes underlined words on board.) Our research activity is designed to help you become familiar with how your textbook is organized and the topics you will be learning about this year in social studies.
>
> Let's begin together by looking at the Table of Contents. What is a Table of Contents?
>
> **Student:** It's at the front of the book. It tells what's in the book, like chapters, and what it's about.
>
> **Teacher:** How many units are in this book? (The teacher writes key words on the board as students respond.) Let's all do an example of what you will be doing with your partners on the board so that we are clear about the directions. On what page does Unit One begin? Let's all turn to that page. What is the title of this chapter? Now quickly read through the pages to find the kinds of information given. How is this information organized? (The teacher writes the responses of the students as they volunteer the information and reacts to their responses as they are given.)

Student: It has two chapters. At the beginning of the chapter, there is a list of words and some questions.

Teacher: Why do you think these words are listed at the beginning of the chapter?

Student: Because these are words we need to know.

Teacher: Yes, these are important terms. What else do you notice about how this chapter is organized?

Student: The title of the chapter is 'The United States: Its Land and Water.'

Student: There are four main sections in this chapter. Some of the pages are different colors. These pages are called Skills for Success.

After a few more quick questions and responses from students, the teacher moves on to give instructions.

Teacher: This is a time to explore your social studies textbook. Write about the kinds of information you discover in the chapter you select and describe how it is organized. If time permits, continue your investigation of this textbook.

You will have about fifteen minutes to read and write. Quickly move to your partner. Even though you will be reading and discussing the assignment, you must each write your own list of kinds of information presented and how it is organized. Begin work. Remember others are working and it is important not to disrupt them. At the end of our reading and writing time, you will have an opportunity for sharing.

(The teacher moves around the room monitoring groups and offering assistance as needed.)

The example given above for teaching Lesson 1 exhibits extensive modeling, which is important at the beginning of the year. Students need this modeling any time new topics or research skills are introduced. This much explanation and group activity will not be necessary as students practice the research process.

RESEARCH PROJECT: READING AND WRITING (15–20 MINUTES)

As students begin to locate and discuss information, the teacher moves among groups to help them with the assignment and to listen to their discussions. This student-to-student and teacher-to-student interaction indicates who needs help, who grasps new ideas quickly, and how students think and process printed information.

A group that is noisy or not on task should be dealt with quickly. The teacher will remind them of the topic and focus, answer questions, and channel behavior in the desired directions. If two students are engaged in an animated discussion, the teacher might ask, "Is this the Chapter you have selected to explore? Tell me what you are finding." The teacher may need to give more direction and perhaps some specific examples to get them

Linda Williams

started. If the students understand the assignment but have gotten off-task because a picture of cowboys prompted discussion of a recent movie, the teacher redirects their attention to the purpose of the lesson: locating and organizing information. Both behavioral and instructional help is most effective when given individually, rather than to the whole class.

The classroom will not be silent, nor should it be chaotic. Students and teachers will decide on the level of activity that allows them to be most productive and how to achieve and maintain that comfortable working level. Some classes and teachers will require more structure than others, depending on learning and teaching styles.

The teacher continues to move around the room, stopping to talk with as many groups as time allows. Each pair of students will be at a different point in their assigned task. Near the end of the time for reading and writing, the teacher should remind the students that they have three minutes until the sharing begins.

SHARING (5–10 MINUTES)

A Sharing time is built into each Research lesson. Most lessons suggest a method for sharing; however, the teacher should decide whether or not this is the most appropriate method for the class. The teacher might introduce sharing by saying, "Today you are going to share with another team the information we have located. When you are sharing, read from your papers the information you have written. Tell why you wrote what you did and what was interesting about that chapter/unit. Then discuss how the information was organized. Discuss the likenesses and differences of your information."

After five minutes, he or she might bring closure to the sharing time by asking the whole class one or more questions: "How many chose Chapter 1? How many Chapter 2? . . . " The teacher might quickly tally these on the board so that the class can see which was the most popular chapter/unit.

"How many found maps in their chapters/units? What about questions at the end of the chapter/unit? How was new vocabulary presented?"

Sharing is an integral and enjoyable part of the module, but students will need guidance on how to use the time effectively. At the beginning of the year they are excited about the freedom to talk, explain, and even debate main ideas. Teachers will need to work with groups to help them focus their sharing on the information and listening to others. Before students share, basic rules and respect for others should be discussed. The teacher should evaluate how sharing time is being used with the students and revise methods and rules if necessary.

At the close of each lesson, students are to write their name and the date on their papers before they are filed in the Research folders.

A REVIEW OF THE STEPS

What happens during this thirty-minute Research module? Every day students will be gathering and organizing information about a topic using the following procedures:

1. The teacher introduces the Research Project: topic and focus, resources, and group structure (5–10 minutes);

2. students read to locate and write information they associate with the Research Project (15–20 minutes);

3. students share their information with other students (5–10 minutes);

4. students date and file papers in Research folders.

▶ Introduce Research Skills

The first fifteen lessons in the Research module introduce the student to a wide variety of resource materials and to the skills involved in effectively choosing and using them. In these lessons students examine and list kinds of information in textbooks and reference materials that they will be using for research during the year. The purpose is to establish that a broad base of information is available to learners and that learning about a topic is enriched by using a variety of materials. Rather than emphasizing the *product* of research, the first series of lessons focuses on the *process* of *researching* to prepare students for the tasks ahead.

After the first fifteen lessons, students will begin to interpret, compile, organize, and present information about a topic in a variety of ways, adding to their own knowledge as well as discovering how to find out what they want to know. Throughout the year, students will be introduced to new research skills and techniques for interpreting information as they collect data on a given topic. It is the continual application and practice of the skills in context that enable the student to successfully locate information.

▶ Research Project Procedures

In Lessons 16 through 180, the Research Projects presented run for either five or ten consecutive days. Usually the project culminates in a presentation of information to the entire class. It is not the final project presentation but the process students use to collect data that is the emphasis. During Research lessons, students read and write for a purpose. Some days they will be taking notes, while on others they will be summarizing, classifying, or analyzing their information. The Research Projects allow them to learn ways to organize and share their information. A summary of the basic steps for completing a Research Project is outlined below.

SELECTING TOPICS

The teacher presents a topic, such as explorers. Students use a resource, for example, a social studies textbook, to brainstorm names of explorers and basic information headings, such as *life, discovery, importance,* and *other.* Students work in groups or with partners. The groups choose topics and collect resources.

David Key

COLLECTING INFORMATION

Students read to locate information and write the important information they find pertaining to the research topic. At the end of the period, the groups meet, share, and discuss information located. This step is repeated for two to six days as the lessons show; it can be changed depending on the amount of time the teacher feels is needed to complete the Research Project.

ORGANIZING INFORMATION

Groups compile their information and decide how best to share and present information to the class. The groups gather materials and prepare research project presentations.

PRESENTING AND EVALUATING

Each group presents its Research Project. The other students respond by identifying strengths of the presentation and suggesting improvements.

▶ Presenting

Presentations have three main ingredients: preparing the audience, sharing the information, and responding to the presentation. Some lessons suggest that the students prepare the listeners for their presentations by forming two or three questions that they think will focus attention on the main concepts to be shared. The presenters may write the questions on the board, and when the presentation has ended, ask the audience to respond, either orally or in writing. Finally, the class might discuss the answers given and whether or not the presentation provided enough information to answer the questions. Some general evaluative questions might include:

Was the information clear and easily understandable?
What techniques were the most helpful?
Can you suggest ways to improve the presentation?
If you were doing this report over, how would you change it?

Although students are usually their own harshest critics, helping them make improvements should be the main objective of this evaluation time. Simple rules of respect enable students to help each other without being hurtful.

GROWING AS PRESENTERS

New SUCCESS teachers need to be prepared! When students begin making their presentations—no matter how much preparation time they have had—some will be disastrous: the students involved in the presentation, the audience, and the teacher will all agree that it just didn't work. The teacher should be patient and allow students time to try out new presentation ideas and methods. They will grow as self-evaluators and communicators only if they have the opportunity to see for themselves how best to share what they know.

As the year progresses and students gain skill and recognize their own strengths, the reports will improve in clarity and content. The teacher should let the students know that improvement is expected and that the whole class is working to help each one become a more effective learner and teacher. Students appreciate a job well done, and the spontaneous outburst of applause that greets a particularly engaging report is genuine.

In order for students to experiment and gain presentation skills, they will need to be introduced to a wide variety of reporting modes and to know that they can make choices and change their minds if they feel the format is not right for their project. Working together to solve problems and assign duties is a crucial part of the presentation planning stage.

TECHNIQUES FOR PRESENTATION

In the course of the year, the following reporting techniques and formats may be included in the lessons. Teachers will find this is only a partial list and will add many ideas from their students.

Charts of main ideas	Letters, journals, or diaries
Tape-recorded information	Graphs, charts, and maps
Books of facts	Surveys and questionnaires
Written reports	Newspaper articles
Oral reports	Bulletin boards and posters
Videotaped reports	Files for authors, presidents, etc.
Interviews	Directions and lists
News broadcasts	Plays, skits, and commercials
Quiz shows	Calendars and time lines
Dramatic role playing	

Sometimes teachers will need to allow extra time (or even days) for presentations or for sharing at the end of lessons. It is important to develop a time structure and help students work toward meeting their deadlines. Guard against letting sharing time run on and on without focus or closure or, in contrast, cutting it short. To emphasize one aspect of the lesson over the other implies that it is more important or meaningful. Preserve the integrity of both the searching and the sharing by maintaining balance between them.

▶ Encourage Student Participation

During the first few days of this program, some students will spend their time reading to locate information and will not have time to write anything. Their papers should be dated and filed with the notation, "Reading—no writing." The teacher should give them credit for the reading part of the module and make a comment orally such as, "Maybe soon you'll not only read, but also have time to write something on your paper before it is filed."

Quantity of writing is not the purpose of this module. The purpose is to teach students how to use a variety of resources to locate information related to a topic, read about the topic, write key information and organize and share that information.

As the year progresses and students become more familiar with this study process, they will locate the suggested information faster and write more than at the beginning of the year. It will take several weeks for some students to start becoming proficient in the Research module. Because of its extreme importance, this module should not be dropped from the program, even though the first days are rather hectic, and some of the students do not "produce" a large quantity of work. Some students may have difficulty getting started for several days. As they begin to realize their papers are to be filed and to adjust to the time limit, they will move into the lesson with less hesitation. Learning to budget study time is a key element in the program.

▶ Helping Students Become Researchers

At the beginning of the year, some students will have difficulty finding information, especially since the teacher will not be giving them specific page numbers, subheadings, etc. Students need praise for finding any information that they can associate, directly or indirectly, with the topic and for anything they can defend as associated with the topic.

If students are having difficulty locating information, the teacher must help them look through the material until they find something that can be associated with the topic. Through conversation they can be helped to make a connection between what they are reading and the research topic. Later, during each conversation the student is asked to locate something in print and to explain how it relates to the topic. Students will often consult classmates during this time before the teacher can get to them for an individual conference. If the student has already located information, the teacher listens to the associations he or she is making before moving on to help another.

Because students are using different materials, they will not all locate identical information and will become frustrated if instructed to do so. Teachers who teach this module are amazed at the kinds of information their students find and at their abilities to make relationships. Even during the first days, the Research module can be a delight to teach if each student is not required to locate a particular item. Teachers need to relax and enjoy teaching this module! It will take time, but it's worth it.

▶ Resources for Research

What if the resources listed in the Lessons aren't readily available? No topic in the Research module should be avoided because "there are no materials on that topic in the classroom." Teachers are conditioned to be natural collectors. Reading future lessons provides a head start for collecting the suggested materials, or for changing the topic to fit the material on hand.

Instead of ordering workbooks, stencils, kits, SUCCESS teachers simply redirect funds to purchase newspaper and magazine subscriptions and paperback books. Notes to businesses, parents, and civic clubs may produce donations of forms, magazines, and other materials. State and federal agencies (departments of transportation and human resources, the forest service, and wildlife commissions, for example) are great resources for materials. Public libraries and professional offices will gladly donate magazines and other print materials that would otherwise be discarded.

Teachers find many creative ways to get the materials they need. In some cases, students can bring in the resources needed for lessons. Other materials may turn up in book storage closets. Teachers working together sometimes pool and share certain resources such as state or local maps, food labels, or telephone books. Addresses for free materials and class sets of information are often shared. Partnerships with local businesses provide not only print materials, such as classroom library sets, but mentors, volunteers, and guest experts as well.

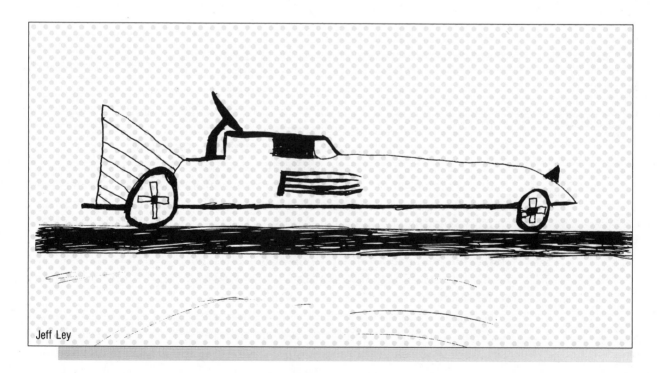

Jeff Ley

The Research module requires a variety of materials on different levels. A concern among many teachers is that the reading level of their science, social studies, health, mathematics, or other textbooks will be too high for the students. As the students use these academic materials during the Research module, they will become more familiar and more comfortable with them. They will cease to look at the science textbook merely as the "time-for-science" book, and recognize it as a resource for learning in general. When texts of different levels are available to students, the less able readers will not hesitate to attempt the assignment. Even the smallest successes will add significantly to their knowledge and their confidence as learners. In SUCCESS students can choose to learn from any level of material, be it their own grade level, below, or beyond. The teacher does not assign a level of text or other resource based on his or her perception of a student's ability. The student's ability to locate and gain information is the primary focus, not the designated level of any text.

Many of the lessons provide options for students working in small groups; this is especially useful when materials are limited in quantity. In most lessons, students and groups will be using such a variety of materials that multiple copies of a resource will not be needed.

As the teacher becomes a teacher/researcher, he or she will develop an awareness of many things as potential resources: the menu or paper placemat at the pizza parlor, the magazine on the airline, the travel brochures at the welcome center, and the job application form at a fast food restaurant can all be used in Research module lessons. Before they know it, teachers have more materials than they ever thought possible.

▶ Adapting the Lessons to the Students

The enthusiasm a teacher conveys to the students about learning new information invites them to explore new topics. Teachers lead them to read and write and become researchers by instilling the idea that learning in and of itself is interesting and rewarding. This excitement begins when teachers are invested in what they are teaching. How does this happen?

Teachers should never underestimate themselves or their students. They have the ability to be the skillful guides students will need to develop competence and confidence as researchers. Students are naturally curious and want to learn. The teacher must provide the opportunities and direct their progress. In the Research module, the questions students ask as a result of a lesson, a national event on the front page of the newspaper, or a local issue become learning opportunities; seize the moment.

When research projects can be connected to real-life problems and concerns, the resulting knowledge and presentations will be the most effective learning experiences for the students. Teachers will find student-initiated topics and school problems arising throughout the year that may become a base for study in the Research module.

For example, in 1989, teachers in South Carolina, when faced with the widespread devastation of Hurricane Hugo, used SUCCESS lessons to help students cope with the tragedy. In a community threatened with a nuclear

*S*UCCESS allows more student-teacher involvement. It is structured yet flexible. SUCCESS gives each child time to think. It teaches to all learning modalities. The children really get involved.

Yolanda E. Mays
teacher

waste disposal site, teachers and students try to understand and respond to the issue through teacher-designed Research lessons. These real life events provide opportunities for designing and implementing a survey, writing a letter to the newspapers, forming debate teams to look at both sides of the issue, and inviting experts to speak to the class. Teachable moments are recognized and honored. Students come to realize that their learning is connected to real life situations.

Just as a teacher's expertise makes a difference in the classroom, the involvement of students with an issue can make a difference. They will recognize the importance of this involvement when they are encouraged to learn about an issue and make an informed decision. In order for this to occur, the teacher must be willing to choose and plan lessons that allow students to explore any issue that could be dealt with during a Research lesson. An issue need not be as dramatic as Hurricane Hugo: perhaps a social studies lesson on longitude and latitude needs to be extended because students are having difficulty with these concepts. By changing topics in the lessons to correlate with content-area topics or current events, the teacher makes the research process more relevant. The students become lifelong learners! Their teachers join them, as the SUCCESS classroom becomes a community of learners!

▶ Research Approaches

DIRECT AND INDIRECT ASSOCIATIONS

In the Research module, students are given opportunities to make both direct and indirect association. In this module reading is not restricted to direct association. Divergent thinking is valued and encouraged. Students often relate information to a specific research topic through an indirect thinking process.

For example, if the module topic is animals, it is conceivable that a student would find a word, a description, or a picture of carrots and associate carrots with rabbits. When a student responds with such an indirect association (carrots), the teacher should ask the student how he or she arrived at that answer, instead of automatically stating the answer is wrong.

Indirect association represents a higher thinking level than direct association. Both kinds of associations and thinking are important. Telling how he or she arrived at an association makes the student responsible for the thinking process, and learning takes on greater personal relevance and importance.

Making direct and indirect associations is an extremely important research skill and should be introduced as early as possible in the academic year. One of the most striking features of this approach is the relief it brings to teachers who no longer have to delay a topic until they have done the physical work of assembling directly related information. Instead, the students are involved in the process of making associations with a topic using any available materials.

▶ Integrate the Research Module

The Research module can be integrated with other modules and with content areas. What does *integration* mean in the context of SUCCESS? A Writing lesson that correlates with a science unit is integrating the curriculum. Introducing social studies vocabulary as the Word Study list is integrating the curriculum. Throughout the year there will be opportunities to introduce the vocabulary of a science, social studies, or health chapter during Word Study, to follow with a Writing lesson related to the topic, to locate information on the topic during Research and to follow with a Recreational Reading lesson that allows students to continue to focus on the topic. The Research lessons are not meant to replace content-area lessons but rather to enrich, extend, and supplement science, social studies, health, or mathematics. Some teachers coordinate Research lessons with music, art, current events, or local issues. When students make connections from content-area subjects to Word Study, Writing, Research, and Recreational Reading they begin to find many ways to examine and understand a subject.

▶ Assess and Grade

Some schools using SUCCESS have developed report cards that include a Research grade. The assessment of progress is based on the behaviors observed and the mastery of research skills. This does not mean that every daily activity or research project presentation is given a letter or numerical grade. If a research grade is to be given, teachers might consider task commitment, cooperative group interaction, ability to locate and organize information, and written and oral presentation skills as important factors for this evaluation.

When there is no research grade, how is the assessment of progress reported? Many SUCCESS teachers use the Research module for reading, writing, and spelling grades. Final Research Projects are sources for these grades. Students should be informed of the specific skills being assessed. For example, students completing posters for an environmental issues project should be told beforehand that spelling is important. If a written report is the form for a final Research Project, students should know that paragraph structure will be important. Assessment is ongoing. Teachers observe and take note of strengths and needs. This continual assessment yields important information for making decisions about all grades and about the student as a learner.

When content-area topics are the focus for Research Projects, assessments may be recorded for these subjects. For example, presentations on the topic of explorers might be included as part of a social studies grade.

Teachers will find ways to incorporate assessment into the Research module, but they will observe many behaviors that have meaning and significance beyond a mere grade.

▶ Decisions

TEACHER CHOICES

Each day during the Research module, the teacher makes several choices, deciding whether to

Mary Beth Burns

1. use the topic and focus suggested in the Lesson plans or change it, based on student interest, other content areas being studied or the occurence of an important event;

2. use the resource suggested or change it;

3. keep or change the grouping suggested in the lesson, allowing for variety in learning styles and abilities;

4. keep or change the report-making sequence to fit the skills and needs of the students, sometimes allowing more time to collect data or materials;

5. use the writing mode suggested or change it;

6. keep or change the way the information will be shared with others.

STUDENT CHOICES

During the Research module, students may make several choices, asking themselves

1. Which resource will be best to use?

2. What information relating to my topic do I choose to write?

3. How will I record the information?

4. With whom will I work on the Research Project?

5. How will my group organize and present information to the class?

▶ Community of Learners

Teachers function as models during the Research module. They must establish themselves as researchers and learners as they share with students how to collect, record, and interpret information to plan classroom activities. The students are allowed to observe that the teacher does not know all the answers, but follows the same steps to learn as they do and joins them in the process. If he or she models the use of a variety of resources for tracking down information, and demonstrates how any and all kinds of questions might be answered, the students will catch on more quickly.

It is essential to be willing to change and to allow students to make their own choices and decisions about the types of topics and materials they will use to answer their questions. All students have a natural curiosity for learning and will be able to become researchers, if the teacher expects and believes that they will.

Ongoing evaluation should be established as part of the Research module. The class can discuss what works and what changes can be made in strategies to help in the learning process. Introducing a wide range of research methods and reporting techniques throughout the year will add variety to the module and accommodate the different abilities and talents of the students. Researchers may be invited to the class to talk about their work and the techniques they use to gather, organize, and present information. Students must be helped to recognize the value of supportive groups, in which every member is important in working toward a common goal. Finally, teachers should accept and encourage divergent thinking by stressing that there are many right answers.

▶ In Summary

Working with others, locating and organizing information, and applying the knowledge to solve problems are important skills for students to develop. The Research Module lays the foundation for these skills. If we think in terms of outcomes, we want all students to be able to read, write, and think critically. We want them to have values and respect for others. We want them to solve problems and address social issues. In short, we expect that after years of education they will be ready to face the world as productive citizens. To accomplish this goal they must become lifelong learners.

Researchers decide what questions to ask and how to find the answer. They explore the world of information. They organize and share their information with others. These lifelong learning skills are the basic elements of the Research Module.

Chapter 3   The Recreational Reading Module

Children in most homes are distracted from spending extended time reading books by an amazing variety of activities. Doing chores, playing with friends, watching television, talking on the telephone, and pursuing hobbies are only a few of them. There is little indication that this situation will change unless there is a concerted and deliberate effort to take action. The daily Recreational Reading module provides thirty minutes for students to explore books of their choice with few interruptions.

▶ The Rationale

Students must have the opportunity to read books at least thirty minutes a day during school time. This module can bring about one of the most significant changes in today's education, with far-reaching positive implications for the future. Indirectly, in this module, students learn science, history, geography, character analysis, value judgments, and much more while reading hundreds of books. They also develop the habit of reading. The habit of reading complete novels and other books filled with information will more likely develop when time for unassigned, sustained reading of library books for pleasure is included regularly in the instructional program.

In some elementary classrooms, students go to the library where each checks out at least one book. When the students return to the classroom, the teacher is likely to say, "Put your library book in your desk and take out your spelling book for a spelling lesson." Any interest the student had in reading the library book is immediately lost.

There are reports of secondary students and adults who have never read a novel. Because many homes do not provide a model of regular extensive reading, the school must make provisions to fill that void. Even if students have a reading model at home, they can increase their knowledge along with their competence through in-school silent reading for enjoyment.

When children begin school, their inborn eagerness to learn can either be enhanced or stifled. How do we enhance rather than stifle this natural desire to learn to read and to become a reader?

▶ Becoming Readers

Some basic principles guide what happens in the Recreational Reading module. Stated simply, students should read for thirty minutes each day, select their own books, be respected as readers, and have opportunities to share books with others. In addition they should have individual conversations with the teacher about reading.

STUDENTS READ FOR THIRTY MINUTES EACH DAY

Reading ability is the obvious foundation for school success, and nothing is more important than developing readers. If students are to *become* readers, they must *think* of themselves as readers. A reader does more than

Catherine Kizer

simply get the words right; a reader constructs ideas and meanings from what is read. It takes time to develop as a reader, uninterrupted time. School is the natural place for this to happen.

STUDENTS ARE FREE TO SELECT THE BOOKS THEY READ

When students are given the chance to select the books they will read each day, the teacher conveys the message, "I trust you to make good decisions." Students who have the freedom to make choices become more responsible for what they read. Removing restrictions allows them to become more spontaneous and genuine in these choices. They soon learn that the teacher is not going to tell them which story, what book, or how many pages to read.

STUDENTS ARE RESPECTED AS READERS

Teachers are often pressured to label students according to a reading level, to assign them to ability groups, and to provide them with "canned" group instruction. The SUCCESS program in contrast supports the theory that the successful reading of any and all materials the student needs and/or wishes to read is more conducive to fostering reading skills development and good reading habits.

Studies reveal that students assigned to the "low" group seldom have the positive feelings about reading that they need to improve their ability. In the SUCCESS Recreational Reading plan, no student is labeled and all students are equal, even though a wide range of reading abilities and disabilities may be present in the classroom.

STUDENTS HAVE CONVERSATIONS WITH TEACHERS

The time spent in a conversation about reading is a meaningful experience for both the teacher and the student. This one-on-one interaction gives teachers the opportunity to learn about their students in an intensely personal way. The focus on the student's reading interests, strengths, and needs provides a wealth of information for future instruction.

STUDENTS SHARE READING EXPERIENCES

Talking about books is fun, and time to share should not be denied students. Adults talk about books they have read or are reading and discuss why they are enjoying a book. Helping students discover this same pleasure in sharing books is important for producing lifelong readers.

▶ Preparing for the Recreational Reading Module

By the time they reach fifth grade, many students are "turned off to reading" because they have not succeeded as readers. The teacher must send a message to students on the first day of school that reading is enjoyable and not threatening. What can teachers do to convey this message? First, the classroom must invite students to read. Second, teachers must prepare themselves and their students to become a sharing, joyful community of readers.

CREATING THE ENVIRONMENT

Teachers must create an environment that says reading is OK in this room. Students learn in the other modules that anything in print may be read. It should be known that during this uninterrupted reading time any book may be read. The room must be "print rich."

Spaces must be provided that are inviting to the reader. A variety of such spaces will honor different learning styles and preferences. For example, many students prefer reading on the floor under a table or even under their desks. Some teachers have managed to provide sofas, pillows, or rocking chairs, which are arranged in a special reading corner for students to use during this time. Students prefer different levels of lighting when they read. The teacher can observe where students choose to read and allow their choices as long as they are involved with their books.

MATERIALS

Organizing materials so that they are easily accessible and manageable invites reading. Students should be given responsibilities for assisting with this task.

For this module, each student should have two file folders. One folder is kept in the student's desk and the second is stored in a permanent file drawer or box somewhere in the classroom. A Reading Log form is duplicated and stapled inside the file folder at their desk. (See Figure 3-1.)

To add to the classroom library, the teacher should make arrangements with the media specialist/librarian to check out two library books per student every three to four weeks (or more often if needed). This is in addition to the students' regularly scheduled visit to the library. The library will welcome suggestions for books to be ordered. For the classroom the teacher can order collections of paperbacks, including multiple copies of titles. (A list of books suggested for reading aloud is found on pages 42–44.)

Figure 3-1

READING LOG

READING LOG FOR _____		
	Started	Ended on
DATE TITLE OF BOOK	on page	page

THE TEACHER'S INVITATION TO BECOME A READER

Teachers should let students see them read and should share books with them. Teachers must model being readers and the joy that comes with reading. The teacher must believe and expect that all students will become readers. One of the most important factors in student achievement is teacher expectations. Unfortunately test scores or other assessments of the students' abilities often limit the goals they might set for their students and for their level of instruction.

BECOMING A CONNOISSEUR OF BOOKS

Collecting and becoming familiar with children's books is a necessity for the SUCCESS teacher. He or she can learn about authors and begin an authors file with the students, consulting them about the best books to read. The expertise and knowledge of the media specialists/librarians will be a valuable asset for the teacher who shares knowledge, interests, and needs with them.

Many special activities exist such as Reading Is Fundamental, book fairs, reading contests, business-sponsored programs, and public library reading programs. The teacher can broaden students' experience by arranging for them to participate or by providing the information they will need to become involved.

SUCCESS is effective for me as a remedial reading teacher because every child can contribute and feel part of every lesson. The most exciting part of SUCCESS to me, personally, is that it gives students many more opportunities to reveal their thinking and learning to me. Therefore, my expectations for my students are much higher.

Sallie Currin, teacher

PARENTAL INVOLVEMENT

Parents, business persons, community leaders, authors and others will enjoy being guest readers or doing "book talks." When parents volunteer time in the class, they can listen to students read and have conversations with the students about the books they are reading. Teachers should communicate with parents about new books and prepare a list of favorite books for possible Christmas and birthday gifts.

Parents need to be aware of the reading expectations for homework. Some SUCCESS teachers ask students to read for fifteen to thirty minutes per night. Parents and their children are asked to keep records of both the time spent reading and the titles of books that are read. Parents should be encouraged to read aloud to their child as often as possible.

CREATING A COMMUNITY OF READERS

Students should be allowed to experience books and to discover the joy of sharing a favorite book. SUCCESS teachers encourage discussion, comparison, and questions about books. Many choose to close the Recreational Reading module each day by having a few students volunteer to tell the class about the books they are reading.

▶ Making the Reading Module Happen

The basic elements essential for making the Recreational Reading module happen are the established daily reading periods, the free choice of fiction and nonfiction books to read, and the teacher as a model. Teachers frequently ask, "How will I know I am covering all the skills? What resources am I going to use? How will the parents react? How will I report progress?" These concerns usually give way to the delightful experience teachers share with their students after they begin the Recreational Reading module. Most teachers report that they know more about their students and their reading abilities, strengths, and weaknesses, than they ever did before.

ESTABLISHED DAILY READING TIME

At the beginning of the year, the teacher is primarily concerned with creating an atmosphere conducive to pleasurable uninterrupted reading. Because they are not used to sitting still and reading, some students will need time to select a book and settle down. They may choose three or four books and flip through them only looking at pictures for a week before they finally begin to feel comfortable with books. Others will know what they want to read, select their books, and not move for the thirty-minute period. Often they will not want to put their book away when the reading time is over.

THE TEACHER'S ACTIVITIES

Nothing is more important to share than a genuine enthusiasm for reading and books. The teacher should share with students why he or she selected a particular book to read, what is best about the book, and something about the thoughts he or she has while reading the book. This is contagious, and students will soon be emulating their teacher's excitement about books. All of a sudden it will be "cool" to read!

▶ The Student-Teacher Conversations

The student-teacher conversations should begin as soon as the teacher has established the model of the quiet reading of self-selected fiction and non-fiction, and the class realizes this thirty minutes is a time to avoid all interruptions.

A suggested guide for focusing conversations is provided for this module in each lesson. The focus is repeated for several days to give the teacher time for a conference with each student in the class about that focus. He or she should adjust the number of days needed for a particular conversation focus, depending on the number of students in the class. Encouraging readers, especially remedial and reluctant ones, should be a part of conversations.

PURPOSES

Each conversation has two major purposes. The first is to provide time for talking with students individually about reading interests and dislikes. Discovering the students' reading interests early in the year is important. The teacher writes notes as he or she talks with the students about what they are reading and why they selected a certain book. Once teachers know the reading interest of their students, they can follow up by locating and suggesting materials a specific student may enjoy. This attention to their reading interests lets students know that they are important. It also sends the message that this module is based on an individual approach rather than the more usual group approach.

This does not mean that teachers become librarians searching for materials; however, when an individual student needs a little extra attention to get involved in reading, this effort may bring large rewards. When the teacher is able to say, "I've found several interesting books about basketball that you might like. I know you enjoy basketball and thought you might want first chance at these," the student usually responds with interest and appreciation.

The second purpose of the conversations is to provide time for the teacher to assess and teach word analysis and reading comprehension with individual students, using their selected fiction or nonfiction books.

SUGGESTED QUESTIONS

The following are some general questions to use in the first few conversations to supplement the specific conversation focus given in the Recreational Reading lessons:

1. What do you like to read about?

2. What is the best book you've read since our last conference? Why was it a good book?

3. What is the saddest book you've ever read? Why was it sad?

4. What is the most exciting book you've ever read? What parts were exciting?

5. What kind of characters do you like best?

6. What kind of books have you never read?

7. What books would you recommend to a friend to read? Why?

8. Do you have any favorite authors? Have you ever read another book by this author?

9. Why do you think the character behaved as he or she did? Have you ever known anyone like this character? What would you do if you were this character?

10. Why did you choose this book? Do you think you will complete it?

11. Have you gained any new ideas or feelings as you've read this book?

12. How much time did you spend reading at home in the last day or two? When do you read at home?

Casey Premo

Some attention and questions will more directly focus on word attack skills and strategies, oral reading fluency, mechanics, writing techniques, and comprehension skills:

1. Summarize the main plot of your book so far.

2. Compare this character to another character.

3. Choose a passage to read to me. What is the main idea of this section?

4. Why do you think the author chose to change paragraphs at this point?

5. Have you found any words that were hard to pronounce, or ones whose meaning you didn't know? How do you try to figure out a word you don't know?

6. What is the most important part, or climax, of this story?

7. Describe what is happening at this point in your book. What do you think will happen next?

8. Describe the setting of the story. How is it important to the plot?

9. What is the theme of the book? What do you think is the author's main message or purpose in this book?

10. Who is telling the story? How might it be different if it were told from a different point of view?

11. Tell me about this illustration. What is happening? How do the illustrations add to this story?

The conversation time should always remain a positive time of sharing between the student and teacher, and the teachers of SUCCESS classes have often found it a time to really get to know a student. Some SUCCESS teachers report that the minutes spent with a student one-to-one have much more meaning than a longer time in the group reading situation. Teachers also report that they are much better able to determine reading deficiencies through the conference approach rather than through testing.

The students do not write during the conversations; however, the teacher records notes at this time. A section on clipboard notes later in this chapter will explain more fully the kinds of notes teachers find helpful.

CONVERSATION PRINCIPLES

Teachers may choose to use the conversation focus suggested in each day's lesson plan or write in one of their own.

During conversation time the teacher should talk with as many students as possible. This focused conversation between two people who love books is powerful. The teacher is letting the students know that they are valued as individuals. It is important to maintain the integrity of this time by sincerely listening to each student and interrupting their reading time as little as possible. There are some basic requirements for maintaining the integrity of conference time. First, the teacher should have a purpose, but guard against turning the time into a testing period. Simply trying to check off skills during this period weakens the conversation. Second, the teacher should sincerely listen and respond to students about their reading. Third, reading time should be interrupted as little as possible. Fourth, a conference with one student should not go on and on at another student's expense. Every student needs and deserves the teacher's undivided attention, and every student needs time to read without being interrupted.

FOUR CONVERSATION MODELS

Conversations will vary in length and style. Four different models are suggested below. Each provides a time for having conversations with students about their reading. Recording observations of a student's reading interests, habits, understanding of written language, and the content of their reading material is an important part of each model.

Teacher-student conversations are the motivational strategy for improved reading competence and love of reading. The model may be changed when necessary to accomplish these objectives.

Model One   The teacher moves among the students having as many two to three minute conversations as possible. If appropriate, the suggested focus for the lesson is discussed. (See Lessons 85–87 for examples.)

This model is especially helpful for finding out the reading interests and general comprehension level of the students. For example, the teacher might ask them to tell why they have selected a particular book or what they like best about the book or if they would recommend the book to a classmate. The observation notes will record these bits of information about the student's reading interests and habits. This information is helpful in locating books to add to the classroom collections or making suggestions about other books the student may want to read.

The main purpose of this type of conversation is to give attention and show immediate interest in the students and their reading. These short interactions will allow teachers to identify students who are struggling with comprehension or having difficultly selecting books, and to give them suggestions of titles or individual help decoding a difficult word. This model is used for three consecutive days with the same focus.

Model Two   The teacher holds seven to ten minute conversations with three or four students individually. If appropriate, the suggested content or language structure focus is discussed. For example, suppose in Writing the students have been composing dialogue. The teacher may focus on finding out if students can recognize the symbols for identifying dialogue in printed materials. The teacher might ask the student to identify a place in his or her book that has dialogue and read it together. If the student cannot identify dialogue, the teacher will give quick instruction and make note of needed follow-up if necessary. The conversation time might then proceed to other points related to plot development, character descriptions and actions, or associations between reading experiences and the life of the student. This model is used for seven days to allow more time for in-depth conversations with each student. (See Lessons 66–72.)

Model Three   For approximately twenty minutes, everyone, including the teacher, reads for pleasure. During the last ten minutes the teacher may choose to talk with some individuals about what they have read. One day out of every twelve this conversation model is suggested. This is a time for modeling the pleasures of reading. The teacher uses this model to reaffirm that reading time is important and valued. Part of this time can be spent observing the reading habits of the students—to "kid watch"—and recording habits that may inhibit or promote the development of reading proficiency. (See the material on clipboard notes.) During the last five to ten minutes, the teacher may decide to have conversations with students who seemed to be engrossed in their reading or to read orally with a few students. (See Lesson 149.)

Model Four   During the first fifteen minutes of this model, students are reading and the teacher is having conferences as needed. During the last ten to fifteen minutes small groups discuss books and stories group members have read. Groups may be organized by book title, topic, or author. These groups can be designated by the teacher or chosen by the students. The teacher should move from group to group monitoring discussions and taking note of the information being shared. When appropriate, the teacher should share his or her own reactions to books being discussed. One out of every twelve days there will be an opportunity for this conversation model. (See Lesson 113.)

▶ Record Keeping and Assessment

Recreational Reading is designed to be both enjoyable and instructional. It is not always easy to create the environment, monitor the progress of students, and focus on the teacher's role. One of the most important things he or she will do is to keep accurate, ongoing records of student responses during conversations and of general observations about the students' reading interests and behaviors. Students will be responsible for keeping a reading record. These records may be reviewed and discussed during the conversations between the teacher and student.

CONVERSATION NOTES

Conversation notes are taken during in-depth individual conversations. A teacher might write the student's responses to comprehension questions, opinions about books, or examples of reading strengths and needs. Some teachers develop forms for recording convenience. The following is an example.

Figure 3-2

CLASS CONFERENCE NOTE FORM

date	student	conference focus/comments	needs

Another example shows a separate form for each student.

Figure 3-3

INDIVIDUAL CONFERENCE NOTE FORM

STUDENT'S NAME_____

DATE	FOCUS/COMMENTS	STRENGTHS/NEEDS

Teachers decide how much to write using either a form such as the examples above or separate reading conversation folders kept at the desk. These records are important for assessment of student progress and instruction because they document the individual strengths and needs of each student. This documentation then becomes the basis for parent conferences and reporting student reading growth; it is also invaluable as a planning guide for further instruction.

Conversations with students are never scripted, and are not predictable, even with suggested questions and skills foci.

Teacher: I see you're reading *Hatchet*. How do you like it?

Student: I think it's good, but at first I almost stopped reading it because the boy vomits so much. It happens right near the beginning of the book.

Teacher: It is something you don't often read in stories. Why do you think the author put it in this story?

Student: Well, Brian, the boy in the story, hasn't had anything to eat or drink, and he's out in the woods. When he gets to water and some berries he can't stop drinking and eating. He gets sick on both of them. I think maybe the berries could have been poison, or just bad for him to eat. I'm not sure. He calls them "gut berries."

Teacher: Why did the author put this part in the story?

Student: I guess it's what really would happen if you ate or drank too much like he did, after being knocked out and all in the plane crash.

Teacher: Writing about real life situations and describing them as lifelike as possible is a kind of writing called *Realism.* Does this story have other details to make the reader feel or sense the scenes in a lifelike way?

Student: Yeah, like the way he describes the mosquitoes, and flies, and when Brian kills and cleans a bird to eat. One thing I know is, it wouldn't be any picnic to be stranded out in the woods with no food or anything. In fact, everything is much harder to do than in most movies or stories. It takes him a lot of work and time to build a fire, or do anything.

Teacher: You said you didn't think you'd like the book at first, but then you changed your mind. What do you like about it?

Student: Well, it's interesting the way he always talks to himself, and you know how he's thinking and feeling. I want to finish the book to find out how he gets saved. I don't think he will die.

Teacher: When the main character tells the story, it's called *first-person point of view,* like you're seeing and feeling everything from his eyes. Is this the best way to tell this story?

Student: I think so. When he says things over and over, like how hungry he is, you really feel it. And when he's scared, he says things to himself to calm down, or just things I have sorta said to myself. He remembers things, too, and it's not like a story, but how things just pop into your mind.

Teacher: Have you ever written like this, using *I* to tell about your thoughts or feelings in a story?

Student: Not like this, but I have written about my brother and how we fight about things and how we play together too. I told some real feelings then, and made it pretty real about how we are. But in *Hatchet,* it's more like he's thinking out loud.

Teacher: Sometimes that's referred to as *stream of consciousness* in writing, when you just write everything you're thinking, as it pops into your mind. Find a section that has him "thinking out loud" that you want to share with me to read aloud.

The conversation continues, with some attention given to pronouncing the word *gratified* correctly, reminding the student to pause at commas, and discussing the meaning of *gratified,* using the context clues in the sentence.

Obviously, in this conversation, the student is a very competent reader, with strong comprehension abilities, and the teacher sees an opportunity to point out several writing techniques and strategies used by the author.

Asking the student to examine the author's techniques and intent not only requires higher level thinking on the student's part and demonstrates mastery of a reading skill included on many standardized tests, but calls attention to a writing model the student might now be able to apply more effectively in his own writing. How the teacher might record the conversation notes is shown in Figure 3–4.

The path taken during a reading conversation depends on many things, and taking notes on conversations also differs greatly from teacher to teacher. The main point is that teachers take the opportunity to document any ability or need a student reveals.

Figure 3-4

FILLED-IN CLASS CONFERENCE NOTE FORM

date	student	conference focus/comments	needs
11/1	Adam S.	Author's intent – Realism Gave examples, good comprehension, uses context clues	Read with feeling commas

CLIPBOARD NOTES

Conversation notes are very specific. Clipboard notes, in contrast, are more general, focus on both individual students and the whole class, and may be recorded at any time during the day. Consistent records of observations reveal learning patterns and other information that help the teacher tailor instruction to meet the needs of the students. These notes may also call attention to behavioral patterns that create barriers to learning. The teacher, as a reflective practitioner, is always watching the students, assessing what is happening, and making decisions based on these observations. The clipboard notes suggested in the Recreational Reading module

Figure 3-5

FORM FOR CLIPBOARD NOTES

NAME	OBSERVATIONS

are suggestions only. They may guide observations for that day, but the teacher will be recording other behaviors as well. Sometimes these notes may simply remind the teacher of changes that need to be made to create a better learning environment.

Here is a sample of some clipboard notes:

"Jonathan—playing under the table."

"Angelia—forgot her books again."

"Mary and Sue took their books to lunch. Sat together and read."

A suggested focus for clipboard notes is included in each daily Lesson. The following is a list of some of these suggestions—things to look for while your students are reading (without interrupting them).

Who reads with whom	Who moves lips or hands
Titles being read	to guide reading
Where students choose to read	Who is searching for meaning
Which students read aloud	Who re-reads the same books
Who is reading the same	Who compares books by author,
book for more than one day	topic, etc.
Which students stay seated	Who reads books read or
Who looks up or daydreams	introduced by teacher
Who prefers which authors	Who loses or forgets book
Who talks eagerly about books	Who reads books by students
Who learns from the pictures	Who recommends books to others
Who tries new books	Who seeks recommendations

Some teachers find it useful to have copies of the class roll with space beside each name for clipboard notes. Blank spaces beside students' names remind the teacher to focus on those students. A sample form used by some teacher to record clipboard notes is shown below. The same form can be used for taking notes when teachers have two to three minute conversations at the students' desks.

STUDENT READING LOGS AND JOURNALS

This is a daily record kept by each student of his or her reading. Each day students record the book title and the number of the first page read that day on a sheet of paper or a printed form stapled to their Recreational Reading folder. (See Figure 3–1.) At the end of the reading time the student completes the record sheet by writing the number of the last page read. The current Reading Log is kept in the folder at the student's desk. When the log is completed, students file it in a folder kept in a box labeled Recreational Reading.

In some classrooms, students use a spiral notebook to keep a record of books being read. This notebook can also be used as a reading journal. Students can record thoughts about reading at the end of the daily Recreational Reading module. The Reading Journal can replace the Reading Log and should be filed in the box when filled. The Reading Log and/or Reading Journal become part of the permanent reading record.

▶ Read-Aloud Books

In 1985, the Commission On Reading issued a report, *Becoming a Nation of Readers,* which stated the following: "The single most important activity for building the knowledge required for eventual success in reading is reading aloud to children."[1] Read-aloud books are suggested every day in the Recreational Reading module. Teachers may read the books suggested or select others. This shared reading experience for the whole class is a non-negotiable part of the daily schedule, not an extra "if-you're-good" or "if-we-have-time" bonus. This ten to fifteen minutes should be scheduled at a time the teacher feels is best. Some teachers find that read-aloud is a great lead-in to the Recreational Reading module. Others like to end the module with sharing and reading aloud.

Below is a list of some of the books included in the lessons as read-aloud titles. These books are suggestions, and teachers are invited to replace them with personal favorites of students, colleagues, and friends.

> *The Great Brain,* John K. Fitzgerald (Dell, 1967)
> *The Secret Garden,* Frances Hodgson Burnett (Dell, 1971)
> *Catwings,* Ursula LeGuin (Orchard/Watts, 1988)
> *The Diamond in the Window,* Jane Langton (Harper, 1962)
> *The Brave Little Toaster,* Thomas M. Disch (Doubleday, 1986)
> *Sign of the Beaver,* Elizabeth George Speare (Dell, 1984)
> *Save Queen of Sheba,* Louise Moeri (Dutton, 1981)
> *Girl From Yam Hill,* Beverly Cleary (Morrow, 1988)
> *Homesick, My Own Story,* Jean Fritz (G. P. Putnam's Sons, 1982)
> *Dear Mr. Henshaw,* Beverly Cleary (Dell, 1984)
> *The Haunting,* Margaret Mahy (Atheneum, 1982)
> *Chocolate Fever,* Robert Kimmel Smith (Yearling, 1978)
> *O Sliver of Liver,* Myra Cohn Livingston (Atheneum, 1979)
> *Sleeping Ugly,* Jone Yolen (Coward, McCann, 1981)
> *The True Story of the 3 Little Pigs!,* Jon Scieszka (Viking Kestrel, 1989)
> *Tattercoats,* Flora Steele (Bradbury Press, 1976)
> *Lon Po Po,* Ed Young (Philomel, 1989)
> *Vasilisa the Beautiful,* Thomas Whitney (Macmillan, 1970)
> *And Then What Happened, Paul Revere?* Jean Fritz (Scholastic, 1973)
> *Where Was Patrick Henry on the 29th of May?* Jean Fritz (Coward, McCann & Geoghegan, 1975)
> *Sarah, Plain and Tall,* Patricia MacLachlan (Harper & Row, 1985)
> *Hey World, Here I Am,* Jean Little (Trumpet, 1990)
> *4-Way Stop and Other Poems,* Myra Cohn Livingston (Atheneum, 1976)
> *Hailstones and Halibut Bones,* Mary O'Neill (Doubleday, 1961)
> *Where the Sidewalk Ends* (1974), *A Light in the Attic* (1981), Shel Silverstein (Harper)
> *The Random House Book of Poetry for Children,* selected by Jack Prelutsky (Random House, 1983)

---

[1]R. C. Anderson et al., *Becoming a Nation of Readers* (Champaign, IL: University of Illinois, Center for the Study of Reading, 1985), p. 23.

Jeremy Knight

The Giving Tree, Shel Silverstein (Harper, 1964)

A Book of Americans, Rosemary and Stephen Vincent Benet (Holt, 1933; reissued 1986)

From Anna, Jean Little (Harper, 1972)

Number the Stars, Lois Lowery (Houghton Mifflin, 1989)

Be a Perfect Person in Just Three Days, Stephen Manes (Bantam, 1984)

Where the Red Fern Grows, Wilson Rawls (Bantam, 1961)

Hatchet, Gary Paulsen (Bradbury Press, 1987)

Einstein, Nigel Hunter (Bookwright Press, 1987)

Two Bad Ants, Chris Van Allsburg (Houghton Mifflin, 1969)

The Wump World, Bill Peet (Houghton Mifflin, 1970)

Mrs. Frisby and the Rats of NIMH, Robert O'Brien (Aladdin, 1971)

A Wrinkle in Time, Madeline L'Engle (Dell, 1962)

Tuck Everlasting, Natalie Babbitt (Farrar, 1975; Bantam, 1976)

El Chino, Allen Say (Houghton Mifflin, 1990)

The Celery Stalks at Midnight, James Howe (Avon, 1983)

Eight Ate: A Feast of Homonym Riddles, Marvin Terban (Clarion, Ticknor & Fields, 1981)

A Chocolate Moose for Dinner, Fred Gwynne (Trumpet, 1976)

What's the Big Idea, Ben Franklin? Jean Fritz (Scholastic, 1988)

The Whipping Boy, Sid Fleischman (Greenwillow, 1986)

The Midnight Fox, Betsy Byars (Viking, 1968; Penguin, 1981)

Motel of the Mysteries, David Macaulay (Houghton Mifflin, 1979)

Pots and Robbers, Dora Hamblin (Simon, 1970)

The Jolly Postman, Janet and Allan Ahlberg (Little Borwn, 1987)

Jumanji, Chris Van Allsburg (Houghton Mifflin, 1981)

Cowboys of the Wild West, Russell Freedman (Clarion, 1985)

The Glorious Flight: Across the Channel with Louis Bleriot, Alice and Martin Provensen (Puffin, 1978)

How a Book Is Made, Aliki (Thomas Y. Crowell, 1986)

The Golden Fleece and the Heroes Who Lived Before Achilles, Padraic Colum (Macmillan, 1921; Scholastic, 1990)

All the Money in the World, Bill Brittain (Harper, 1979)

Abel's Island, William Steig (Sunburst/Farrar Straus, 1976)

Who Stole the Wizard of Oz, Avi (Alfred A. Knopf, 1981)

From the Mixed-Up Files of Mrs. Basil E. Frankenweiler, E.L. Konigsburg (Alladin, Dell, 1967)

The Kid in the Red Jacket, Barbara Park (Alfred A. Knopf, 1987)

In the Year of the Boar and Jackie Robinson, Betty Bao Lord (Harper,
1984)

▶ Integrate Reading Throughout the Day

The most obvious connection is the reading and writing connection. In conferences with students, the teacher is learning about the books they read.
He or she will also discover excellent examples in their books that can be
used to illustrate what is being taught during the Writing, Word Study,
and Research modules. The conversations about books often call attention
to outstanding examples of language usage and writing skills. Many students start to look at books differently – as writers – and to consider how
a writer uses words.

Lesson 93 illustrates how books can be used during the Writing module.
Point of view is the focus for the mini-lesson. *Ben and Me* by Robert Lawson
or *Two Bad Ants* by Chris Van Allsburg is used to introduce this writing
technique to the students.

Library books and read-aloud books are often suggested as the resource
in Word Study. Students begin to see the connections between vocabulary
growth and reading.

In the Research module, students might choose to base their presentations on a literature model such as a question-and-answer format. A theme
or unit of study can provide opportunities for integrating the lessons in
all four modules. For example, Lessons 51 through 55 develop the theme
of fairy tales throughout the four modules. In Word Study students select
words related to fairy tales for the chart. They choose writing activities
related to this theme in Writing such as rewriting a fairy tale with a different point of view or setting; they might also write about their favorite fairy
tale. A Research lesson uses fairy tales for surveys and making charts and
graphs. In the Recreational Reading module, the read-aloud book suggested
is a fairy tale book. Literature can be the central focus of lessons in all
the modules. Books are presented to students as the source of many kinds
of learning.

▶ Shared Reading Experiences

If students always choose their own books, is it possible for the whole class
to read the same novel as part of the SUCCESS Recreational Reading module? Of course. Shared reading experiences, oral discussions of novels, and
reading and writing activities about a book are important parts of a reading plan. Teachers will want to help students select books for and work
together in whole-class novel studies and in "book clubs," smaller groups
choosing to read the same book.

WHOLE-CLASS NOVEL STUDY

Some teachers initiate a whole class shared reading experience by introducing some novels to the students in the first few minutes of the reading time, or during read-aloud time. Students are given time to examine the books and make a selection for class reading. A class set of copies of the book is then purchased so each student has a copy for individual reading.

Many teachers enjoy beginning a class novel study by reading aloud at the beginning of the period, discussing some aspect of what was read, and then allowing students to continue reading individually or in pairs. Reading along with the teacher or a partner gives some students the opportunity to read books they could not read alone. Many students are motivated to complete a book after they have "gotten into" the plot.

Some teachers include whole-class reading experiences in their classroom once or twice a semester and often correlate the book choice to a theme of study. While studying Indians in social studies and Research, one fifth-grade class chose a book from this group to read together: *Indian in the Cupboard, Save Queen of Sheba, Sign of the Beaver,* and biographies of Indian leaders.

Whole-class book reading is fun. It provides limitless opportunities to develop oral discussion abilities, appreciate an author's style, laugh out loud, and even shed tears.

Dustin Spencer

BOOK CLUBS

Many classes enjoy reading books in smaller groups sometimes called book clubs. Teachers allow students to choose a book from several sets of books, such as Beverly Cleary books, fantasy or science fiction books, mysteries, multiple copies of the same book, or stories from story collections. Students choose which "book club" they will join and which book they will read during Recreational Reading. Students will read individually; they might also have "partner days" for reading together. Book clubs may meet for sharing discussions at the close of the reading time or give "book talks" about their selections. These clubs are based on student choice and interest, not on books preselected by the teacher and assigned to match reading levels. Shared interests build bonds between readers. Books make friends.

▶ Spreading the Word about Books

SHARING TIME

Like adult readers, students enjoy and profit from talking about books with their friends. Sharing books is important in producing life-long readers. Sharing can be done at the end of the Recreational Reading module. Students are given a few minutes to find a partner and share what they have been reading.

When a student is particularly excited about a book, he or she should be allowed to share the excitement with the rest of the class. If a reluctant reader suddenly discovers that reading can be fun, the student may be immediately asked to share what he or she is enjoying. The teacher should always be watchful and sensitive to the perfect moment when sharing can bring personal pleasure and can motivate others.

BOOK TALK SESSIONS

Even though students learn to enjoy the Recreational Reading module, the familiar complaint may still be heard in the classroom: "I can't find any good books." Often this stems from the student's lack of a reading habit, rather than book selection itself. However, it might pay a teacher to "advertise" some books.

Book Talks for Small Groups   Many teachers choose to boost interest by inviting a small group of students to a corner of the classroom for a short book talk. He or she briefly introduces several books from the library, students' homes, a personal collection, or the classroom library, making the selection as varied and as interesting as possible. Somehow, these "special" books end up being quickly chosen, even by reluctant readers. The teacher may wish to invite students, parents, or other school personnel to present a book talk. If the book talk takes place at the beginning of Recreational Reading time, it should be presented quietly, taking no more than five to ten minutes. At the end the teacher should return to the regular conference schedule.

Whole-Class Book Talks   Sometimes the teacher or a student might choose to introduce a selection of books to the entire class. The books might be new to the class or relate to the topic or theme of another module. For example, when students are writing poetry, the teacher might read some favorite poems from poetry collections available for students to choose during Recreational Reading. A tub of science fiction books may call attention to that genre when the students are writing fantasy and science fiction stories. A particularly exciting book talk was given by a student during the Research module study of flying things (Lessons 141–150). She brought her personal collection of "pop-up" books to school. Many of the books were about flying things: birds, planes, balloons, and Leonardo da Vinci's inventions. The class and the teacher were in awe. Her classmates carefully examined and read these books.

Nonfiction books related to Research topics give students the opportunity to read for information as well as for pleasure. In addition, before introducing a new unit in science, social studies, or health, the teacher should ask the librarian to pull books related to the topic and share with the students one of the collection during their library time. The books can then be taken to the classroom for the students to read.

Only a few minutes are used for book talks. Often the book talks are done during the regular read-aloud period, and the teacher or student might read short passages from the books. Book talks suggested in the lessons in the Recreational Reading module are optional.

▶ Reading Levels

It is often the case with fiction and nonfiction books for adults that some are more difficult to read then others. Adult books are not classified according to their reading level. In contrast, attempts have often been made to place numerical reading levels on chidren's books; this practice could deprive students of opportunities to read some books because they are "above" or "below" a certain reading level. Students may automatically disregard books someone has deemed too hard and be ashamed to read books someone else has called too easy. Some students like to reread old favorites even though they know they are capable of reading much harder material. The content of the book is more important than any predetermined "reading level." When discussions and assessments of progress are based on what a student is reading or has read, rather than on what magic "reading level" the student has attained, real progress will become evident, expectations of students will be higher, and students will think of themselves as true readers and not occupants of some level.

Teachers are often pressured by schools and parents to identify students' reading levels. If it is necessary to assign reading levels, short, informal diagnostic reading tools of a common-sense nature, coupled with conversation notes and observations by the teacher, are recommended. These tools should be used within the framework of the Recreational Reading module, not on a group basis, and should always emphasize the individual's reading abilities and interests.

Joel Townsend

▶ Reading Interests

Reading interests will change within a day, week, month, and year when students are given opportunities to expand them. Some students' reading interests are temporary and highly subject to change. Other students may read books by only one author until they have read them all, or they may want to concentrate on books about only one topic.

Introducing new topics and kinds of literature will expand the reading interests of students. The teacher is the key to opening a door for many students when he or she helps them explore the exciting and real world of books and literature. Teachers can remove the barriers present in many schools that prevent students from reading beyond predetermined, restricted confines.

In some schools where basal readers are required, the students are not allowed to take the basal reader home because they might read the next story, or they might read a story before the teacher has introduced the new words or properly motivated the students to read it.

In schools where students may check out only one library book per week (a maximum of 36 books per academic year), a starvation diet is under way. In schools where the "Great Books" are carefully preserved until the students are old enough, it is certain that fifth-graders will not encounter any Shakespeare or Tennyson.

As long as numerical reading levels command what students will or can read, students will be at a disadvantage and will continue to not read.

▶ Non-Readers and Reluctant Readers

Through observations and conversations teachers can quickly identify the students who are reluctant or nonreaders. These students will require some special attention as the teacher establishes a community of readers. They must not be ignored. Teachers may want to consider the following suggestions for developing a plan to help these students become readers and enjoy reading.

CLASSROOM LIBRARIES AND BOOK CHOICES

Just as students in one classroom will have a wide range of reading interests and abilities, so the book selections available for the Recreational Reading module must offer a wide range of topics and reading difficulty. Every level of reading from wordless books to adult-level reading may be included. Indeed, some wordless books will be quite sophisticated and yet allow students who have not yet mastered word-attack strategies to successfully complete a book.

Picture books are an important part of the classroom collection and are often suggested for read-aloud selections or as models in the Writing module. If the teacher gives these books the respect they deserve, students who may be overwhelmed by long pictureless chapters, thick books, or even a page full of text will not be embarrassed to choose them. Collections of poems or riddles also provide less threatening text, as well as clues of rhythm and rhyme.

STUDENTS HELPING STUDENTS

Students who are poor readers need more attention and encouragement to develop reading strategies and positive feelings about books. Yet, the teacher will not be able to read with these students every day during the thirty minutes of Recreational Reading. Many teachers are discovering that students are a great resource for helping each other. When readers read together, they practice new strategies for analyzing words and using context clues. Through their discussions of the reading, they increase comprehension skills. Teachers should carefully plan "student-helping-student" situations. The teacher may suggest a partner for a student, but both should be open to the arrangement. The first approach might be to identify an interest that the pair have in common, collect books on that topic, and ask them to select a book to read together. The teacher will have a conference with the students to discuss working together.

RECORDED BOOKS

Tape recorded books may be another strategy for increasing a student's reading abilities. Many students benefit from the sound of the language pattern in books when they listen to them as they look at the words in print. Repeated exposure through recorded books increases their sight vocabulary. The student should know the goal of the taped reading time will be independent reading and discussion of the story. When the student has listened enough, he or she will read the story to the teacher.

▶ Evaluate and Grade

The assessment and evaluation of students as readers is a very complex task. Teachers will consider observations, conversations, and records kept by themselves and the students for determining student progress and needs. Assessment should reflect what a student can do. Evaluation is ongoing and supports instruction.

When deciding grades or preparing for student and/or parent conferences, teachers should consider the clipboard notes that document each student's reading abilities, difficulties, and progress during a specific time period. This documentation is cumulative, and growth can be charted. Plans for instruction should grow from this documentation. Taping students reading during a conversation session is another way to document growth and progress.

At the beginning of the year the teacher should let parents know that they will be partners in the assessment of their child's reading progress. They should be encouraged to read with their child as often as possible and to have their own conversations with him or her about reading.

The more teachers listen to and observe students reading the more confident and competent they will become as evaluators of their strengths and weaknesses. A grade should not be the most important consideration. The development of the students as readers should always take priority.

▶ Decisions

TEACHER CHOICES

Every day during the Recreational Reading Module the teacher will decide

1. whether to use the Conversation focus suggested in the Lesson plan or change it;

2. whether to use the Conversation model suggested or change it;

3. with which students to have conversations;

4. what they will record as clipboard notes and what to write about each student;

5. what basic behavioral rules will be in effect;

6. when to do book talks;

7. when students will read together;

8. which content-area topics to integrate;

9. how and when to allow students to share.

STUDENT CHOICES

Students make the following choices each day in Recreational Reading:

1. what book(s) to read;

2. where to read;

3. with whom to read if partner reading is suggested;

4. which book to discuss in conversations with the teacher;

5. how to share their reading experiences with other students;

6. whether to finish a book or exchange it for another one.

▶ In
Summary

Recreational Reading is the backbone of the SUCCESS program. Students who become readers through it discover that reading is a source of pleasure, information, ideas, and shared experiences. This module recognizes the dignity of all learners regardless of their reading abilities. It builds on the assumption that every student can and will become a reader.

Chapter 4 The Writing Module

"My book is about moving. I wrote it because we moved this year and it tells how I felt about it. I added some things that are not true, but mostly it is true."

The student spoke nervously as she shared her story. She picked up her book and explained, "I'm going to read one part because it tells about my true feelings. It starts right after my mother told me we were moving.

'I ran up to my room. I yelled, "I don't want to move!" When I got to my room, I laid on the bed, put my head on the pillow, and I didn't want to, but I cried. All I could think about was my friends. I don't know how long I cried. I don't remember any more until I woke up the next day. I must have cried myself to sleep.'"

When the student closed her book, there were tears in the teacher's eyes, and the room was silent. One student quietly said, "We're glad you moved here."

▶ The Rationale

Why write? Once students personally experience the power of writing, as the girl above did, the answer to this question becomes obvious. When given the opportunity, students can respect and appreciate each other's writing. They will discover that writing can make others laugh, cry, think, and question. They learn to clarify their thoughts and become better able to communicate their feelings, their hopes, fears, and fantasies.

The Writing module is designed to create the environment for this discovery. For thirty minutes each day, students are thinking, composing, and sharing their thoughts. The emphasis in the SUCCESS Writing module is where it should be—on helping students experience the rewards and pleasures of written expression while encouraging accuracy in the mechanics of writing. Each lesson has a proofreading focus that allows the teacher to incorporate the mechanics of writing, but only in the context of the students' writing and not as isolated skills.

▶ Becoming Writers

In the last decade much research and writing has been done on the writing process. The basic components of the SUCCESS Writing module reflect what this research documents: Through consistent effort and daily practice students can become writers. The following elements produce an environment that supports writing growth.

STUDENTS HAVE OPPORTUNITIES TO WRITE EVERY DAY

Writers improve their writing by writing. They learn to do what they have the opportunity to do. Writing is an important, valuable skill that is validated through the daily emphasis. Each SUCCESS module offers an opportunity for writing; at least thirty minutes each day is devoted to the

Jaime Smithie

Writing module. The ability to write is not developed without consistent effort and time to plan, think, and compose. When students know they will be involved in some stage of the writing process every day, they think ahead about topics and begin the first step of composing—thinking about how to say what they want to say.

STUDENTS ARE GIVEN CHOICES

Writers are more motivated to write about the things they know best; they are more comfortable writing about the things they know best. When students are given choices about topics to write about, they see themselves as writers and become more motivated and vested in their writing. Students will also be making decisions about who will proofread their papers, what they will publish, and how it will be published.

STUDENTS LEARN THE WRITING PROCESS

Writing, sharing, revising, and editing are necessary steps for developing a final work. In the Writing module, students are given many opportunities to develop their writing skills and become comfortable and competent writers. They begin to feel at ease with writing.

STUDENTS WRITE FOR VARIED AUDIENCES

Writers must have a focus and purpose for their writing. When students are given opportunities to write for varied audiences, they have a greater understanding of the value and power of writing. This means that the teacher is a coach and facilitator of writing and not the main audience.

STUDENTS SHARE THEIR WRITING EVERY DAY

Each lesson includes time for peer sharing. Some days this will be one-on-one. Other days the student will be sharing with a small group or the entire class. Sharing is designed to offer support for the development of the student as a writer. This sharing allows students to receive help, give help, and appreciate each other as writers.

STUDENTS HAVE OPPORTUNITIES FOR PUBLICATION

Students will have regular opportunities to write for publication. The Lessons are designed to lead them through this process. In addition to classroom presentations, revised student publications are shared with others in a variety of formats including books, filmstrips, plays, and articles. Through publishing, students are recognized and validated as authors. They take great pride in this recognition.

Writing lessons are designed to incorporate the elements described above. Each day the Writing module begins with prewriting activities. Students write; students share; students proofread. In SUCCESS lessons, learning the process of written expression receives priority over learning the details of grammar and mechanics. This does not mean that standard English is not introduced and reinforced. It means that the students learn the elements of standard English in the most effective way—within the context

As a veteran administrator who has been involved in *SUCCESS in Reading and Writing* for eleven years, I am just as excited and enthusiastic about the program today as I was eleven years ago. I have seen what it has done for students and teachers in our school district. The learning environment now focuses on children and allows teachers to take charge and to decide what students need to help them become adults who can read and write.

Dr. Joanne Jumper, assistant superintende

of their own writing. With SUCCESS, students learn to write clearly and coherently, to feel comfortable expressing themselves, and to enjoy writing as they learn the form of written language.

▶ Prepare for the Writing Module

Two things should happen before teachers begin the Writing module. First, they should create a writing environment for their students. Second, they must prepare themselves to be teachers of writing.

CREATING AN ENVIRONMENT

When children are learning to speak, their auditory environment supports their development as effective communicators. Coaching, modeling, and constant positive feedback from others are necessary to reinforce this newly developing communication skill. Children who experience the positive responses of others to their language development feel comfortable and motivated. When parents clap and make a big fuss over new words in the child's vocabulary or call grandparents on the phone to share the latest word learned, the child learns that speaking is a rewarding activity. When children do not receive positive feedback or reinforcement for learning to speak, they often become reluctant and unwilling to risk failure; therefore, their oral language development is thwarted.

The oral language development model shows that learning to write requires coaching, modeling, and positive response to student efforts. A supportive environment that allows students to experience the rewards of oral and written communication helps them feel comfortable and willing to take risks as developing writers.

The physical environment of the classroom must also support writers. Materials are easy to obtain and should be in place before the module begins. Each student needs two file folders. One is kept in the student's desk, and the second is stored in a permanent file drawer or box somewhere in the classroom. Extra pencils and paper should be easily accessible for students who may have forgotten or can't provide them for themselves. Dictionaries and thesauruses should be available.

Teachers need to arrange desks to facilitate composing and sharing. This might mean designating some places as quiet areas and others for peer conferencing. Teachers should

- create a language-rich environment by reading aloud daily from books that contain interesting words and descriptions;
- call attention to the richness of language;
- share details about writers and how they came to be authors;
- show obvious pleasure in the written word.

TEACHERS AS WRITERS AND TEACHERS OF WRITING

Most teachers are not Judy Blume or Ernest Hemingway! Very few people are accomplished first-draft writers. Most probably go through the process of writing, deleting, adding, and marking through words as they try to express their thoughts in the most meaningful ways. Even when composing a thank-you note, writers may put down their thoughts on scrap paper before actually writing the words on stationery. A letter recapping an entire year for friends and family usually goes through several revisions before being stuffed inside the Christmas card. Teachers write letters to parents, memos to colleagues, notes to students, and comments on report cards. Each of these writing activities requires careful thinking about what should be said and how best to say it. Teachers are, in fact, writers.

Practice the Process   Teachers of writing must understand the process of writing. Practicing this difficult process leads to understanding through experience. Teachers who learn to write by writing are better able to relate to the problems and joys students will encounter as developing writers.

Know the Literature   Another way to develop as a teacher of writing is to know the literature. Much has been written describing the writing process and the experiences of teachers, students, and researchers in their quest for what works. Teachers should expand their knowledge by learning what these people have discovered. A personal philosophy for teaching writing is important if teachers are to believe in what they are doing.

Develop Resources   Developing resources is part of becoming an effective teacher of writing. Often teachers will use examples of writing to model author techniques and language patterns. Teachers need to establish a strong supportive relationship with the school librarians. Librarians are eager to share their knowledge and to assist the classroom teacher by introducing them to the latest books and professional collections of information. Teachers will want to find out about the services provided by their state department of public instruction. Many times consultants can provide the names of authors and others who are willing to speak to students about their experiences as writers. Universities and public libraries are other places to find resource persons.

Read Through the Lessons   It is important to read through the lessons in the SUCCESS book and be familiar with suggestions for the topics and for proofreading. Teachers may decide to change and write in their own topics or proofreading focus for some lessons. Whenever possible, many teachers also integrate lessons with content-area subjects such as science, health, and social studies. Teachers will need to plan ahead to incorporate books in the writing activities.

▶ How to Teach the Writing Module

The basic components of the Writing module are Mini-Lesson, Composing, and Sharing.

MINI-LESSON (5 MINUTES)

During the Mini-Lesson the teacher introduces a writing topic and the proofreading focus. The main purpose of this time is to help students start

They had just walked in the door, when the telephone rang. Leah yelled, "I'll get it!" She said, "Hello?"

Her grandfather said, "Would you like to go to the lake for a week with us?"

She said, "Hold on and let me ask mom." She quickly returned to the phone and said, "Yes, I can. What time do you want me to be ready?"

He said, "7:30"

She replied, "Ok, bye."

Jennifer Meadows

THE UNEXPECTED MOVE

Written and Illustrated by Jennifer Meadows

Moving Meadows Inc. Hillsborough, NC

thinking about and discussing the chosen topic or focus. This prewriting time should create the energy and excitement that will motivate the students to write. Teachers should not dominate this time with their own "stories to tell," but share just enough to get the students thinking about their experiences and eager to write about them. Rather than extending this time, teachers find that less is better. As teacher and students become more comfortable with the structure of the Writing module, they will want to get started on their writing. The mini-lessons vary from discussions on students' feelings about the opening day of school to the revision process to editing techniques.

The proofreading focus is meant to turn student attention to mechanics, such as punctuation, or to content, such as adding detail or using descriptive language.

It is useful to write the proofreading focus suggested for the lesson in a box on the chalkboard and give one or two examples of it. The teacher should not hold all students back for a lengthy discussion of the proofreading focus. Additional explanations can be made to individual students at their desks with specific references to something they are writing (or could write). Reviews and other reinforcements can occur on other days. In fact, each focus will be repeated in other lessons throughout the year. Students should not be forced to include the proofreading focus in their writing, but rather reminded of the correct way to use the focus if it occurs naturally. The main reason for the Writing module is to provide time for students to write. They expect to write, and their eagerness will force the teacher to limit "instruction" so that they can get on with the task.

COMPOSING (20 MINUTES)

Most students will begin writing immediately. A few will need extended "think time," but will get started on their own. Still others will sit and stare out the window not knowing where to begin. The teacher will probably want to move to these students first and have a conversation with them about the topic to help them see that they do have something they would like to write about. This may or may not be directly related to the topic you have just introduced and discussed.

Justin was still angry about the kickball tournament earlier in the day and was unable to focus on writing poems about animals. Being aware of his mood, the teacher immediately moved to Justin's desk to have a conversation about what he would write. Realizing that Justin could not focus on the topic suggested in the Lessons, she asked if he would like to write about how he was feeling about the kickball tournament. Justin's immediate response was an adamant "Yes." Justin wrote a very detailed play-by-play, descriptive paragraph of the kickball game. In the same classroom after the Mini-Lesson on poems about animals, one student wrote a poem about baseball and another about his girlfriend.

Allowing students to write what they want and need to write is to be encouraged, and the teacher should never force students to write about the same topic. What is important is that each student writes.

A few minutes before writing time is to end, the teacher may ask students to read over their papers silently and place a check mark over any example of the proofreading focus which appears in their writing. As the students are reading their papers, they may spontaneously make changes such as adding punctuation, correcting spelling, or substituting more interesting words. Students should know that they are the first and foremost proofreaders of their writing.

SHARING (5 MINUTES)

During the last five to ten minutes of the Writing module students will have a conversation about their writing with another student or students. Each one will take a turn reading his or her paper to another student or to the group and answer any questions from peers concerning the content of the writing. During this discussion the listeners may assist the author by suggesting ways to make the writing more effective.

Before this session ends, students exchange papers and check for correct use of the proofreading focus, if the writing has examples of it.

Some teachers ask students to call attention to examples of incorrect uses of the proofreading focus and to check (✓) examples of correct usage. After the proofreading, students should date and file their papers in their writing folders located in their desks or stored in a box in the classroom.

In the beginning, the teacher might need to monitor carefully the time allotted to each section of the Writing module. Once students are familiar with the structure of the module, they will learn how to pace themselves in order to accomplish these tasks.

A REVIEW OF THE STEPS

What happens during this thirty-minute Writing module? Every day the basic procedures are the same. The following outlines these lesson procedures.

1. The teacher begins with the Mini-Lesson: topic and proofreading focus;

2. students write;

3. the teacher moves from student to student having conversations about writing;

4. students share, proofread, and make additions and corrections to their writing;

5. students date and file papers.

▶ Respond to Students

The most important role for the teacher during the Writing module is responding daily to the students' writing. The teacher should move among the students, engaging in conversations about their writing. The three main purposes for these mini-conferences are to give positive feedback, to identify areas of need, and to document progress.

GIVING POSITIVE FEEDBACK

As discussed earlier in reference to oral communication development, nothing works like praise and recognition for motivating students to continue writing. This feedback about their writing needs to be specific and sincere.

"When you used the words *old* and *twisted* to describe the tree, I could really see it."

"I can see you understand how to use quotation marks."

This is the applause. This short response should leave the student with affirmation of a skill or thought that gives value to his or her efforts. For many students, this response will motivate them to continue writing.

IDENTIFYING AREAS OF NEED

The teacher should note needs that can be responded to by immediate instruction or will require additional follow-up instruction.

The teacher might begin a conversation about needs by asking, "Tell me about your writing." It is important that the teacher not ask the student to read the entire composition. He or she should assist the student in identifying one thing that could be changed or added to make the composition even better, and leave the student with a positive comment.

Teacher: What exciting time did you choose to write about, Catherine?

Catherine: I'm writing about a family trip.

Teacher: Tell me the exciting part.

Catherine: Right now, I'm writing about the night before when I couldn't sleep and my stomach was all fluttery.

Teacher: Is most of this piece about the night before your trip?

Catherine: Yes.

Teacher: I don't know where you are going. Did you put it in your paper?

Catherine: No, I'm saving it for the end . . . when we get to Texas to see my grandparents.

Teacher: I think you are right. It really works at the end.

When the teacher questioned Catherine about an important detail in her composition, she realized there was indeed a well thought-out plan.
  Another conference might go this way.

Teacher: Aaron, would you read the beginning of your paper.

Student: I'm telling about when I got hit by a car. "We were playing basketball and Jerod missed his shot. I seen the ball bounce high in the air. When I ran for it, I suddenly heard the tires squeal."

Teacher: I know this must have been a frightening time for you and I'm glad to see that you want to describe and share this experience. Read your second sentence to yourself and look at the verb *seen*. Does this sound correct to you?

Student: Oh, I remember! Should it be *saw?*

Teacher: Yes, *saw* would be correct. When you use the verb *seen*, it must always be with a helping word such as *have, had,* or *has.* Now, read your sentence again using *saw* instead of *seen.* Sound correct?

Student: Yeah, that sounds better.

Teacher: You are off to a good start. I can't wait to read the rest of your story.

During this conference, the teacher has responded to the student's sharing of his experience, helped him identify an area of need, provided instruction, and given him an opportunity to correct his writing. The teacher leaves with a positive comment. These short student/teacher interactions are the backbone of the skills instruction for the SUCCESS program. The skills are taught and learned within the context of the students' own writing.

DOCUMENTING STUDENT PROGRESS

Teachers are encouraged to keep daily records of observations they make about each student's writing so that they can monitor student progress and document competencies and needs for further instruction or practice. Some teachers use a clipboard or composition notebook daily to record the skills being learned and those needing further instruction. The teacher may also decide to change a proofreading focus for a few days after observing that many students are having trouble with a particular skill.

Figure 4–1 is an example of a filled-in form that can be used to record what the teacher is finding out about students through conferences.

Figure 4-1

STUDENT SKILLS ASSESSMENT AND OBSERVATION FORM

DATE: *Feb. 15*

NAMES OF STUDENTS	OBSERVATIONS
1. *Aaron*	*"I seen." Corrected with teacher's help.*
2. *Julie*	*Used quotation marks correctly.*
3. *Lonnie*	*Not focused, had trouble getting started.*

The teacher who filled in this form also observed that several students had misused verbs and decided to do a mini-lesson on verb tense the next day. It is important to note mastery of skills as well as to identify areas for additional instruction. Some teachers will make brief, coded notes and others will write more detailed statements.

▶ The Teacher as Model

WRITING

One of the most important ways teachers can convey to students the joys and struggles of writing is to write and share their writing. This modeling includes thinking through how to best express thoughts, writing, rewriting, changing directions, and searching for the best word or words. It establishes that the teacher is a person who, having experienced the process, understands students' frustrations and pleasures as they emerge as writers. Teachers should be sincere, legitimate, and honest with their writing. They shouldn't intentionally set up examples. Sometimes sharing this writing is necessary to introduce a concept, to teach a technique, or to show how to make editing symbols. This can be done on the overhead projector or on chart paper.

Teachers might want to consider the following suggestions for modeling:

On the first day, model writing the entire time the students are writing.

On the second, write only for a few minutes.

By the third day, students will begin to need your response to their writing.

In order to preserve your image as a writer, return to the modeling whenever you have a need to write. Let your students see you write.

I like the way SUCCESS teaches children at a young age that by reading, you can learn things either of necessity or just for enjoyment and opens the world up to them.

Robert K. Beckwith
parent

It would be nice if the teacher could spend every day writing, sharing, and discussing his or her writing as a member of the class writing community. This is not possible. The teacher must guide the students as they become writers.

REVISION AND EDITING

The students have written for several days and have had peer conferences to discuss content and to proofread. Some have made notes and have returned to pieces of writing they want to complete and revise. One effective way to introduce the editing process is to model it, with the teacher as editor.

The teacher can present a sample written during a writing period using a piece of chart paper or the overhead projector. It should be an honest, unplanned, and imperfect first draft, one that may be messy or awkward, but free of faked errors for students to correct. During the time for composing, the teacher has modeled the process of creating and has written quickly to get thoughts on paper, sometimes striking through false starts and using carets to insert new words or phrases. After the teacher finishes writing, he or she should read silently over the paper to make any obvious corrections. This is the piece to be shared with the class to demonstrate the editing process.

The teacher reads the writing aloud and asks the students to focus on the writing and make suggestions for improvements. Some questions to prompt them might be:

"Do you have any questions about this piece of writing? Is there any part you don't understand?"

"Do I need to tell more?"

"Did the opening bring you right into my story, or does it need some changes?"

"Are there any words that don't seem to fit in, or that you're not sure what they mean?"

As students ask questions and suggest changes, the teacher discusses them aloud, and adds to the paper those changes he or she feels are needed. It is important that the writer make the final decisions about what will be changed. The teacher should demonstrate the use of carets to insert material, use margins to note words being considered for replacements, and mark through unwanted words and phrases. The students should see that their suggestions are welcomed and cause the writer to rethink the writing, producing a better piece. When the teacher is satisfied, he or she should read the piece aloud to hear the finished result.

As soon as the editing of the writing is complete, the teacher should lead students into their own editing conferences with partners. Revision and editing will develop over time and will need to be modeled over and over as the teacher moves among writers who are conferring with each other in sharing sessions. Establish the idea that authors are willing to listen, ask questions, make suggestions, and work together to help each other grow as writers.

The teacher may decide to demonstrate revising and editing at the end of a writing lesson. If this modeling exercise is done with the whole class after writing time, there will be no time for student revision conferencing that day. The next day students should choose a piece of their writing to share with a partner or small group for help in editing and revision, following the basic steps used in the whole-class activity.

▶ How Often Do Students Revise?

Many teachers will start the year using the writing process cycles outlined in the Writing module. In the lessons there are two models or cycles for introducing students to the writing process and helping them feel comfortable with it. One is a shorter cycle during which the students write on days one, two, and three; revise one selection on day four; and share their final draft on day five. The other cycle lasts for about ten days. Every eight to ten days students are given the opportunity to select one of their compositions for revision and editing. The ninth and tenth days are spent rewriting and sharing compositions selected by each student.

Even though this process is outlined in the lessons, the frequency of revision and publishing is determined by the teacher and the students. Some students will choose to revise and rewrite papers on their own and should be encouraged to do so. These steps are repeated often to give students the experience necessary to feel comfortable with the revision process and to use it for developing their best works. Later, revision and editing may occur whenever a student decides that a piece needs them. Teachers might set definite deadlines for certain pieces, but many times the student will initiate the revision process. A minimum number (established by the teacher and the students) of revised and edited final drafts are the basis for evaluation of growth in writing.

▶ Students Helping Students

For decades, teachers have collected student papers, taken them home, spent hours reading and marking them, and returned the papers. Some students glanced at the marks, and that was about it. The teacher did the proofreading and checking; few students benefited because they did not go through the process and internalize the "pseudo-instruction." If students are to develop as writers, they must have daily and immediate feedback about their work and an audience besides the teacher that is responsive to their writing.

Current research and literature about writing suggests that students helping students is a realistic and effective method for providing daily

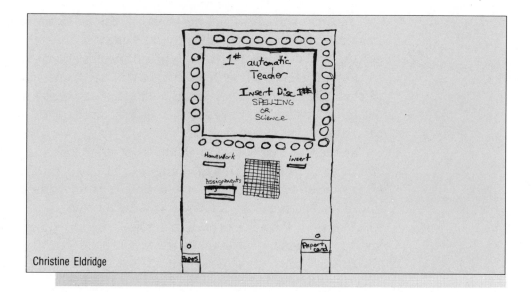

Christine Eldridge

responses to writing. These daily conversations between students lead to greater clarity in written work and cause each author to question, justify, and reexamine how his or her thoughts have been expressed.

In each Writing lesson, a method for sharing is suggested. Teacher and students must decide if this is appropriate for their particular situation. For example, the lesson may suggest that students meet one-on-one to share their writing. The teacher may decide that several students should meet in a group, others one-on-one, and still others in different arrangements. On some days whole-class sharing is suggested (Share Day). This day is usually suggested after students select a paper, revise, and edit it. This can always be changed should the teacher decide it is not appropriate.

PREPARING STUDENTS TO HELP EACH OTHER

Before students can help other students, they must know how to go about it. They tend to be excited about the simple idea of getting together to talk, and talk they will. A few straightforward directions from the teacher will start them on the right track. The teacher might say, "Your most important job is to listen to your partner's paper. Don't be looking around or working on your own paper. Listen, then ask any questions you have about the writing, or just tell what you understand about it. You are not trying to grade the paper."

After giving instructions, teachers may see some students more interested in being on the floor or under a table than in conferring, others chatting endlessly, and some papers returned with big *A*s or teacherlike comments from peer partners. It will take time for students to learn how to respond to writing. One way to help them is to model the correct procedure each time a student reads to the class. For this reason, the teacher may want to choose whole-class sharing at the beginning of the year. After a student reads work aloud, the teacher follows up with a few simple comments or questions about it. The respect given to the writer when the teacher listens carefully and responds specifically to the words will set the desired tone for the students' conversations about writing. They will catch on. Still, it will take time.

PEER CONFERENCES

The point of sharing is not just show-and-tell for an audience, but to let writers know if they have succeeded in communicating their ideas, and to help them solve problems.

One student, when asked to share her poem with the whole group, replied, "I'll read it, but one line is stupid."

Her poem about her rabbit ended with these lines:

Funny Bunny eats like a pig,
But he doesn't wear a wig.

The student said, "I just couldn't think of anything to rhyme with pig that I liked."

The teacher empathized with the problem of sometimes getting stuck in a poem that rhymes. Then she turned to the class to ask them how they would deal with this problem. Some suggestions were

"Well, all poems don't have to rhyme, so you could just forget about rhyming, and write your ideas."

"I start listing all the rhyming words I can think of in the margins or at the bottom of my paper. Sometimes I ask someone to help me think of them. Usually, I can come up with one I like."

"When that happens to me, I just skip that next line and go on with other ideas. Sometimes I don't even need it, or I find a way to rearrange it."

Without being asked for suggestions, some students quickly offered,

"What about big, or dig?"

"Is Funny Bunny fat? Is that what you mean?"

"Maybe he eats all day, or just use the words *eats* and *eats* for your rhyme."

These comments were made in response to one student's writing problem. It only took a few minutes for the other students to come up with suggestions to help her.

Do Peer Conferences Help?   After students have had some experience in whole-group sharing and responding sessions, the teacher might need to ask them what they are doing that is helpful to them as writers. A Writing Mini-lesson could be used for them to tell how conferring is useful or what kinds of responses make them think about ways to be a better writer. Specifically, the teacher needs to know what works and what does not. Such a Mini-lesson will give students an opportunity to talk about how some of their partners ask silly or unimportant questions or just say, "I think it's O.K." Helping writers is not easy, nor is it easy to teach. Yet, when students realize they can develop some strategies to prod another's thinking, they often will use the same strategies when they are thinking and writing. If students ask for more details in the description of a character upon hearing a peer's story, they will be more likely to include details in their own character descriptions.

What About Peer Sharing Groups?   Adding variety to the peer sharing will enable students to continue developing as helpers of others. This might mean changing partners regularly or forming larger groups of students to listen and respond to each other's writing. Writing groups of three or four students may be especially useful when they are engaged in longer writing projects, like books or stories, and need consistent response to help them as their writing develops. It is always up to the teacher considering the individual makeup of the class to decide how to establish groups, and when and if changes will be made. Meeting in groups, each student should read and talk with others about his or her paper; any necessary attention to proofreading should be handled quickly. Content is the main focus of the conferring time. Only when time comes for the final draft will helpers turn their main attention to checking spelling and the mechanics of writing.

▶ The Reading-Writing Connection

One of the most effective ways to improve students' writing skills and style is to let them learn from the best. When teachers use literature examples in the Writing Mini-lesson, they present models and patterns that students might use as guides for their own writing.

When the focus for the Writing Mini-lesson is point of view, the teacher might quickly read a few paragraphs from a book, such as *I, Houdini* (told by a hamster) by Lynne Reid Banks, to introduce the lesson, and ask students to suggest a point of view they might like to take in a composition.

When beginning a Writing lesson with poetry, the teacher might ask students to identify elements of poetry after listening to some of Jack Prelutsky's poems. Hearing examples of rhythm, rhyme, and alliteration generates more interest and response than listening to definitions of those terms. Students who have difficulty getting started may be prompted by another writer's style or ideas on the way to developing their own.

When teachers discuss writing styles and techniques in the books students are reading in Recreational Reading conversations, they are calling attention to writing strategies in context. When asked to describe the setting of a book in a reading conversation, students begin to notice how authors introduce and describe settings in stories. A writing lesson about describing settings is connected with an example from the student's reading experience.

Patterns for class writing projects might be suggested by an unusual format or title. One class chose to write and illustrate an ABC book titled *Athens to Zeus* during a research project on ancient Greece, after discovering the book *Ashanti to Zulu: African Traditions* by Margaret Musgrove.

Teachers may introduce books during Recreational Reading that are related to a topic in another module. When students are writing poetry in the Writing module, the teacher may introduce several poetry books by reading from them during read-aloud time. Suddenly poetry books become popular during the Recreational Reading time. The continual exposure to quality writing in books helps students recognize, appreciate, and apply effective writing skills.

▶ Integrate the Writing Module

OTHER MODULES

SUCCESS Lessons are designed to allow teachers to include any topic in any module to produce a natural integration of ideas and skills. Some Lessons use the same general theme in all four modules for several days, such as Fairy Tales in Lessons 51–55. In these Lessons, the students might list fairy tale titles or characters in the Word Study module, rewrite fairy tales in the Writing module, design a survey of fairy tale favorites and graph the results in Research, listen to fairy tale selections in the read-aloud period, and have the option to read fairy tales in Recreational Reading.

CONTENT AREAS

Topics included in the Lessons often occur in fifth-grade curriculum content areas; examples are Native Americans, wars, environmental issues, nutrition, and American colonial life. When these topics are included in the modules, they reinforce and extend the social studies, science, or health unit being studied. Many Writing module lessons correlate with these content-area topics. Students might write essays, letters, or editorials about an environmental issue, compose poems about Native Americans, or write diary entries reflecting life in colonial times. In such writing lessons students have a chance to express clearly what they know and think about these topics rather than completing an unrelated language activity.

▶ Evaluate and Assess

Since teachers are held accountable for the progress and growth of their students, a question often asked is, "Where do the grades come from?" They have not put grades on daily student writings, nor administered language arts textbook tests. They have not graded duplicated skills worksheets. The grade book looks empty. What do they have for grades? A lot!

Teachers have a Writing folder of daily compositions for each student, daily observation notes, selected (edited and revised) final writings for grades, students' evaluations of their own writing progress, and their writings from other modules. Writing folders provide powerful documentation of a student's writing progress. This longitudinal record becomes the basis for evaluating their progress.

PROCEDURES

At the beginning of each grading period the teacher should tell students that their writing is being evaluated with the emphasis on the skills covered during this time. During the first six weeks of school, he or she might be observing whether they are using capital letters to begin sentences, ending sentences with correct punctuation, writing properly developed paragraphs, using more descriptive language and so forth, depending on the lessons introduced.

The observation notes made during this grading period will be helpful as the teacher determines the progress made by each individual. For example, if Aaron was having trouble with verb tense at the beginning of the grading period, is he still making verb tense errors? Is he making them less frequently, or has he learned to use tenses properly?

Every two to three weeks the teacher asks the students to select a writing that they will revise and hand in for a grade. Before they begin the revision process, the teacher should tell them what he or she will be looking for to determine their grade. The teacher might say, "We have been studying subject and verb agreement and how to write clear, concise sentences with correct punctuation. For this grade, I'll be noting whether or not you have used these writing skills correctly." After this paper has been graded, the teacher will want to hold a brief conference with each student to answer any questions they may have about their grades. Students then file these papers in their Writing folders.

All revised writings, publications, reports, and completed presentations from other modules are potential sources for grades.

SELF-ASSESSMENT

At certain intervals, teachers will want to ask students to do a self-assessment of their writing progress. One way to introduce the procedure to determine their language or writing grade is to ask students to look over their writing for a period of two to three weeks and see if they think their writing is improving. They should be specific and give examples of ways their writing has improved. If students are keeping their daily writing in a folder in their desks, when they transfer these writings to the permanent Writing file folder, they should go through these steps of self-assessment.

1. Arrange papers in order by date. Never discard a writing.

2. Staple or clip the papers together.

3. Include a cover page that is duplicated and given to each student to put with their papers. See Figure 4–2 for an example of such a form. Through this process, the students grow more aware of their development as writers and begin to accept responsibility for continually assessing their progress.

▶ Decisions

TEACHER CHOICES

Each day during the Writing module, the teacher decides whether to

1. use the topic suggested as part of the mini-lesson or change it, based on student interest, other content areas of current interest, or individual student choices;

Figure 4-2

SELF-ASSESSMENT COVER PAGE

```
MY WRITING FROM _____ TO _____
                     (date)              (date)

*   Things we have been working on
    _____

*   I'm improving on
    _____

*   I need to work on
    _____

*   My progress as a writer is
    _____
```

2. use the day's Proofreading focus or replace it with a skill or concept identified as more appropriate for the students;

3. have revision and editing at intervals suited to students' needs or revise and edit when suggested in the lessons;

4. allow self-selection of partners for peer sharing or assign partners when necessary;

5. restructure and/or change writing response groups;

6. use the writing mode suggested in the lesson or change to another.

STUDENT CHOICES

During the Writing module, the students may decide the following:

1. Whether to write about the topic presented in the lesson or select another;

2. Whether to compose using the mode suggested in the Mini-lesson or try a different mode of writing;

3. Who to choose as a partner for peer sharing. (Occasionally, the teacher will need to assign partners for a specific reason);

4. Whether to continue a previous day's writing, revise a writing, or start a new one;

5. What papers to revise and publish, and hand in for evaluation.

▶ In Summary

Writing is challenging. Learning to write is not easy. It takes practice, guidance, and time. Through the Writing module teachers and students learn to appreciate the writing process. They develop a respect for the difficult work of an author. Students begin to understand that writing is a way to communicate their thoughts, dreams, and fears to others. They learn the power of words.

Chapter 5 The Word Study Module

During the Word Study module, students explore the world of words. They read in a variety of materials to locate words related to a topic and/or a spelling pattern. Discussions are focused on the associations and connections the students make between the words they locate and the topic. Each day a class chart is developed from the words the students volunteer. This word list becomes the springboard for individual writing and partner spelling activities. From beginning to end, the students are actively involved in discovering the meanings of words, and how they are formed and used. Word Study is a fast-paced, exciting thirty minutes.

▶ The Rationale

This module is designed to allow students the freedom to discover words, use them in writing and conversations, and enjoy the benefits of a growing vocabulary. Students learn words when they attach meaning to them. Through repeated exposure and usage, words become tools for communication. The variety and excitement of the materials used and the choices students are given become powerful motivators. Lively discussion, creative and critical thinking, and exploration of word meanings are the key features of the Word Study module that keep students involved with words. Students want to use and write words that are important to them. This is the reason many children learn to write and spell such "difficult words" as *Dustin, Blake,* and *Katherine*—their own names—even before they begin school.

Traditionally, teachers have taught spelling by identifying a phonetic rule and producing lists of words that demonstrate the rule. Rarely do these lists provide examples of exceptions to the rule. These lists also control and limit the vocabulary development of students. Students concentrate only on words "appropriate" to their grade level, regardless of the word knowledge they have previously acquired.

For years American school children have been taking a spelling test each Friday for thirty-six weeks of the school year. Every lesson in the spelling book is supplemented with exercises, sentence writing, word copying, puzzles, and other mimeographed work sheets as practice for learning the twenty words in each week's lesson. Parents expect the spelling book to come home almost every night so that they can diligently call out the words and make certain their child knows them for the test. Students may complete all these activities and may spell all words correctly on the weekly spelling test, and then ironically show a lack of transfer when they use the same words in their compositions the following week. Should teachers continue to use what has been demonstrated to be a flawed pattern of learning?

Teachers' excitement and enthusiasm for helping their students explore new words and their meanings will be one of the most important elements

Jeremy Gossett

in establishing an inviting setting for Word Study. When the teacher first announces, "This year we will be reading many different materials and resources to explore and learn about words: what they mean, how they are used, and how they are spelled," he or she is setting the stage for students to become active learners. After the first few lessons, students discover that they are making decisions and are in control of their learning. They quickly discover that the lists on the charts are more interesting and provide more opportunities for real word study than traditional spelling books and exercises.

▶ Becoming a Master of Words

What is learned during the Word Study module? Students learn to recognize spelling patterns and word structure. They increase their vocabularies as they discuss word meanings and associations. They become creative and critical thinkers. Word selection for writing, handwriting, and dictionary skills are also studied during the Word Study module. The parts of the module address the different ways in which students learn.

SPELLING PATTERNS AND WORD STRUCTURE

Each lesson contains criteria for the selection of words for that day. Even at the fifth-grade level, after years of phonics instruction, students still need exposure to many different words so they can apply their knowledge of letter sounds as they encounter new words. Combinations of letters are guides to pronunciation and word recognition.

The sounds of letters in words are not always as simple as phonics rules might suggest. Sounds made by some letters may be changed by the letters that surround them, and by their position in a word. Repeated exposure to words in print builds visual word recognition and spelling skills.

The lessons contain Spelling Emphases that ask students to focus on certain letter combinations as they choose words for the day. The combination may occur anywhere in the word, allowing students to recognize the similarities and differences both in sounds and positions within words. When students discover spelling relationships in words that have meaning for them, retention is more likely to take place.

Lessons 1 through 65 emphasize two-letter combinations, such as *br, ie,* or *gn.* Lessons 66 through 90 emphasize more phonetically complex three- and four-letter combinations. In Lessons 91-130 the focus changes to word structure: how words are formed, base words, and affixes and their effects on meaning and usage. Finally, Lessons 131-180 allow teachers and students to choose any letter combination or word-structure feature they decide is appropriate for the spelling emphasis for that day.

VOCABULARY DEVELOPMENT

Another criterion for word selection in the lessons is called the Other Emphasis: it is usually a topic such as plants, entertainment, or politics. These are presented as a springboard for discussion and generation of words the students associate with the topic.

*T*eachers have a right to enjoy the classroom along with the children. SUCCESS classrooms are exciting, challenging, child-centered, and every day is different. The message is: "We'll all work and learn together."

Jean Weaver, teacher

Because there is no controlled list of words and students are at different stages in their vocabulary development, the Word Study module allows them to learn from each other. They are exposed to a greater number and diversity of words. In the context of their reading to find words that pertain to a topic, students will select words that are familiar to them. A word that is familiar to one student may be unfamiliar to another. When students explain the connections of the words they find to the chart topic, other students have the benefit of listening, adding to the discussion, and questioning. This interaction provides meaningful reinforcement to help students remember what may be an unfamiliar word. In this module, learning a new word can happen at any time. It can happen through a discussion; it can happen through an association, or just because a student is intrigued with the length of a word.

CREATIVE AND CRITICAL THINKING

In Lesson 14 the Spelling Emphasis is *an* and the Other Emphasis is Earth. Students use science or social studies books as the resource. When students are seeking words related to the chart topic, they must think about the meaning of the word and how it relates to the topic.

"My word is *escape*. You can't escape from earth because of gravity. It holds you down."

"*Hemisphere* is my word. Hemisphere means half of the earth."

Their experiences allow them to make many different associations and connections. They are challenged to expand their thinking by justifying the connection.

This sharing of one's knowledge in unique ways is, for many, the most exciting feature of the module. It reveals to students that there is not always "just one right answer" but often many—depending on their own experiences and creativity. Students begin to enjoy the challenges and complexities of thinking. Thinking becomes fun.

USING CHART WORDS IN WRITING

Understanding words in the context of one's own thoughts and writing promotes confident spellers and builds students' vocabularies. When they use and spell words correctly in their writing, students are not simply learning letter arrangements but are incorporating words as concepts into their own thinking. The importance of the writing time is that it lets students focus on the words and their meanings, not on repeated drills such as using each word in a sentence, copying the complete chart, or writing words over and over. During writing time in this module, the students should be encouraged to develop their imaginative and creative thinking processes. The key words are *think* and *write,* not *copy.*

HANDWRITING

Some teachers choose to emphasize handwriting during the Word Study module. As they write the spelling emphasis on the chart each day, they call attention to the letter formations and ask the students to practice making these letters correctly. Handwriting can be integrated into each lesson and takes the place of separate, unconnected, and repetitious drills.

DICTIONARY SKILLS

Dictionaries are resources to be used during this module. At any given point in the lesson, a student may quickly look up a word to check a spelling or meaning before the teacher writes the word on the chart. Dictionaries are used when they are needed. Through this incidental, functional use of dictionaries, students develop an appreciation of this resource. They choose to use it; it becomes a learning tool for them.

▶ Prepare for the Word Study Module

Before beginning to teach this module, the teacher will need to do two things; gather the materials and review the lessons.

GATHERING THE MATERIALS

The following is a list of steps for gathering materials prior to the Word Study Module.

1. Provide a file folder for each student labeled Word Study, which is stored in a permanent box in the classroom.

2. Make several dictionaries and thesauruses available and easily accessible.

3. Gather supplies such as chart paper (at least one sheet for each day), masking tape, and magic markers.

4. Have students bring or make a Word Study notebook. This can be a spiral notebook or five sheets stapled together weekly.

A variety of real-life print materials are suggested as resources in each lesson. The following list is a guide for assisting teachers with their preplanning. These materials are suggested in the Lessons over the course of the year.

newspapers	brochures and pamphlets
magazines	advertisements
textbooks	maps and globes
reference books	school handbooks and guides
catalogues	library books

Teachers who do not have the resources suggested should ask students to bring newspapers and magazines from home. Businesses and other organizations are often glad to contribute some of the suggested resources. Parents and volunteers can be enlisted to assist with the collection of these materials. It should be noted that teachers always have the choice to change a resource they lack to one that is available. Many have discovered that sharing and recycling materials with other teachers gives them greater access to a variety of resources.

REVIEWING THE LESSONS

In the Word Study module the basics are the same throughout the year. Even with this consistency, every lesson involves making decisions. Each lesson suggests a Spelling Emphasis, Other Emphasis, and a Resource. Even though these are listed in the lesson, a blank is provided for substituting a different letter combination, topic, or resource. Choices about the emphases and resource should be made before beginning the lesson.

▶ How to Teach the Word Study Module

The basic components of the Word Study module are Chart Development, Writing, Spelling, and Homework. Following is a description of each of these components.

CHART DEVELOPMENT (12–15 MINUTES)

Step One: Introducing the Emphases and the Resource   The Word Study module begins with the introduction of the letter or letters for the Spelling Emphasis, the topic for the Other Emphasis, and the Resource. The Emphases are written on a piece of chart paper attached to the chalkboard with masking tape. Students write these along with the date in their Word Study notebooks. If teachers are reviewing handwriting skills, the students should practice the letter combinations for that day.

Step Two: Students Read to Locate Words   After the introduction, students read in the designated resource to locate words they can associate with the emphases. Some teachers introduce the Spelling Emphasis and the Other Emphasis at the same time.

> "Today we will be locating words which have the letters *by,* or relate to the topic, *leisure.* You might find some words that relate to *leisure* that have a *by* in them. You will be using newspapers as today's resource."

Students can choose to look for one or both.

Other teachers decide to introduce one emphasis and give students time to locate words before introducing the next. This allows the students to concentrate on each emphasis equally. When this method is used, it is important to allow only three to five minutes for each emphasis. Some teachers use a timer, and students soon learn to switch from one emphasis to the other when the timer signals the change.

In some SUCCESS classrooms, students circle the words in the newspapers or magazines as they find them. In others, students write the words in their Word Study notebooks. When nonexpendable resources are used, the students should obviously write the words on a separate piece of paper or in the notebooks.

Figure 5-1

CLASS CHART

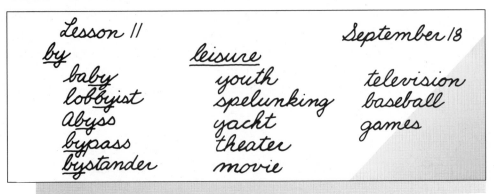

Lesson 11   *September 18*

<u>*by*</u>
   baby   <u>*leisure*</u>
   lobbyist   *youth*   *television*
   Abyss   *spelunking*   *baseball*
   bypass   *yacht*   *games*
   bystander   *theater*
                   movie

Step Three: Students Volunteer Words for the Chart After approximately five to ten minutes, students volunteer words for the chart, explaining why they selected the words. As quickly as possible, the teacher writes the words volunteered by the students on the chart. Some students will not be able to pronounce the words they have located. They should be encouraged to attempt to pronounce each word and spell it aloud as the teacher writes it on the chart. Pronouncing the word and discussing its meaning will involve other students.

As students volunteer words for the Other Emphasis, they explain the associations they make between the word and the emphasis. Sometimes the associations will be direct and easily understood by all class members. Other times, the associations may be indirect. Any valid association explained by the student should be accepted. This acceptance of the student's thoughts is a powerful builder of self-esteem.

Words containing the Spelling Emphasis are written on the chart. Most teachers underline the letters of the Spelling Emphasis and briefly call attention to any similarities and differences in the sounds of the letters that may appear in the words.

The following is an example of how the Chart Development for Lesson 11 might unfold. The letters *by* are the Spelling Emphasis and *leisure* is the Other Emphasis. The following words appear: *baby, youth, lobbyists, abyss, spelunking, bypass,* and *yacht.* When the teacher introduces *by* and *leisure* using newspapers as the material, students volunteer these words because they make an association or connection between the word and *leisure.* For example, one girl gives the word *yacht,* which she located in the classified ad section of the newspaper. Another student gives the word *abyss* from the entertainment section because it is the name of a movie. A third student locates the word *youth* and explains that youths seem to have a lot of leisure time. Each student has found a word containing a *by* and/or relating to *leisure.* By making such connections, students find relevance in learning to spell any or all of these words. This list also illustrates the diversity of student responses.

The words on this chart also demonstrate the similarities and differences of the *by* sound in words. Students begin to recognize that the position of the letters in words often dictates how the word is pronounced. These discoveries come from examples of words from their speaking, reading, and thinking vocabulary. Students begin to formulate their own strategies for spelling the words relevant to their learning.

The class has now a completed chart with lots of words and excited students. Their enthusiasm and eagerness about real word study leads to an invitation to write.

WRITING (5–10 MINUTES)

Each lesson provides an opportunity for a written response to the chart focus. Students decide what they will write. They may decide to add words from their reading that were not included on the chart; they may decide to write about the vocabulary emphasis making the associations and connections they choose to make; they may respond by writing sentences with some of the words; they may write a paragraph or a poem using one word from the chart as the focus of thought. These responses reflect the associations and connections the students make to the words on the chart or to other words. With such an open-ended writing assignment, students have opportunities for creative and critical thinking as they write. They may decide to do this writing in their Word Study notebooks or on a separate sheet of paper which will be filed in their Word Study folders.

The consistency of the steps in each day's lesson helps students develop time-management skills. During the first week, while the students are getting comfortable with the procedures, their written responses may not be extensive. As they become familiar with the structure, they will be able to move more easily through the steps of the module and will be ready to respond in many different ways.

While students are writing, the teacher is moving among the students having one- to two-minute conversations about their writing. The teacher seizes every opportunity to teach myriad skills, from phonics and spelling patterns to cursive handwriting skills or word meanings and clearly ex-

Figure 5-2

WORD STUDY RECORD SHEET

	SCORE	
DATE	WORDS/LETTERS	REVIEW WORDS
October 5	*2/16*	*space*

SUCCESS fits my personality and my style of teaching—flexible, fun and meaningful!

Linda Pickard, teacher

pressed thoughts. This one-on-one attention is the teacher's best opportunity to deal with individual student needs in the context of their language development.

SPELLING (5 MINUTES)

With the daily spelling activity students challenge and expand their spelling vocabularies. Growth is based on the words students select to spell. The selected words are spelled with a partner, may be used in writing, become a spelling resource list, and are reviewed as a homework assignment.

Selecting the Words   Students select words from the chart that they want to learn to spell and write them in their Word Study notebooks. There is no set number of words for each student to spell. Sometimes teachers encourage students to challenge themselves with their word selection and the number of words they select. Because of time constraints, teachers may suggest to some students that they should be more realistic in the number of words they select to spell. Students can include more words on their homework list. After a short time, students will find a reasonable range for both the difficulty and the number of words they select to spell. They are becoming responsible decision makers.

After the students have selected their words to spell, they find a partner, exchange notebooks, and team test. Partners check each other for correct spelling.

Scoring the Team Tests   The student receives one point for each letter in every word that is spelled correctly; however, if the student misses any part of a word, no points are given.

As soon as students become aware that the longer the word, the more points they receive, most want to spell longer words. The following are examples of scoring on the spelling test:

1. gravity (*gravity spelled correctly*)   =   7 points
2. spaice (*space spelled incorrectly*)   =   0 points
3. astronaut (*astronaut spelled correctly*)   =   9 points

TOTAL = 16 POINTS

Students score both the number of words spelled correctly and the number of letters in the words spelled correctly. From the example above, the student would record the data on the Word Study Record Sheet (Figure 5–2). This Word Study Record Sheet is stapled to the inside of the Word Study folder. Each day the student records the number of words spelled correctly and the number of letters in the correct words. Misspelled words are listed in the Review Words column.

Some teachers prefer an oral test to the daily written test. Students find partners, exchange notebooks, and spell their selected words orally. As one student spells a word orally, the partner makes a small check above each letter said in the proper sequence. This checking is done in the Word Study notebook.

HOMEWORK

The minimum nightly homework assignment is for students to team test the spelling words selected for that lesson. Students should be encouraged to study the words in their review list column. When students design their own homework assignments, they gain a greater sense of control over their learning activities. Some students will accept responsibility for challenging themselves with words not on the chart completed in class. Others will only want to spell the words they selected to spell in class. Still other students, who spelled the chart words correctly, should be encouraged to select new words from their reading, other chart words, or words that the teacher might suggest. To trust in a student's competence as a decision maker helps motivate him or her in the strongest way possible.

Beyond the nightly spelling test, there are suggested homework extension activities in many of the lessons. These activities offer a variety of ways to involve students and their parents/partners in Word Study. Teachers may decide to change, elaborate, replace, or omit these extended homework activities. Homework can be individualized to meet the needs of students and to address their ability to study independently. Homework assignments are meant to be not only concise and easy to check, but meaningful.

Remember, homework is more than just spelling words correctly. Homework assignments should include the use of a variety of materials easily accessible to children at home, such as cereal boxes or bread containers, magazines, newspapers, and books. An example of expanding an activity could be asking students to list the names of plants found in their house, classroom or yard when the topic is plants.

Each night students complete the assignment in their Word Study notebooks. These notebooks should be signed by their study partner. A study partner may be a parent, another relative, or any significant adult in their lives. Not only does this person take an active role in the student's learning experiences, but he or she also is able to observe each day's work as it is recorded in the notebook and to monitor the child's progress. Parents/partners become familiar with what is expected and appreciate the suggestions for assisting with the student's learning. Whether they give a short oral test of that day's word list or only sign the child's homework, parents/partners are positively reinforcing the child's learning. (See Chapter 6 for a fuller discussion of homework and the selection of partners.)

Some teachers ask students to open their notebooks to the previous night's homework the first thing each day, and they quickly check it. After a few weeks this will become routine; because students know what to expect, the responsibility for being prepared becomes theirs.

A REVIEW OF THE STEPS

What happens during this thirty-minute module? Every day the basic procedures are the same. The following outlines these lesson procedures.

1. The Spelling and the Other Emphases are presented.

2. The reading material to be used in the lesson is distributed.

3. Students read to locate words they can associate with the focus.

4. Students volunteer words and teacher writes them on a chart. Class discusses words.

5. Students practice handwriting.

6. Students respond in writing.

7. Students select words to spell.

8. Students team test.

9. Students score, record test results, and file papers in folders.

10. Homework is assigned.

▶ Other Things to Consider

DECIDING THE SPELLING EMPHASIS FOR LESSONS 131–180

Beginning with Lesson 131, there will not be a suggested Spelling Emphasis. Teachers may choose to review a letter cluster or focus on new letter combinations that do not appear in earlier lessons. Some classes find that after the class chart is made, some letters or other features of the words suggest an emphasis. Such choices broaden the opportunities for student involvement in the lesson design. The chart in Figure 5–3 was developed by students using newspapers to locate words related to *flight*, the Other Emphasis for Lesson 141.

During the chart development, students pointed out the fact that certain words had to be capitalized as they were written on the chart. This prompted a discussion of proper nouns as naming particular persons, places, or things. After the chart had been completed, the teacher asked volunteers to underline the words on the chart that were proper nouns. The words on the chart revealed an emphasis (Proper Nouns) that had not been planned beforehand. Other options for the Spelling Emphasis might have been compound words or suffixes. In Lessons 131 through 180, the decision to have a spelling emphasis is made by the teacher and the students. This decision

Figure 5-3

CLASS CHART

March 5 Flight		
military	tower	aviation
crews	Domestic Airlines	US Air
smoking	competition	British Airways
KLM Royal Dutch Airways	rise	above
	combat	airport
Northwest Airlines	United Airlines	
traveling	transportation	

is made either before the chart is developed or during the chart development. Sometimes the teacher may choose to have no Spelling Emphasis and only use the Other Emphasis suggested in the lesson.

WORD STUDY NOTEBOOK

A spiral notebook for each student is suggested. Each day students will use a new sheet to list the selected test words and do the writing assignment. If the test is taken orally, the checked words are in the notebook with the classwork; if the test is written on a separate sheet of paper, the checked test paper is filed each day in a folder designated for Word Study. The classwork and homework assignments remain in the notebook until the notebook is completely filled, at which time it may be stored in the student's file in a box labeled Word Study Module. After a notebook has been filled, the student begins a new one.

INAPPROPRIATE WORDS

What about inappropriate words? If a student suggests a word that he or she cannot relate to the vocabulary emphasis or one that does not have the spelling emphasis, what happens? Often, teachers write the word on the chalkboard beside the chart and explain why this word is not appropriate. Through discussion, students will understand the reasons for not putting the word on the chart. Teachers should quickly move on with the chart development and follow the same procedure for unacceptable language or profanity.

PACE AND TIME MANAGEMENT

John Thomas

Chart making is fun; teachers and students both enjoy this part of the lesson. Experienced SUCCESS teachers acknowledge that it is tempting to continue a lively lesson, and yet, they caution teachers to remember the schedule and try not to spend extra time on the chart. There are other modules and other subjects to be taught during the school day. Spending more than thirty to thirty-five minutes on any one module will be at the expense of others. Those wonderful "teachable moments" will arise often. Students frequently have more words to volunteer than time permits for writing on the chart. Encourage the students to put these words on their spelling lists to study or include them in their writing.

ENCOURAGING STUDENT PARTICIPATION

If some students are not volunteering words, the teacher needs to encourage (not threaten) them privately: "Find a word today. I'd like to call on you to help make the chart."

Perhaps he or she might suggest, "Tomorrow, I hope you will find a word for the chart. Let me know if you do, so I'll be sure and call on you." For students having more difficulty, the teacher may need to move to their desks and quietly assist them in locating words for a few days until they develop the confidence to do this on their own.

Toby Edwards

CHART REVIEW TEST

An option in the Word Study module is the Chart Review Test suggested every fifth day. The teacher may suggest a particular focus for the review test, asking students to select the words they think are most important for the review or those they did not select previously as test words. The lists are almost always individual tests with each student selecting his or her words; the teacher may select some of the words occasionally. The number of words spelled for the Review Test varies from student to student.

After the words for the list have been identified, the students should be given the opportunity to study the words either as partners or in small groups. If the test will be for grades, the teacher may decide to let the students study the words at home before giving the test. The Review Tests can be checked by either the teacher or by student partners following the same procedure as for daily spelling test. These Chart Review Tests can be used as a measurement tool for grades since the students have selected their own lists and have had exposure to them.

The Chart Review Test is optional and is used at the teacher's discretion. The frequency of the test is also up to the teacher. It is included in the SUCCESS program as a built-in review of the words being introduced to the students.

WHAT TO DO WITH THE CHARTS

The charts generated each day should be displayed for a minimum of five days as individual charts, each one visible for students to use. After five days the charts may be stapled together to form a week of charts. These in turn may be stapled together as a month of charts and displayed permanently for students to refer to when they need to spell a word on a previous chart. Some teachers have space to hang more than five charts. Others find unique ways to display more charts, such as stringing wire or clothesline across the room and using clothespins to hang the charts. The more visible and accessible the charts are for the students, the more useful they become. "We live in a dictionary," declared a student in a SUCCESS classroom. The charts become part of the print-rich environment and are an additional resource for the students to use in all other classwork.

The charts also become prized possessions. Some teachers wait until the end of the year to give the charts to students. Others give them out at the end of a grading period. Some teachers write the name of a student on each daily chart and later present it to the student.

▶ Adapting Word Study to the Needs of the Students

Because the students are reading from a variety of materials to find words, the charts represent a broader range of words than would be found in a spelling book. The range in difficulty meets the needs of both the most academically gifted students and most reluctant learners without limiting any student.

MAKING CHANGES

SUCCESS teachers are encouraged to be decision makers who trust their abilities and professional knowledge to direct student learning. This means that on any given day the lesson presented in the SUCCESS manual may be freely adapted to students' needs. The teacher is the decision maker and, within that context, the professional willing to justify what is right for the students.

How does this work? The teacher has been using SUCCESS for several weeks and is feeling comfortable with the basic, nonnegotiable structure of the lessons. The class is beginning a science unit on space. Word Study, Lesson 38, gives *authors* as the Other Emphasis and *or* as the Spelling Emphasis. The teacher decides instead of the Other Emphasis to introduce the vocabulary words for the science unit on space, while keeping the Spelling Emphasis suggested in the Lesson. The material for this first day might be the science textbook. Students would read to find the vocabulary words the teacher writes on the chart; or he or she may ask the students to read pages in the textbook to locate words they think are important in this unit. After the chart is completed, the teacher decides which words are basic for understanding the subject of space and words the students will be expected to know. The teacher might identify these words as important and suggest that each student include some of them in their writing and spelling activity. The teacher has made decisions that help students direct their learning without taking away their ownership of the words they will learn. During the writing part of the lesson, the teacher might suggest that students write the meanings for each word they do not know and write a sentence demonstrating their understanding of the words they do know.

Because of the importance or number of words to be learned, on the second day of this sequence of lessons, the teacher decides to continue using space as the Other Emphasis. He or she might add the Spelling Emphasis *ph* to introduce words relating to space study, such as *atmosphere, troposphere, exosphere,* and *hemisphere.* The selection of *ph* is a deliberate decision because the teacher has noticed many words in the unit with *ph.* He or she wants to introduce the *ph* as a unique letter combination with a sound different from the separate letters. The base word *sphere* was also clearly important to understanding the content in this science unit.

BENEFITS

In other lessons, the Other Emphasis suggested might include words related to the oral reading selection, words about an important news event, words that relate to a suggested writing topic, or words from another content-area subject. This integration of vocabulary from other modules and subjects offers opportunities for students to make connections and for the teacher to tailor each lesson to students' needs. Teachers decide what is immediate, relevant, and useful for their classes.

What does this integration with other subjects or modules accomplish? Students become more aware of the importance of vocabulary development. They begin to see the words on the chart as something more than just a list of words to spell. Students are provided with opportunities to use these words in both their oral and written communication. Students begin to feel ownership of their vocabulary and a sense of control and security from their increased understanding. Once they feel at ease with their vocabulary, the applications and connections they will make are endless. These student applications and connections signal real learning.

▶ Evaluate and Assess

By far, the most important measure of a student's learning is observed in all written work throughout the day and, indeed, throughout the year. Daily spelling tests filed in the folders and the writing in Word Study notebooks are sources for grades. These sources reveal a student's ability to learn to spell words and use them properly. Students should know that the teacher is assessing word usage in their daily writings. Some teachers write the following messages:

"I am looking for the difficulty of the words you select to spell. Don't always select the easiest words. Challenge yourself."

"I am looking to see how you use these words in other assignments."

"I will be determining whether or not you can recognize misspelled words in your compositions and make corrections when you revise and edit."

Revised and edited compositions and reports should also be considered as sources for spelling grades. Students again need to understand that spelling in the context of one's own writing is something that counts. The importance of spelling is not a test list on Friday. In and of itself the mechanical skill of spelling is totally useless if students cannot think and make connections from the word to ideas and concepts.

▶ Decisions

TEACHER CHOICES

On any given day, the teacher makes the following choices:

1. to use the Spelling Emphasis suggested or change it to meet other identified needs of the class;

2. to use the Other Emphasis suggested or change it to correlate with a content area or any topic of interest;

3. to let the students have an open response or make specific suggestions for written responses;

4. to add words to the chart for the students to spell or not;

5. to have students take written or oral tests;

6. to use the suggested resource or change it;

7. to assign partners for spelling tests or let the students select their own;

8. to give additional homework assignments or not;

9. to have whole-class chart review tests/assessments or individual chart review tests/assessments;

10. to allow students to include words not on the chart or not.

STUDENT CHOICES

In the course of each daily Word Study lesson, the students decide

1. which words to volunteer for the chart;

2. the associations and connections they will make to the Other Emphasis;

3. which words to spell and how many words to spell;

4. how they will respond to the chart in the writing activity;

5. their partner for the spelling test;

6. to take an oral or a written test;

7. their homework lists for team testing.

▶ In Summary

The main focus of this module is, as the title indicates, Word Study. The value of this module is expanding vocabularies, building new concepts, and encouraging creative thinking, not simply putting every letter in every word in its proper place. Of course, phonics will be learned through the Spelling Emphases and oral pronunciation and discussion, but phonics is not the primary focus. The SUCCESS program is building thinking communicators, not just spellers.

Chapter 6 Evaluation, Communication, and Materials

An interesting thing happens when teachers dare to take control of their classrooms and the curriculum. They accept that teaching is their responsibility, and they are willing to be accountable for the results of their efforts. When teachers believe in what and how they are teaching, they have an added edge. Commitment shows in their teaching. They have made the decisions about how to work with their students and see the results in their classrooms. When these results are positive, it is easy to spot. When the results are less than hoped for, teachers revise their plans, search for different strategies with some credible basis of success, and try again.

When SUCCESS teachers get together at conferences and workshops, they show renewed interest and enthusiasm for their profession. They are upbeat, intensely involved, and anxious to know more about the latest research and how to improve as professionals. They want to share their latest children's book discovery, writing projects that generated excitement, and how a research topic led to integrated learning. They ask for suggestions for handling instructional and behavioral problems. Through interaction with their colleagues, personal efforts, and knowledge about how their students learn, a program evolves which is their own. They have a great interest in making it work.

This chapter is all about what happens as teachers move from the basics of how to teach the modules to making SUCCESS their own. Some of the topics and issues most frequently discussed when SUCCESS teachers get together for conferences, workshops, and teaching seminars are presented.

▶ Assess and Evaluate

One of the most frequently asked questions is "Where do I get the grades?" The record-keeping emphasis in this program is on performance, evidence of progress, and positive self-concept on the part of students who realize they are enjoying learning.

Ideally, assessment begins with allowing students to demonstrate their strengths and weaknesses through their reading and writing. Teachers then facilitate learning opportunities that allow students to build on their strengths and to improve areas of weakness through consistent feedback. More simply stated, on the first day of school a teacher looks at a class and asks, "What do these students know? What do they need to know? What do they want to know? How will I help them learn?"

Through consistent observation and documentation of demonstrated applied knowledge, the teacher is able to determine a student's needs and progress more accurately. After a few days in a SUCCESS classroom, the teacher has several pieces of writing, observation notes, and conversations with students that are clues to what students already know, to what they need help to learn, and to how they learn.

SUCCESS teachers address these needs through the lessons provided or they change the lessons. Each interaction with a student offers an op-

Ben Bridwell

portunity for individual instruction in response to his or her needs. With this approach to instruction, assessment and reporting are backed up with concrete evidence of student performance. The student folders from each module, records of books read, research presentations, and published writings are all sources for evaluating student progress. Combined with teacher observations and notes, these provide more information about each student's reading and writing abilities and progress than any standardized, criterion-reference, or fill-in-the-blank tests.

In Chapters 2 through 4 are specific suggestions for evaluating student progress. (See Evaluate and Assess sections in Chapters 2–4.) Teachers will choose what is important for evaluation and develop their own system for dealing with grading requirements. SUCCESS recognizes the importance of the teacher's professional judgment. Teachers new to SUCCESS may feel uncomfortable and unsure about this aspect of the assessment process. With experience and constant interaction with students, teachers will find themselves looking more closely at students and their work and less at artificial numbers in a grade book. They will come to trust themselves.

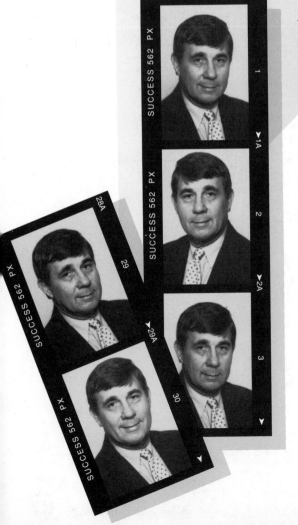

As a school administrator, I have seen the SUCCESS program literally "light up" children. When children sense that their interests and contributions are important in the learning process, they tend to try harder. The use of everyday materials (newspapers, magazines, library books, etc.) enhances the world of reading for children and helps them to understand that reading is something you do everywhere, not just in school during reading class.

Dr. Thomas J. Silvester, superintendent

▶ Talking to Parents

SUCCESS, in all likelihood, is different from the way most parents were taught to read and write and from how their child may have been taught in the past. It is important that parents know and understand the *SUCCESS in Reading and Writing* approach to helping their child grow as a reader, writer, and thinker. Communication between parents and teacher should be consistent and ongoing throughout the school year.

On the first day of the school year, most SUCCESS teachers send a letter to parents such as Figure 6-1. In the letter they explain the SUCCESS philosophy and briefly describe what will be happening in each of the module lessons.

Figure 6-1

LETTER TO PARENTS

Dear Family,

Your child is involved in an innovative and creative program for teaching language arts—SUCCESS in Reading and Writing.

This program does not depend on a basal reader alone to teach reading skills. Working as a class and individually, students participate each day in two hours of language arts instruction. During this time they both read a wide variety of materials and produce their own writing.

The program consists of four modules, or lessons. These modules are

RESEARCH
This lesson helps students become familiar with all types of printed materials by reading and workng with magazines, newspapers, encyclopedias, and textbooks. Students learn how to look for important information and make use of that information. Comprehension skills are also sharpened.

RECREATIONAL READING
This lesson allows students to read in a variety of printed materials on an individual basis. These include readers, other textbooks, library and paperback books, and newspapers. The teacher holds individual and group conferences to check on and develop comprehension skills.

WRITING
This lesson teaches students skills involving listening, speaking, reading, and writing. The main emphasis is on writing in many forms. Including sentences, paragraphs, stories, letters, poems, and factual articles.

WORD STUDY
This lesson teaches students word attack skills, spelling, sentence structure, thinking skills, vocabulary development, and handwriting.

Parents and friends are always welcome in the classroom, either to help out or just watch. Please let me know when you would like to come and visit. Also, if you have any questions about the program, please call me.

Sincerely,

Allison L. Gardiner

P.S. We are in need of magazines, especially news magazines such as <u>Time</u>, <u>U.S.</u> <u>News</u> <u>&</u> <u>World</u> <u>Report</u> and <u>Newsweek</u>. If you have any you would like to send to school, they would be greatly appreciated. (<u>Better</u> <u>Homes</u> <u>&</u> <u>Gardens</u>, <u>Country</u> <u>Living</u>, etc.)

Figure 6-2

NEWSLETTER

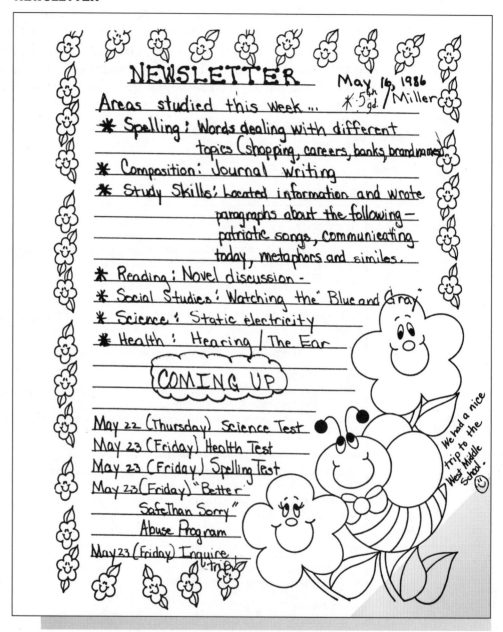

Some SUCCESS teachers invite parents to a Parents' Night at the school. There, the teacher explains the four SUCCESS modules, gives a brief demonstration in which the parents play the roles of students, and lets parents examine their child's work. The teacher responds to questions and comments.

A weekly class newsletter that includes examples of student writing, the research topics, and lists of books being read is another way SUCCESS teachers and their students keep parents informed about what is happening. Suggestions to parents on how they can reinforce classroom activities may be included, also. Figure 6–2 is an example of such a newsletter.

During parent-teacher conferences, the teacher will be using the folders of student's writing and other work to help parents understand the progress and needs of their child. This is the clearest, most important reporting that takes place. Most parents find more meaning in a conversation about their child's work with the teacher than looking at grades on a report card.

Teachers need to show parents their notes, checklists, and other records. Teachers must communicate to parents the extensive knowledge they have about their children. Videotaping SUCCESS lessons is an excellent way to help parents and others understand what happens in a SUCCESS classroom. Some schools have produced school or school district videos with parents as participants.

There are many opportunities to involve parents directly with SUCCESS and the daily activities in the classroom. Parents can help secure materials and resources. They can listen to students read. They can assist with book publishing. The invitation to participate is often all that parents need to become involved with and supportive of what is happening in the classroom. Parents can even be involved in an evaluation of SUCCESS. Figure 6–3 shows a letter written to a fifth-grade SUCCESS teacher.

Parents appreciate being informed of what is happening in the daily school life of their child, but more important, they appreciate a happy, motivated learner. A teacher's best communication to parents comes through their child.

▶ Homework

SUCCESS homework is intended to be HOMEFUN! It emphasizes vocabulary development and the rich, exciting world of language usage. A sense of familiarity and comfort with words only develops through usage—oral, written, and visual. Homework assignments are designed to be concise, simple to check, and most important, meaningful. The SUCCESS program supports the concept of homework each night of the school week (or at least Monday through Thursday nights). For this reason, a suggested basic assignment appears with each lesson in the Word Study module.

Many lessons at the beginning of the year have specific suggestions for homework assignments beyond the team test with a partner. For example, Lesson 11 suggests that, in addition to team testing words, students make a list of family members and their favorite leisure activity. This homework assignment ties into both the Word Study lesson and the Writing lesson. It is always understood that students team test words and have their Word Study notebooks signed nightly.

Beyond the nightly spelling test in Word Study, teachers and students may design homework extension activities in other modules. Teachers may add homework assignments in any module as needed.

It is important to encourage parents/partners to read with students and to have conversations about what they read. Discussing the meanings of words and doing activities like word games that facilitate language development are also suggested. Parents and students sharing a pleasant learning time is the most important goal.

Figure 6-3

LETTER TO A SUCCESS TEACHER

Dear Mrs. Miller,

Thank you for introducing our child to Success. Hamil loves to read. Her comprehension of the material has given her the self-confidence to express her feelings in writing.

Because of the use of many media — newspapers, magazines, etc., Hamil seems to accept reading as an intricate part of many daily activities and doesn't shy away from written material in other fields. Instead, she faces them as new and interesting challenges. Her mastering of vocabulary furthers her confidence in pursuing more difficult reading material.

In summary, this program in our opinion has led the way for a non intimidated desire to learn through reading for our child. Our only disappointment was that it was not available when we were in school.

Sincerely,
Mr and Mrs. W. P. Pearsall Jr.

It is necessary to understand the students' home situations and to suggest appropriate times and places for homework study as well as suitable partners. When parents are not available to be active partners in their child's learning experiences, substitutes might include older brothers or sisters; after-school care-givers or baby-sitters; business people or community volunteers; volunteer retirees.

Including the parent or other adult is very significant, since not only will they take an active role in the student's learning, but they also will observe each day's work and monitor the child's progress. SUCCESS teachers may wish to explain the important role of parents/partners during parent-teacher conferences or in a letter sent to each one at the beginning of the year. The actual time required of the parent/partner need not be lengthy because the homework is designed to be short, with clear directions, and easily shared with others.

Letting students design their own homework gives them ownership of their learning activities. When students are doing research projects, they may want to make models and posters or develop other extensions of their reports as homework in addition to their group project. Students should be encouraged to read material of their own choice each night. For many students, this trust in their competence as decision makers is a greater motivation than grades.

▶ Building a Community of Learners

In SUCCESS, working together as a class or in nonthreatening and non-competitive teams and groups (cooperative learning) is a basic instructional strategy. It is integral to each SUCCESS lesson, not a frill or a reward. SUCCESS provides numerous opportunities for students to interact with each other in helpful, meaningful, and supportive ways. The emphasis is on students developing an understanding of what is required for people to work together.

Current research suggests that cooperative learning allows for the following:

- Greater mastery and retention of material (Cooperative discussion of reading passages increases retention of reading content.)
- Positive attitudes toward the experience (Cooperative groups produce more and better ideas than do individuals working alone or competitively.)
- Improved intergroup relation: "People who cooperate learn to like and appreciate each other." (Cooperative discussion improves problem solving behavior. People enjoy working together.)
- Increased self-esteem
- Greater acceptance of mainstreamed students

"One for all and all for one" becomes an understood motto for such classrooms. In the Word Study module, developing the chart and team testing spelling lists is a time for students to learn from and help each other. The proofreading and sharing in the Writing module also involves reciprocal learning. The many different kinds of team and group work in Research and the book talks and sharing in the Recreational Reading module are all examples of times when the classroom becomes a community of learners.

▶ SUCCESS and Technology

Many teachers already incorporate computers into the daily SUCCESS plan. There is a wide range of software and technology available for creative teaching. However, the final gain will be determined by *how* the student and teacher *interact* and utilize the technology.

WORD PROCESSING AND DESKTOP PUBLISHING SOFTWARE

Word processing programs would seem to be a natural way to develop the reading/writing connection in the SUCCESS classroom. Virtually any

Writing lesson can be completed at a computer, and both teachers and students are usually excited about the possibilities. Many programs address the obvious advantages of editing on the computer and producing more legible first drafts, as well as elevated self-esteem and pride in the final publication. With regular computer use and well-designed software, elementary students can use word processing effectively, especially in the revising and editing stages. The students need the writing time to think, to formulate their ideas, and to share their experiences in their own words. Teachers will still need to move among the students at the computers to respond to their writing and to help them clarify their thoughts.

Desktop publishing programs extend word processing capabilities. Teachers find it useful to have students use these programs to create books, magazines, newspapers, posters, and pamphlets, complete with mastheads, headlines, columns, and graphic designs. The computer does the time-consuming work of layouts and column structure. Some SUCCESS teachers might very well find that students can produce their articles in the Writing lessons and then use the desktop publishing program to type the final drafts for a professional-looking publication, ready to be copied, displayed, and distributed. Student-written newspapers are great for communicating with parents and administrators.

ENCYCLOPEDIA/RESEARCH SOFTWARE

The increasing availability of technology products has opened new doors for student researchers. Extensive video libraries and computer software on nonfiction topics are a part of many media centers today. Complete encyclopedias are computerized, and laser videodiscs offer a multimedia approach to a wide range of topics for Research lessons. Student presentations may be enhanced by Hypermedia programs that can compile and integrate video, text, graphics, and sound into exciting final products. Interactive software allows students to create time lines, graphs, crossword puzzles, word finds, and charts to present their information. The combination of the motivational appeal of computers and the up-to-date information available in quality software programs adds an extra dimension to research resources. SUCCESS teachers have discovered the power of the electronic page as partners work at computers during the Research module.

Chris Held, a SUCCESS teacher in Bellevue, Washington, assisted students in creating a database of books read by the class in Recreational Reading (*SUCCESS Stories,* Spring, 1988). Students decided on what information they wanted to enter, including their name, the title of the book, author, number of pages, and their evaluation of the book. Students created scales for rating the book and its readability. Students would then use the database to help them select a book. (They entered 587 books!)

Libby Pollett and Debbie Head, SUCCESS teachers from Shelbyville, Kentucky, have had enthusiastic responses from their class when using the computer monitor as an electronic Word Study Chart, typing the words students volunteer and then printing copies for writing and spelling activities.

Kristy Kay Cheatwood

LANGUAGE AND READING SOFTWARE

SUCCESS teachers might find some language and reading skills programs useful for diagnostic purposes, for lesson design, and as a management tool. A teacher could identify and insert proofreading skills into the Writing mini-lessons based on the results of student performance on language usage programs. Such performance might also help determine areas on which to focus in Recreational Reading conversations.

However, because most of these programs isolate language and reading skills from the natural speaking and writing of the student, they seldom reflect a student's true understanding. When a student uses the skill successfully in his or her own writing and speaking, then mastery is demonstrated. Such mastery will be best observed by the teacher throughout the day in the students' progress in writing, spelling, and reading of real-life printed matter and books.

Specific computer applications for special needs students as well as for regular students can be integrated into every classroom. The creative use of technology can be a part of any instructional program, and student-generated products connecting stories and research reports from the word processor, computer graphics, and videotaping and/or slide shows are realistic products that blend well with the SUCCESS philosophy.

▶ Materials and Resources

There are some basic materials needed to begin using *SUCCESS in Reading and Writing*. A detailed description of what is needed is also given in each module chapter. Here are the basics:

- a minimum of four manila folders per student for storing their work;
- chart paper, magic markers, masking tape;
- one spiral notebook per student for use in the Word Study module;
- writing materials available to students at all times—paper and pencils;
- project and special presentation materials—poster board, glue, scissors, colored pencils, and markers;

- two copies of *SUCCESS in Reading and Writing* for the teacher—one for home and sharing, and one for use as the daily lesson guide;
- storage boxes for folders.

Resources must come from all facets of real life. They should be varied in both reading difficulty and content. The purpose is to teach students to read any material they encounter and need or want to read.

CLASSROOM RESOURCES

The following is a list of the resources found in most SUCCESS classrooms:

- one adult dictionary for each student;
- various mathematics, science, social studies, health, and music textbooks—grade levels two through six;
- at least two to three subscriptions to a newspaper per school day, August through May;
- magazines and journals on various subjects and topics;
- one set of encyclopedias per classroom;
- thesauruses;
- maps, catalogues, telephone books, forms, "survival" reading materials such as contracts, leases, and applications;
- a minimum of fifty library books every three weeks should be checked out in the name of the class;
- multi-media resources such as videos, computer software, and filmstrips.

Some teachers will have resources available that other teachers will not have. Not all schools or classrooms are equally funded. The teachers of some SUCCESS classes ask friends, parents of students in their classes, and others to save and donate newspapers, magazines, telephone books, maps, encyclopedias, and other needed resources for their classes. With the current trend for businesses to become more directly involved with education, a source for resources might be local or regional companies.

Teachers should never omit a lesson or a module because of a lack of resources. It is better to substitute what is available or borrow from and share with colleagues. Looking ahead and planning for future lessons is a big help.

FILING AND STORING STUDENT WORK

The use of file folders is a convenient method for keeping up with students' work in each of the four modules. Some teachers have students use spiral notebooks instead of file folders for organizing work.

In some SUCCESS classrooms the students keep the folders in their desks for daily filing and then move their work to boxes of folders at the end of the week or the end of a grading period. In other classrooms, the students file their papers after each lesson in boxes where their folders are kept. The number of boxes provided per module is a teacher decision. Here are some helpful tips from veteran SUCCESS teachers:

SUCCESS reaches everyone; the students are enthused and genuinely like school. Busy work and grading are *past*—evaluation is easier because every moment you are *teaching*.

Margaret H. Turlington, teacher

- Divide the boxes alphabetically so that the traffic flow around each box is not so hectic.
- Place the storage boxes in different areas of the room to control traffic flow.
- Use colored file folders to separate the modules or groups.
- Designate (and rotate) student representatives to file papers for an entire group.

The most important thing is for teachers to design a method that is workable for them and their students and allows for efficient filing.

▶ Extensions

The creativity of SUCCESS teachers is forever abundant. Once they grasp the basics of SUCCESS, they are off and running with ways to expand and enrich the reading and writing experiences of their students. The ideas that follow are examples of such extensions of SUCCESS.

WORD OF THE WEEK

A student's vocabulary is always growing. Vocabulary development evolves naturally when students are exposed to words and a print-rich environment. With SUCCESS, vocabulary development takes place in each of the modules. Many teachers can create additional opportunities for vocabulary expansion by introducing new words daily or weekly and giving a brief two- to three-minute Word Talk on the Word of the Week. As the students learn this technique for introducing words to the class, they can be encouraged to give the Word Talks. Words such as *capitalism, rendezvous,* and *tempestuous* are examples of Words of the Week from different SUCCESS classrooms. The teacher or student explains why the particular word was selected, what the word means, and gives an example of the use of the word in context with other words. Students are encouraged to introduce the word to their families each time there is a Word Talk.

Some teachers set aside special bulletin board areas to display these words. After the words are presented, they are displayed for students to use in their writing and speaking. Some students also choose to include them in their spelling list. If tag board, sentence strips, and markers are available, some students might make a word card to take home with them.

SUCCESS WRITERS' CONFERENCES

Students need a purpose for writing, an audience, and response to their published works. A natural extension of the Writing module has been the creation of Writers' Conferences. In SUCCESS classrooms the first such conferences take place when students have completed works that are shared in groups of three to five. Students learn to appreciate the recognition and rewards of being an author. After some classroom experience, the students want to expand their audience. This may lead to sharing with other classes or a special evening for parents and other invited guests. Some school systems invite students to participate in district Writers' Conferences.

Teachers who are interested in providing experiences beyond the classroom for their students will want to plan ahead. Some guidelines for arranging Writers' Conferences include the following:

1. Practice author sharing strategies with the students. Ask *why* they chose to write on a topic, *how* they get ideas, and to *tell about* their writing techniques.

2. Form a planning committee of teachers, students, and parents.

3. Invite published authors to attend the conference and share their writing and experiences as authors with students and guests.

4. Arrange to have one adult per six to seven students to facilitate discussion. These people need to meet prior to the conference for some discussion of their roles and the goals of the conference.

5. Invite businesses to be partners in this effort. Ask them to provide such things as pencils, pens, tablets, and gifts for participants. Businesses can also provide spaces for public displays of students' work.

6. Involve newspapers, radio, and television in the publicity of the SUCCESS Writers' Conference. Students can make posters for display throughout the school community.

The Wisdom Pearl

Written and Illustrated
by: Brian Hauser

You are hiking in the woods. You come to a thicket and try to climb over it. Instead, you seem to fall ~through~ the thicket and find yourself falling in an unknown world. You land on a funny-looking man who tells you to come with him. If you decide to go with him, turn to page 10. If not, turn to page 7.

About the Author

Brian Hauser lives in Carrboro N.C. This is his 2nd book. He likes choose-your-own-adventure books. Brian likes the fact that you can control some of your actions in them If he writes any more books, one of them will probably be the choose-your-own-adventure type.

Brian Hauser

7. Arrange a location that is easily accessible, provides adequate spaces for small groups to read and discuss their writings, and a space for a larger group to meet.

Teachers can be creative in designing opportunities for students to share their writing. Vary the types of programs and audiences. Tailor the conferences to meet the needs of the students as developing authors.

STUDENT PUBLICATION CENTERS

Throughout the year, students will be revising and publishing writings. Anything that is edited, revised, and rewritten and then shared or displayed is considered published writing. This varies from the simplest form of publications—the student or class booklet stapled together with a cover—to the bound book complete with illustrations and hardback covers. Because making books becomes an exciting way for students to share their writing and creativity, a publication center motivates students to work toward authorship. Parent volunteers are a valuable resource for setting up this center and providing assistance when students are ready to publish. When students have a completed manuscript, parents can help them put together the hardback cover, plan page breaks and illustrations, and sew the pages. In some publication centers, typewriters and computers are available to students and parents. More detailed instructions are outlined in Figure 6–4. This is only one suggestion for binding hardback books.

NEW WAYS WITH CHARTS

"Do students get tired of making a Word Study chart each day?" Surprisingly, they do not. On the surface, the structure of the Word Study module does not change. What does change is the student response to new words, spelling patterns, and ideas.

New emphases for charts will often be suggested by students and by class events. A particularly involving read-aloud selection will prompt a chart to record characters, interesting phrases and descriptions, or an exciting sequence of events.

A class field trip to the art museum might prompt a before-and-after list of interesting sights and events on the trip. Such a list is a way to prepare students on what to expect and to find out what impressed them after the trip.

Sometimes students want to use one day's chart to list important words, phrases, or concepts from a unit of study as a review before a test. Students become involved in making their own study notes and practice spelling and using the content words before the test. Asking the students to volunteer and elaborate on important ideas learned during the unit helps the teacher evaluate comprehension and effectiveness of the learning, while making the students responsible for their own review.

Special class projects also lend themselves to chart emphases, such as a class alphabet book about space, or "our town." Teachers become comfortable with the basic idea that words used in the classroom, found in print,

Figure 6-4

BOOKMAKING INSTRUCTIONS

Materials for Hardback Books

2 pieces cardboard or packing board, 6" x 9"
plastic book tape or binding tape
wallpaper or other covering paper
rubber cement glue
5-10 sheets of paper (ditto, bond, etc.)
needle and thread or dental floss

ruler
scissors
paper clips
cellophane tape, optional

Bookmaking Steps:

1. *Cover the cardboard pieces with wallpaper.*

    Line up the wallpaper with one edge of the cardboard and glue with rubber cement. Cut the corners off and glue edges to the inside of the cardboard, pulling the covers tight to make smooth edges and sharp corners. Use tape to help hold the edges in place as they dry (optional).

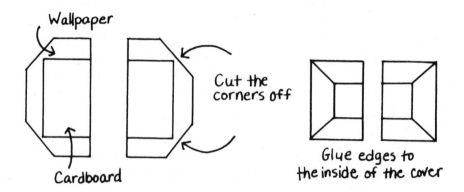

2. *Tape the covered cardboard pieces together.*

    Cut a piece of book tape about 13-14" long and tape the cover pieces together, leaving about 1/4" space between the covers for the gutter of the book. (The number of pages in the book will determine how much space is needed for the gutter. Usually about 1/4" is ample.)

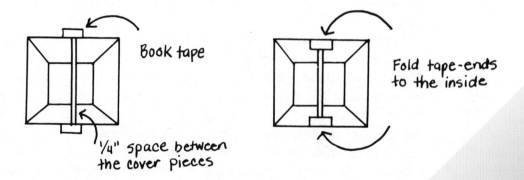

BOOKMAKING INSTRUCTIONS

3. *Sew together the pages and end pages to make a booklet.*

Fold the sheets of paper for the pages of the book in half to form a booklet (5 1/2" x 9"). Put the pages together, one inside the other.
Fold 2 pieces of construction paper into a 6" x 9" rectangle and put the pages inside the construction paper sheets, forming a cover for the booklet of pages.

Open the booklet flat. Use paper clips to help hold the pages firmly so that the fold stays together as you punch holes down the centerfold about 1" apart. Use a large darning needle or other needle. The holes should go through the pages and the construction paper.

Thread a needle with heavy thread or dental floss, about 20-30" long. Begin on the back of the construction paper side of the pages at one end. Tape the knotted end of the thread to the construction paper to keep it from pulling through as you sew. Sew to the end of the pages, and then continue sewing to return to the starting place, using an over under stitch, pulling the thread tight after each stitch. End the sewing on the back side of the booklet with a knot, and tape the knotted thread for extra strength.

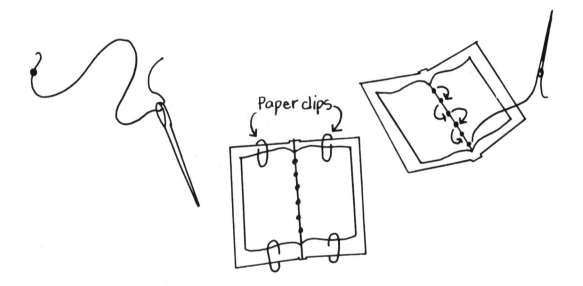

Paper clips

4. *Glue the pages and end pages booklet to the cover.*

Before you glue the booklet of pages into the book covers, put it into the book covers to make sure it will fit exactly. Sometimes trimming on a paper cutter will adjust any edges that are slightly long.

Put glue on the inside of the front cover and in the tape gutter of the book. Glue the construction paper cover to the cardboard, forming the inside of the cover. (The other piece of construction forms the end pages and is not glued.)

Press out any wrinkles, and glue the back cover in the same way. Glue completely to the edges to insure sharp edges that will last. Let dry.

and suggested by the students are worth learning. It is not difficult to adapt the chart, making time for the needs and interests of the class and keeping student involvement and motivation high.

Some SUCCESS teachers use simple variations in materials for making special charts. These might include using orange and black markers at Halloween, using colored paper for charts, using shape charts, letting students occasionally illustrate words or whole charts. Teachers can be creative. If a teacher decides a variation is appropriate, is a meaningful addition to Word Study, and doesn't interfere with the basic goals of this module, he or she should add the personal touch. Sometimes students will have great ideas to extend chart making.

▶ In Summary

SUCCESS promotes high expectations for students and teachers. Every day students read books of their choice. They write about things they choose to write about. They develop lifelong learning skills through research projects. The student is respected as a learner, and the teacher is respected as a professional who is capable of making myriad decisions throughout the day to direct the learning of the students. These basic premises foster a joyful community of learners. Welcome to a natural way of learning!

SUCCES**S**
in Reading and Writing
Second Edition

These lesson plans were designed as daily suggestions and starting points for each of the four modules described in the previous chapters. Teachers should use, adapt, or replace them as necessary. Blank lines indicate many opportunities for teachers to substitute different themes for the ones suggested. What should remain is the basic objective and structure of each module described below.

Research
In the Research module students practice the processes of locating, organizing, and sharing information. They learn to use a wide range of resources as they expand their knowledge.

Recreational Reading
Students read books of their choice and have conversations with the teacher and other students to share their growth as readers and their joy of reading. The Lessons suggest books for a regularly scheduled Read-Aloud time, or teachers may choose favorite books of their own.

Writing
Students write each day. Teachers and students make choices about writing topics. They practice the steps of the writing process and share published works.

Word Study
Students expand their vocabulary and thinking as they select the words they associate with a topic. They learn to recognize spelling patterns and develop spelling strategies.

Lesson 1

Research

LEAD-IN
Teacher introduces the Research Project:
Topic and Focus: Kinds of information/Textbooks or _____
Resource: Social Studies textbooks or _____

RESEARCH PROJECT
Read the Table of Contents. Skim textbook to find different kinds of information. Look through the book to find the section(s) you think will be the most in-teresting. With a partner, list different kinds of information you locate in text-book. Choose the most interesting topics you find in Table of Contents. What is lo-cated at the end of the book?

SHARING
Discuss what you found with other teams, and compare information listed. Tell why you chose your most interesting section.
 Papers are dated and filed.

Recreational Reading

For approximately 30 minutes, all stu-dents read books.

CONVERSATIONS
No conversations; teacher models reading for pleasure.

CLIPBOARD NOTES
Teacher notes who gets involved in a book quickly or _____.

READ-ALOUD BOOK
The Great Brain by John D. Fitzgerald, *Skinnybones* by Barbara Park or _____

Writing

MINI-LESSON
"First Day" or _____. Teacher shares feelings about the first day of school. Students share their "first day" feelings as teacher writes main phrases or key words on the chalkboard.
 Proofread for capital letters in a title.

COMPOSING
Write about how you felt today, and/or what you did to get ready for today. Or another "First Day" experience or _____.

SHARING
Read your paper to a partner. Discuss your ideas.
 Check for correctly capitalized title.
 Papers are dated and filed.

Word Study

CHART DEVELOPMENT
Spelling Emphasis: *en* or _____
Other Emphasis: School supplies or _____

Resource: Newspaper, magazines, or _____

WRITING
Write associations with chart focus. Stu-dent choice

SPELLING
List words to spell in Word Study note-book. Exchange notebooks with a partner for a written team test. Check and file in folder.
 Papers are dated and filed.

HOMEWORK
Team test words on spelling list. Make a list of school supplies you have bought this year, and their costs. How much have you spent?
 Notebook signed.

Lesson 2

Research

LEAD-IN
Teacher introduces the Research Project:
Topic and Focus: Kinds of information/Textbooks or _____
Resource: Science textbooks or _____

RESEARCH PROJECT
Read the Table of Contents. Choose one chapter or unit of study to look over carefully. List different parts of a chapter or unit in book. What kinds of information are included, what is at the end of the chapter? Tell what you like or dislike about the book.

SHARING
Discuss and compare your lists, questions, or comments about the book. Did you agree or disagree with another team?
Papers are dated and filed.

Recreational Reading

For approximately 30 minutes, all students read books.

CONVERSATIONS
Teacher models reading for pleasure.

CLIPBOARD NOTES
Teacher notes who gets involved in a book quickly or _____.

READ-ALOUD BOOK
Continue current selection or _____.

Writing

MINI-LESSON
"Expectations for this Year" or _____. Teacher asks students what they hope school will be like this year and writes main words/phrases volunteered on the chalkboard.
Proofread for correct use of capital letters at the beginning of sentences and punctuation at the end.

COMPOSING
Write about your hopes and ideas for making this a great year or _____.

SHARING
Read paper to a partner, discuss similarities/differences of ideas.
Check correct use of capital letters to begin sentence and punctuation to end.
Papers are dated and filed.

Word Study

CHART DEVELOPMENT
Spelling Emphasis: *ie* or _____

Other Emphasis: School place words, or _____
Resource: Newspaper or school handbooks or _____

WRITING
Write associations with chart focus. Student choice

SPELLING
List words to spell in Word Study notebook. Exchange notebooks with a partner for a written team test. Check and file in folders.
Papers are dated and filed.

HOMEWORK
Team test words on spelling list. Share your writing about a place at school. Describe a place at home.
Notebook signed.

Lesson 3

Research

LEAD-IN
Teacher introduces the Research Project:
Topic and Focus: Kinds of information/Textbooks or _____
Resource: Health textbooks or _____

RESEARCH PROJECT
With a partner, skim the parts of the book to find the different kinds of information included. Choose one unit or topic to look at closely.

SHARING
Share with another team the list you made. Compare preferences and try to convince others to see your point of view. Be ready to share your first choice of unit with the class.
  Papers are dated and filed.

Recreational Reading

For approximately 30 minutes, all students read books.

CONVERSATIONS
During last ten minutes of reading time, teacher talks to individual students about reading interests and habits or _____. (One to three minute conversations)

CLIPBOARD NOTES
Teacher notes who gets involved in a book quickly, or _____.

READ-ALOUD BOOK
Continue current selection or _____.

Writing

MINI-LESSON
"Who Am I?" or _____. Teacher tells some information that describes what he/she is like, including physical and nonphysical traits. (Avid reader, loves to cook/eat, talkative, blonde)
  Proofread for capitalized pronoun *I*.

COMPOSING
Write to tell about yourself, without revealing your identity. Try to include both physical and nonphysical traits. Write your name or initials on the back of your paper.

SHARING
Teacher collects papers. Redistributes them, not showing name side. Students read "mystery" paper, then locate the writer by asking questions to match the writer to paper. Return to seat when paper is returned to its writer.
  Proofread.
  Papers are dated and filed.

Word Study

CHART DEVELOPMENT
Spelling Emphasis: *so* or _____
Other Emphasis: School subjects or _____

Resource: All textbooks or _____

WRITING
Write associations with chart focus. Student choice

SPELLING
List words to spell in Word Study notebook. Exchange notebooks with a partner for a written team test. Check and file in folders.
  Papers are dated and filed.

HOMEWORK
Team test words on spelling list. Share your ideas about your favorite subject. List favorite subjects of other family members.
  Notebook signed.

Lesson 4

Research

LEAD-IN
Teacher introduces the Research Project:
Topic and Focus: Kinds of information/Textbooks or _____
Resource: Math textbooks or
_____

RESEARCH PROJECT
Skim the entire textbook with a partner. Find the different kinds of information in this text. Did you locate any unexpected information? List information found. What will be most useful to you, and why? What parts look most interesting, or most challenging?

SHARING
Share and compare your lists.
  Papers are dated and filed.

Recreational Reading

For approximately 30 minutes, all students read books.

CONVERSATIONS
Teacher moves among students having two to three minute conversations with as many individuals as possible, discussing reading interests, habits, book choices and/or _____.

CLIPBOARD NOTES
Teacher notes students' reading interests and/or _____.

READ-ALOUD BOOK
Continue current selection or _____.

Writing

MINI-LESSON
Revision Process, "Guess Who?" or _____. Using papers from previous lesson, the class will create a bulletin board display. ("Guess Who?" or other title) Teacher introduces the revision process by showing how to revise and edit a paper he or she has written. (See p. 61)
  Proofread using dictionaries to check spelling. Make sure interrogatory sentences end with a question mark.

COMPOSING
Read your paper. Make changes or additions/improve the paper. Underline spell-ings you need to check. After sharing your paper with a partner, make further changes and/or corrections. Recopy paper in best handwriting. (Two days may be needed.)

SHARING
Choose a partner for revision. Read your paper. Answer questions about it. Make notes of needed corrections/suggestions for improvement. Listen and respond to partner's paper. Check spellings with a dictionary. Make sure title is correctly written.
  Papers are dated and filed.

Word Study

CHART DEVELOPMENT
Spelling Emphasis: *ea* or _____
Other Emphasis: Teachers/school personnel or _____
Resource: School handbooks, printed rosters, or _____

WRITING
Write associations with chart focus. Student choice

SPELLING
List words to spell in Word Study notebook. Exchange notebooks with a partner for a written team test. Check and file in folders.
  Papers are dated and filed.

HOMEWORK
Team test words on spelling list.
  Notebook signed.

Lesson 5

Research

LEAD-IN
Teacher introduces the Research Project:
Topic and Focus: Kinds of information/Textbooks or _____
Resource: Spelling textbooks, reading books or _____

RESEARCH PROJECT
Skim with a partner to find the different kinds of information in the material. List the different kinds of information, and where it is located in the book. What part would you find most useful, and why?

SHARING
Share and compare list and ideas with another team. Did you find any unexpected information?
  Papers are dated and filed.

Recreational Reading

For approximately 30 minutes, all students read books.

CONVERSATIONS
Teacher moves among students having two to three minute conversations with as many individuals as possible discussing reading interests, habits, book choice and/or _____.

CLIPBOARD NOTES
Make notes about the above, or
_____.

READ-ALOUD BOOK
Continue current selection or _____.

Writing

MINI-LESSON
Share Day: Discuss responses to shared writings, courtesy, and listening skills. Set time for all drafts to be ready for sharing. Suggest final draft format (title, indented paragraph, legible handwriting, any illustrations desired).
  Review proofreading lessons 1–4 (optional). Double check spelling.

COMPOSING
Complete all final editing and drafts. Proofread your paper.

SHARING
Whole group sharing, or divide students into groups of five or six to share papers before mounting on bulletin board.
  Papers are dated and filed.

Word Study

CHART DEVELOPMENT
Spelling Emphasis: *oi* or Chart Review Day
Other Emphasis: Lunch or

_____

Resource: Newspaper or spelling textbooks or _____

WRITING
Write associations with chart focus. Student choice

SPELLING
List words to spell in Word Study notebook. Exchange notebooks with a partner for a written team test. Check and file in folders.
  Papers are dated and filed.

HOMEWORK
Team test words on spelling list.
  Notebook signed.

Lesson 6

Research

LEAD-IN
Teacher introduces the Research Project:
Topic and Focus: Kinds of information/Reference books or _____
Resource: Dictionaries or _____

RESEARCH PROJECT
Choose any word (or an *ex* word from the word study chart). Locate it in the dictionary and read the information given. Look through the dictionary to find the different types of information included. List the different kinds of information you and a partner found about your word.

Put your information on tagboard to share and display.

SHARING
Share your information and word with another group. Which word had the most information given in the dictionary? Compare dictionaries and the different kinds of information they include. Talk about how they are alike or different.
 Papers are dated and filed.

Recreational Reading

For approximately 30 minutes, all students read books.

CONVERSATIONS
Teacher moves among students having two to three minute conversations with as many individuals as possible discussing reading interests, habits, book choice and/or _____.

CLIPBOARD NOTES
Make notes about student reading interests/habits or _____.

READ-ALOUD BOOK
The Secret Garden by Frances Hodgson Burnett, *Harriet the Spy* by Louise Fitzhugh, or _____.

Writing

MINI-LESSON
Brainstorm "Exciting Times" (or "Funny Times"). Teacher shares short phrases naming exciting personal events, explaining that all of these could be possible topics for writing. Students volunteer examples.
 Review listening and responding skills in sharing conferences. Proofread for correctly capitalized titles.

COMPOSING
List some exciting times in your life, using phrases or sentences. Suggest titles for these events.

SHARING
With a partner, read over your list of events and titles. Share a few details about each exciting time and underline the most interesting topics, at least the top two.
 Check correctly capitalized titles.
 Papers are dated and filed.

Word Study

CHART DEVELOPMENT
Spelling Emphasis: *ex* or _____
Other Emphasis: Emotions or

_____

Resource: Newspaper, spelling textbooks or _____

WRITING
Write associations with chart focus. Student choice

SPELLING
List words to spell in Word Study notebook. Exchange notebooks with a partner for a written team test. Check and file in folders.
 Papers are dated and filed.

HOMEWORK
Team test words on spelling list.
 Notebook signed.

Lesson 7

Research

LEAD-IN
Teacher introduces the Research Project:
Topic and Focus: Kinds of information/Reference books or _____
Resource: Encyclopedias or

_____

RESEARCH PROJECT
Locate a famous person in the encyclopedia and skim the information to find out why that person is famous. What other kinds of information is given about that person? Working in groups of two or

three, write one sentence to tell your person's "claim to fame." List other kinds of information given about the person. Try to locate one especially interesting fact to share.

SHARING
Share your information with another group. Which person had the most information in the encyclopedia? Share an interesting fact with the whole class.
   Papers are dated and filed.

Recreational Reading

For approximately 30 minutes, all students read books.

CONVERSATIONS
Teacher holds seven to ten minute conversations with three to four students individually; discuss sequence of plot, the most exciting part so far or _____.

CLIPBOARD NOTES
Teacher notes who moves around during reading time, or _____.

READ-ALOUD BOOK
Continue current selection or _____.

Writing

MINI-LESSON
The first class publication will be a collection of writings of "Exciting Times" or _____. Choose an event from your list to write about. Thinking of and discussing a possible topic is a writer's strategy you used yesterday to help you plan what you want to say. A first draft is the first writing of your thoughts.
   Proofread for declarative sentences that usually end in periods, and exclamatory sentences that end with exclamation marks.

COMPOSING
Write the first draft of the exciting time you selected from your list, or a new one you have recalled or _____.

SHARING
Read your paper, and respond to a partner's paper. Check for correctly punctuated exclamatory sentences, if used. Make any notes for additions or changes in your paper.
   Optional: Group share: a few students read aloud the most exciting part of their paper. (Teacher may have previously prepared them for this.)
   Papers are dated and filed.

Word Study

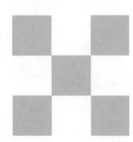

CHART DEVELOPMENT
Spelling Emphasis: er or _____
Other Emphasis: Famous persons or

_____

Resource: Newspaper or magazines or

_____

WRITING
Write associations with chart focus. Student choice

SPELLING
List words to spell in Word Study notebook. Exchange notebooks with a partner for a written team test. Check and file in folders.
   Papers are dated and filed.

HOMEWORK
Team test words on spelling list.
   Notebook signed.

Lesson 8

Research

LEAD-IN
Teacher introduces the Research Project:
Topic and Focus: Kinds of information/Reference materials or _____
Resource: Newspapers or _____

RESEARCH PROJECT
Read to locate all the different kinds of information found in newspapers. Work either individually, or in groups of two or three. List the different kinds of information in the newspaper. Tell where each is found. Underline the part of the newspaper you would read first.

SHARING
Share and compare information with another person or group.
   Papers are dated and filed.

Recreational Reading

For approximately 30 minutes, all students read books.

CONVERSATIONS
Teacher holds seven to ten minute conversations with three to four students individually; discuss sequence of plot, the most exciting part so far or _____.

CLIPBOARD NOTES
Teacher notes who moves around during reading time, or _____.

READ-ALOUD BOOK
Continue current selection or _____.

Writing

MINI-LESSON
"Exciting Times" or _____, continued. Often students have more than one story to tell on a topic. Writing about another idea will give them a choice of the one they like best for the class book.
   Proofread for capitalized proper nouns (names of particular people, places, or things).

COMPOSING
Choose a different topic/title from your list of exciting times, continue writing on previous first draft, or add a new exciting topic for today's writing. (Or teacher may choose to begin a revision of the writing from the previous lesson to give more time for revising and editing.)

SHARING
Read your paper to a partner, discuss and make notes for any changes. Listen and respond to partner's writing.
   Check partner's use of capitals for names of particular people, places, and things.
   Papers are dated and filed.

Word Study

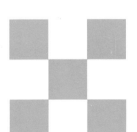

CHART DEVELOPMENT
Spelling Emphasis: *sh* or _____
Other Emphasis: Proper names (people) or _____
Resource: Current read-aloud selection, library books, or newspaper or

_____

WRITING
Write associations with chart focus. Student choice

SPELLING
List words to spell in Word Study notebook. Exchange notebooks with a partner for a written team test. Check and file in folders.
   Papers are dated and filed.

HOMEWORK
Team test words on spelling list.
   Notebook signed.

Lesson 9

Research

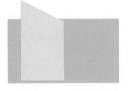

LEAD-IN
Teacher introduces the Research Project:
Topic and Focus: Kinds of informa-tion/Reference materials or _____
Resource: Atlases and almanacs or _____

RESEARCH PROJECT
Look through the material to find the different kinds of information given. List with a partner the different kinds of in-formation found in material. Underline any surprising information you located. Tell when you would find this resource useful.

SHARING
Share and compare information with an-other team. Were you surprised at any kind of information included in the resource?
Papers are dated and filed.

Recreational Reading

For approximately 30 minutes, all stu-dents read books.

CONVERSATIONS
Teacher holds seven to ten minute con-versations with three to four students in-dividually; discuss sequence of plot, the most exciting part so far and/or _____.

CLIPBOARD NOTES
Teacher notes who moves around during reading time, or _____.

READ-ALOUD BOOK
Continue current selection or _____.

Writing

MINI-LESSON
Revision and editing conferences–Teacher reviews revision and editing steps or models the steps for revising and editing paper for the class publication, "Exciting Times." (See p. 61) Quickly review proofreading thrusts for lessons 1–8. (Optional)

COMPOSING
Select the paper you will revise. Read your paper, making additions and changes for improvements. After meeting

with a partner, make any further changes, and check spellings. Meet to dis-cuss your writing with a partner several times, if needed.
Begin final draft or _____.

SHARING
Read and discuss your paper with your partner, making notes for changes. Listen and respond to your partner's paper.
Check spellings with the dictionary.
Papers are dated and filed.

Word Study

CHART DEVELOPMENT
Spelling Emphasis: *ch* or _____
Other Emphasis: Proper names (places) or _____
Resource: Newspaper or magazines or _____

WRITING
Write associations with chart focus. Stu-dent choice

SPELLING
List words to spell in Word Study note-book. Exchange notebooks with a partner for a written team test. Check and file in folders.
Papers are dated and filed.

HOMEWORK
Team test words on spelling list.
Notebook signed.

Research

LEAD-IN
Teacher introduces the Research Project:
Topic and Focus: Kinds of information/Reference materials or _____
Resource: Magazines, guides to magazine articles, or _____

RESEARCH PROJECT
Read to locate different kinds of information in a magazine. When would you find this magazine useful? Who is this magazine mainly designed to reach? Or locate articles on a topic in magazine guides from the library. List with a partner or team the kinds of information found, and answers to the questions.

SHARING
Discuss and compare your list and preferences with another group.
Papers are dated and filed.

Recreational Reading

For approximately 30 minutes, all students read books.

CONVERSATIONS
Teacher holds seven to ten minute conversations with three or four students individually, discussing sequence of plot, and the most exciting part so far, and/or _____.

CLIPBOARD NOTES
Teacher notes titles being read, and/or _____.

READ-ALOUD BOOK
Summer of The Monkeys by Wilson Rawls, *In The Year of The Boar and Jackie Robinson* by Bette Bao Lord or

Writing

MINI-LESSON
Share Day: Students choose a title for the class collection. Set time for sharing. Or _____.
Proofreading: check final draft format (Title, complete sentences, legible handwriting, etc.).

COMPOSING
Complete final draft, proofreading your paper. Add illustrations, if desired. Or _____.

SHARING
Share in whole group or smaller groups. Did the writings make you feel the excitement of the writer?
Papers are dated and filed.

Word Study

CHART DEVELOPMENT
Spelling Emphasis: *io* or Chart Review Day
Other Emphasis: Writing or _____
Resource: Magazines or _____

WRITING
Write associations with chart focus. Student choice

SPELLING
List words to spell in Word Study notebook. Exchange notebooks with a partner for a written team test. Check and file in folder.
Papers are dated and filed.

HOMEWORK
Team test words on spelling list. Make a list of things you like to write about that you might use for composition.
Notebook signed.

Lesson 11

Research

LEAD-IN
Teacher introduces the Research Project:
Topic and Focus: Kinds of information/Schedules or _____
Resource: TV Guides and/or other schedules, or _____

RESEARCH PROJECT
With a partner read to find the different kinds of information in the materials. List different information in the material, or use the TV schedule to plan two hours of leisure, or write your daily schedule from morning to night.

SHARING
Compare and discuss your list or viewing schedule with another team or individual.
   Papers are dated and filed.

Recreational Reading

For approximately 30 minutes, all students read books.

CONVERSATIONS
Teacher holds seven to ten minute conversations with three or four students individually, discussing sequence of plot, and the most exciting part so far, and/or _____.

CLIPBOARD NOTES
Teacher notes titles being read and/or _____.

READ-ALOUD BOOK
Continue current selection or _____.

Writing

MINI-LESSON
Paragraph structure: "Leisure Favorite" or _____. Teacher reads aloud a paragraph from any fiction book or a teacher-written paragraph about a leisure activity. Students state what the paragraph is about, or find topic sentence. Teacher lists the elements of a well-constructed paragraph with the students.
   Proofreading for complete sentences that relate to one topic, a main idea or topic sentence, and indention.

COMPOSING
List your favorite leisure activities. Choose one to write a paragraph(s) about, telling what you like about the activity, or _____.

SHARING
Partners share and exchange for proofreading, or whole class shares. Read aloud topic sentence, or underline it and then check to see that other sentences relate to it.
   Papers are dated and filed.

Word Study

CHART DEVELOPMENT
Spelling Emphasis: *by* or _____
Other Emphasis: Leisure activities or _____
Resource: Newspaper, magazines, or _____

WRITING
Write associations with chart focus. Student choice

SPELLING
List words to spell in Word Study notebook. Exchange notebooks with a partner for a written team test. Check and file in folder.
   Papers are dated and filed.

HOMEWORK
Team test words on spelling list. List family members and their favorite leisure activity.
   Notebook signed.

Lesson **12**

Research

LEAD-IN
Teacher introduces the Research Project:
Topic and Focus: Kinds of information/Schedules or _____
Resource: Calendars, travel brochures, or other schedules, or _____

RESEARCH PROJECT
Read with a partner to find different kinds of information given. List kinds of information. Write statements of facts you learned from this material. Was any information given that you found surprising or unexpected? Underline the most interesting fact found.

SHARING
Share listed information and facts of interest found. Give your most interesting fact for whole class sharing.
  Papers are dated and filed.

Recreational Reading

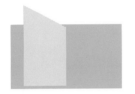

For approximately 30 minutes, all students read books.

CONVERSATIONS
For the last ten minutes, small groups discuss books they are reading. Groups may be organized by topic, author, same book, or any other appropriate criterion.

CLIPBOARD NOTES
Teacher notes how students listen and respond in discussion groups or _____.

READ-ALOUD BOOK
Continue current selection or _____.

Writing

MINI-LESSON
Paragraph structure: Nonfiction topic or _____. Teacher reads aloud a nonfiction paragraph to help students identify elements of good paragraphs. (For example, from a nonfiction book about spiders if class is studying insects in science.)
  Proofread for indention, complete sentences, topic sentence.

COMPOSING
Write a paragraph or paragraphs related to the mini-lesson topic (such as spiders), or write a paragraph about any chosen nonfiction topic, or _____.

SHARING
Read and discuss paragraph(s) with a partner.
  Proofread for good paragraph structure. Ask some students to share with the whole group.
  Papers are dated and filed.

Word Study

CHART DEVELOPMENT
Spelling Emphasis: *ee* or _____
Other Emphasis: Calendar words or _____

Resource: Newspapers, magazines, calendars or _____

WRITING
Write associations with chart focus. Student choice

SPELLING
List words to spell in Word Study notebook. Exchange notebooks with a partner for a written team test. Check and file in folder.
  Papers are dated and filed.

HOMEWORK
Team test words on spelling list. Practice spelling the months and days. Make a list of the ones you need to practice more.
  Notebook signed.

Lesson 13

Research

LEAD-IN
Teacher introduces the Research Project:
Topic and Focus: Choosing resources/Earth or _____
Resource: Globes and/or world maps or _____

RESEARCH PROJECT
Read and locate information on the maps and/or globes. Locate the continents and oceans. Write two or three fact statements and two or three questions you can answer by reading information on the globe or map. Work in groups of three or four.

SHARING
Point out and share your fact statements, then ask your questions to another team to have them find the answer on the maps or globe. Be able to prove your answers are correct.
　Papers are dated and filed.

Recreational Reading

For approximately 30 minutes, all students read books.

CONVERSATIONS
Teacher moves among students having two to three minute conversations with as many students as possible. If appropriate, discuss any unfamiliar words in today's reading, and/or _____.

CLIPBOARD NOTES
Teacher notes which students have difficulty selecting an appropriate book, and/or _____.

READ-ALOUD BOOK
Continue current selection or _____.

Writing

MINI-LESSON
"Learning Memory" or _____.
Teacher shares a memory of something he or she has learned to do, such as riding a bicycle. Students volunteer things they learned how to do, as teacher writes some of the phrases on the board.
　Proofreading: Correct use of past tense verbs.

COMPOSING
Write about a learning experience from your past, or write about any past experience, or _____.

SHARING
Read and discuss papers with a partner.
　Check correctly used past tense verbs.
　Papers are dated and filed.

Word Study

CHART DEVELOPMENT
Spelling Emphasis: *ed* or _____
Other Emphasis: Actions/words that show action or _____
Resource: Newspapers, magazines, or _____

WRITING
Write associations with chart focus. Student choice

SPELLING
List words to spell in Word Study notebook. Exchange notebooks with a partner for a written team test. Check and file in folder.
　Papers are dated and filed.

HOMEWORK
Team test words on spelling list.
　Notebook signed.

Research

LEAD-IN
Teacher introduces the Research Project:
Topic and Focus: Choosing
resources/Earth or _____
Resource: Social studies or science
textbooks (student choice) or _____

RESEARCH PROJECT
Choose one resource to locate information
about the earth. Write facts and/or questions you can answer using your resource.

SHARING
Compare with others to share facts and
ask questions. Do you think one resource
was more informative than the other?

Recreational Reading

For approximately 30 minutes, all students read books.

CONVERSATIONS
Teacher moves among students having
two to three minute conversations with as
many students as possible. If appropriate,
discuss any unfamiliar words in today's
reading, and/or _____.

CLIPBOARD NOTES
Teacher notes which students have difficulty selecting an appropriate book,
and/or _____.

READ-ALOUD BOOK
Continue current selection or _____.

Writing

MINI-LESSON
"I'm working on getting better at
_____," or _____. Students dis-
cuss things they say they are working to
improve. Teacher writes examples on the
board as they suggest them.
   Proofreading: Use verbs in the present
tense to write about things going on in
the present.

COMPOSING
Write about something(s) you are trying
to improve now, or _____.

SHARING
Read and discuss with a partner. Underline and check correctly used present
tense verbs. Or whole-group shares: Read
the first two sentences of your paragraph
to the whole class.
   Underline examples of correctly used
present tense verbs. Exchange papers to
check underlined verbs.
   Papers are dated and filed.

Word Study

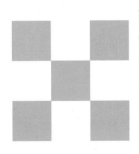

CHART DEVELOPMENT
Spelling Emphasis: *an* or
_____

Other Emphasis: Earth or
_____

Resource: Newspapers, science, social
studies textbook, or _____

WRITING
Write associations with chart focus. Student choice

SPELLING
List words to spell in Word Study notebook. Exchange notebooks with a partner
for a written team test. Check and file in
folder.
   Papers are dated and filed.

HOMEWORK
Team test words on spelling list. Using
only the letters in the word earth, how
many words can you make?
   Notebook signed.

Lesson 15

Research

LEAD-IN
Teacher introduces the Research Project:
Topic and Focus: Choosing resources/Earth or _____
Resource: Encyclopedias and/or nonfiction library books or _____

RESEARCH PROJECT
Read to locate factual information about our earth. Write two or three facts you located, and two or three questions that you can answer using your resource.

SHARING
Compare information and ask questions with partners or another team. Which resource do you think was the most useful? Over the last three lessons, which resource did you like the best, and why? (Whole class shares orally the last question.)

Recreational Reading

For approximately 30 minutes, all students read books.

CONVERSATIONS
Teacher moves among students having two to three minute conversations with as many students as possible. If appropriate, discuss any unfamiliar words in today's reading, and/or _____.

CLIPBOARD NOTES
Teacher notes which students have difficulty selecting an appropriate book, and/or _____.

READ-ALOUD BOOK
Catwings by Ursula Le Guin, *Five Children and It* by E. Nesbit or _____

Writing

MINI-LESSON
"Pets," or _____. Teacher tells about a pet, or a pet he or she would like to have. Teacher writes phrases as students volunteer feelings and ideas about pets.
   Proofreading: Use verbs to tell of past, present, or future time. (May use book *Kites Sail High* by Ruth Heller. This is a book about verbs.)

COMPOSING
Write about your pet now, in the past, or one you'd like to get in the future, or write about any event in the future, or _____.

SHARING
With partners, or small groups, read papers and discuss.
   Proofread for correctly used verbs and well-constructed paragraphs.
   Papers are dated and filed.

Word Study

CHART DEVELOPMENT
Spelling Emphasis: *il* or Chart Review Day
Other Emphasis: Pets or _____
Resource: Newspapers, magazines, or _____

WRITING
Write associations with chart focus. Student choice

SPELLING
List words to spell in Spelling notebook. Exchange notebooks with a partner for a written team test. Check and file spelling test paper in folder.
   Papers are dated and filed.

HOMEWORK
Team test words on spelling list. Ask family or friends, if you could have any pet, what would you choose? List the people and responses.
   Notebook signed.

Lesson 16

Research

LEAD-IN
Teacher introduces the Research Project:
Topic and Focus: Taking
Notes/Invertebrates (or any animal group)
or _____
Resource: Teacher reads from an encyclopedia or other nonfiction source
aloud about an animal (about five
minutes).

RESEARCH PROJECT
Listen to read-aloud material. Take notes
after the reading has ended. Work individually or with partners to write notes
about information read aloud, discussing
what you think is important.

SHARING
Volunteer information recalled in note
form as teacher makes a chart of important facts. What are the most important
facts? Was the resource useful and clear?
  Papers are dated and filed.

Recreational Reading

For approximately 30 minutes, all students read books.

CONVERSATIONS
Teacher holds seven to ten minute conversations with three to four individual
students. If appropriate, discuss paragraph changes and topic sentences in
paragraphs in their books, and/or
_____.

CLIPBOARD NOTES
Teacher notes who daydreams or looks at
the teacher, and/or _____.

READ-ALOUD BOOK
Book Talk: Teacher may introduce books
about animals, fiction and nonfiction, for
reading choices. Or continue current
selection or _____.

Writing

MINI-LESSON
"Make-Believe Animals" or _____.
What characteristics would you include?
Teacher lists student suggestions on the
board. (How it eats, moves, physical
description, habitat, helpful or harmful to
man) Book: Jack Prelutsky's poems "The
Quossible," "The Gibble," etc.
  Proofreading: Changing paragraphs
when topics or subtopics are changed.

COMPOSING
List characteristics of your make-believe
animal. Group together ideas you think
will go in one paragraph. Add notes after
sharing.

SHARING
Discuss ideas with a partner, as well as
how to group ideas into paragraphs. Did
you include enough information about
your animal?
  Papers are dated and filed.

Word Study

CHART DEVELOPMENT
Spelling Emphasis: al or _____
Other Emphasis: Animals or
_____
Resource: Newspapers or _____

WRITING
Write associations with chart focus. Student choice

SPELLING
List words to spell in Word Study notebook. Exchange notebooks with a partner
for a written team test. Check and file in
folder.
  Papers are dated and filed.

HOMEWORK
Team test words on spelling list. Write: If
you could be an animal, which would you
choose to be, and why?
  Notebook signed.

Lesson 17

Research

LEAD-IN
Teacher introduces the Research Project:
Topic and Focus: Taking
Notes/Invertebrates (or any animal group)
or _____
Resource: Encyclopedias, library
books, science books, or _____

RESEARCH PROJECT
Choose one resource to locate information
about an animal you or your team selects
to study. Read information individually.
Take notes on the main ideas you read.
Select your most important fact or facts
to share.

SHARING
Share your resource and the facts you
found with other members of your group.
Compile information on a group chart
without repeating information.
  Papers are dated and filed.

Recreational Reading

For approximately 30 minutes, all students read books.

CONVERSATIONS
Teacher holds seven to ten minute conversations with three to four individual
students. If appropriate, discuss paragraph changes and topic sentences in
paragraphs in their books, and/or
_____.

CLIPBOARD NOTES
Teacher notes who daydreams or looks at
the teacher, and/or _____.

READ-ALOUD BOOK
Continue current selection or _____.

Writing

MINI-LESSON
Continue topic of make-believe animals.
Some students volunteer their main ideas
for grouping their notes in paragraphs.
Teacher writes suggestions on board, or
_____.
  Proofreading: Changing paragraphs to
signal a topic or main idea change.

COMPOSING
Review and add to your notes for your
created animal, begin writing paragraphs
for each main idea you present about
your creation; or _____.

SHARING
Discuss ideas with a partner, and check
for clear main ideas and needed changes
in paragraphs.
  Papers are dated and filed.

Word Study

CHART DEVELOPMENT
Spelling Emphasis: *st* or _____
Other Emphasis: Animal body fea-
tures or parts or _____
Resource: Encyclopedias or other non-
fiction library books or _____

WRITING
Write associations with chart focus. Student choice

SPELLING
List words to spell in Word Study notebook. Exchange notebooks with a partner
for a written team test. Check and file in
folder.
  Papers are dated and filed.

HOMEWORK
Team test words on spelling list. Choose
one body feature that humans don't have
that you think would be useful, and tell
why.
  Notebook signed.

Lesson 18

Research

LEAD-IN
Teacher introduces the Research Project:
Topic and Focus: Taking Notes/Invertebrates (or any animal group) or _____
Resource: Encyclopedias, science textbooks, library books, any science/animals reference books available, or _____

RESEARCH PROJECT
Choose one resource to locate information about the animal your team selected to study. Read information in your group or individually. Take notes on the main ideas you read. Select your most important facts to share. Write the name of your resource.

SHARING
Share your resource and the facts you found with other members of your group. Compile information on a group chart without repeating information. Group discussion: Which resource(s) are the most useful to your group?
Papers are dated and filed.

Recreational Reading

For approximately 30 minutes, all students read books.

CONVERSATIONS
Teacher holds seven to ten minute conversations with three to four individual students. If appropriate, discuss paragraph changes and topic sentences in paragraphs in their books, and/or _____.

CLIPBOARD NOTES
Teacher notes who daydreams or looks at the teacher, and/or _____.

READ-ALOUD BOOK
Continue current selection or _____.

Writing

MINI-LESSON
Booklet publication with tape recording or _____. Teacher presents the idea of preparing an illustrated booklet of make-believe animals with a tape recording of each entry to be used by students in lower grades or another classroom.
Proofreading: Consistent verb tense usage throughout the composition. Is your animal existing in the present time, or did you write it as though it were living in the past?

COMPOSING
Complete your rough draft. Meet to begin revision when you are ready. Make notes for changes and/or additions. Or _____.

SHARING
Partners discuss and review paragraphs and consistent verb usage. Begin revision and editing, checking spellings with a dictionary.
Papers are dated and filed.

Word Study

CHART DEVELOPMENT
Spelling Emphasis: _sk_ or _____
Other Emphasis: Invertebrates or
_____
Resource: Science textbooks or
_____

WRITING
Write associations with chart focus. Student choice

SPELLING
List words to spell in Word Study notebook. Exchange notebooks with a partner for a written team test. Check and file in folder.
Papers are dated and filed.

HOMEWORK
Team test words on spelling list. Share the facts you know about invertebrates with someone at home.
Notebook signed.

Lesson 19

Research

LEAD-IN
Teacher introduces the Research Project:
Topic and Focus: Taking
Notes/Invertebrates (or any animal group)
or _____
Resource: All available resources on
topics being studied, including
newspapers and magazines.

RESEARCH PROJECT
Choose a different resource to locate information about your topic. Take notes on
any new information found on your topic.
Write two to three questions about the
main points of your topic. Write the title
of the resource you used.

SHARING
Add final notes of new information to the
group chart. Group decides on two or
three questions to ask after material is
presented to the whole class. Eliminate
irrelevant information from chart. Plan
presentation of chart information.
   Papers are dated and filed.

Recreational Reading

For approximately 30 minutes, all students read books.

CONVERSATIONS
Teacher holds seven to ten minute conversations with three to four individual
students. If appropriate, discuss paragraph changes and topic sentences in
paragraphs in their books, and/or
_____.

CLIPBOARD NOTES
Teacher notes who talks about books
spontaneously, and/or _____.

READ-ALOUD BOOK
Continue current selection or _____.

Writing

MINI-LESSON
Teacher presents materials for illustrations of make-believe animal for booklet,
shows illustrations from class library
books, makes and posts a schedule for
completing taping, final drafts, and illustrations. Or _____.
   Proofreading: Review final draft format
and paragraph structure guidelines.

COMPOSING
Complete revisions, write final draft, begin illustration. (Some students may be
scheduled for taping their entries during
this time.) Or _____.

SHARING
Work with a partner to discuss and edit
final draft and illustration ideas.
   Proofread for spelling, capitalizations,
and clear handwriting.
   Papers are dated and filed.

Word Study

CHART DEVELOPMENT
Spelling Emphasis: gr or _____
Other Emphasis: Television or
_____

Resource: Newspapers, magazines, library books, or _____

WRITING
Write associations with chart focus. Student choice

SPELLING
List words to spell in Word Study notebook. Exchange notebooks with a partner
for a written team test. Check and file in
folder.
   Papers are dated and filed.

HOMEWORK
Team test words on spelling list. Work on
the illustration of your make-believe animal. Label the body parts.
   Notebook signed.

Research

LEAD-IN
Teacher introduces the Research Project: **Topic and Focus:** Taking Notes/Invertebrates (or any animal group) or _____
Resource: Student-made charts of compiled information or _____

RESEARCH PROJECT
Each group reads their collected information to the whole class. Presenters will write two to three questions on chart paper or chalkboard for class to answer following each presentation.

SHARING
Evaluate resources. Which were most useful to each group? Evaluate presentations. Were they clear, interesting, and main ideas included?
 Papers are dated and filed.

Recreational Reading

For approximately 30 minutes, all students read books.

CONVERSATIONS
Teacher holds seven to ten minute conversations with three to four individual students. If appropriate, discuss paragraph changes and topic sentences in paragraphs in their books, and/or _____.

CLIPBOARD NOTES
Teacher notes who talks about books spontaneously, and/or _____.

READ-ALOUD BOOK
Continue current selection or _____.

Writing

MINI-LESSON
Class selection for booklet title. Set time for whole class sharing. Or _____.
 Proofreading: Review Proofreading focus lessons on paragraph structure, if needed.

COMPOSING
Proofread final draft, tape-record, complete illustration, as scheduled. Or _____.

SHARING
Students present compositions to whole group, choosing their best paragraph to tell about their made-up animal. (Tape and booklet set up for all students to enjoy before they are lent to another class.)
 Papers are dated and filed.

Word Study

CHART DEVELOPMENT
Spelling Emphasis: *re* or Chart Review Day
Other Emphasis: Proper names (things or titles) or _____
Resource: Newspaper, magazines, or _____

WRITING
Write associations with chart focus. Student choice

SPELLING
List words to spell in Word Study notebook. Exchange notebooks with a partner for a written team test. Check and file in folder.
 Papers are dated and filed.

HOMEWORK
Team test words on spelling list. Use the newspaper or any source to write correct titles of books, movies, etc.
 Notebook signed.

Lesson 21

Research

LEAD-IN
Teacher introduces the Research Project:
Topic and Focus: Choosing resources/Automobiles or _____
Resource: Class library and media center, printed or overhead copy of the Dewey Decimal System, or _____

RESEARCH PROJECT
Read the headings of the Dewey Decimal System with a team of three to four to suggest where you might locate informa-tion about automobiles in the media center. List possible resources for automobile research. Go to the media center and work in teams to locate, skim, and choose resources for class use.

SHARING
Share the materials you found with an-other team (or whole class) and tell why you selected the materials.
Papers are dated and filed.

Recreational Reading

For approximately 30 minutes, all stu-dents read books.

CONVERSATIONS
Teacher holds seven to ten minute con-versations with three to four individual students. If appropriate, discuss para-graph changes and topic sentences in paragraphs in their books, and/or _____.

CLIPBOARD NOTES
Teacher notes who talks about books spontaneously, and/or _____.

READ-ALOUD BOOK
Book Talk: Teacher calls attention to books about automobiles (or somehow related to automobiles) that may be cho-sen to read.
The Diamond in the Window by Jane Langton or _____

Writing

MINI-LESSON
Complete sentences: "Dream Car" or _____. Teacher describes dream car. Writes several sentences on the board, in-dicating the parts of complete sentences in the examples.
Proofreading: Complete sentences have a subject and a verb and express a com-plete thought.

COMPOSING
Write about your idea of a dream car, or _____.

SHARING
Discuss your writing with a partner, and check for complete sentences. (Indicate subject and verb orally or underline.)
Papers are dated and filed.

Word Study

CHART DEVELOPMENT
Spelling Emphasis: *au* or _____

Other Emphasis: Automobiles or _____

Resource: Newspapers, magazines, or _____

WRITING
Write associations with chart focus. Stu-dent choice

SPELLING
List words to spell in Word Study note-book. Exchange notebooks with a partner for a written team test. Check and file in folder.
Papers are dated and filed.

HOMEWORK
Team test words on spelling list. Ask a parent or other driver to tell about their favorite car or driving experience. (Writ-ing is optional.)
Notebook signed.

Lesson 22

Research

LEAD-IN
Teacher introduces the Research Project:
Topic and Focus: Choosing
resources/Automobiles or _____
Resource: Encyclopedias, library
books, social studies textbooks, any reference materials or _____

RESEARCH PROJECT
Work with a partner or team of three to
four. Read in any reference material to
locate information relating to automobiles. Brainstorm a list of different kinds

of automobile information you might try
to locate (history, main manufacturers,
costs, etc.) List different kinds of reference materials you think will be useful.

SHARING
Discuss lists. As a whole class, compile
the two lists to make class charts of (1)
automobile subtopics and (2) automobile
references. Choose one subtopic you
would like to research.
 Papers are dated and filed.

Recreational Reading

For approximately 30 minutes, all students read books.

CONVERSATIONS
During the last 10 minutes, small groups
discuss books they are reading. Groups
may be organized by topic, author, same
book, or any other appropriate criterion.
Or _____.

CLIPBOARD NOTES
Teacher notes how students listen and respond in discussions or _____.

READ-ALOUD BOOK
The Brave Little Toaster by Thomas M.
Disch, *The Lady's Chair and Ottoman* by
Noel Tennyson, or _____

Writing

MINI-LESSON
Personification: "My Life, by A. Car" or
_____. Teacher presents subject:
What if you were a car? Tell about your-
self. Use descriptive words to give your-
self personality, form and feelings.
 Proofreading: Include words that show
feelings or give life to the car.

COMPOSING
Write about an automobile or any other
thing using the technique of personification and first person point of view (*I*).
 Proofread to underline the words or
phrases that give life to the subject or
_____.

SHARING
Discuss your paper with a partner or
group. Discuss the main words that gave
life to the subject.
 Papers are dated and filed.

Word Study

CHART DEVELOPMENT
Spelling Emphasis: *es* or _____
Other Emphasis: Problems related to
automobiles or _____
Resource: Science textbooks,
newspapers, or _____

WRITING
Write associations with chart focus. Student choice

SPELLING
List words to spell in Word Study notebook. Exchange notebooks with a partner
for a written team test. Check and file in
folder.
 Papers are dated and filed.

HOMEWORK
Team test words on spelling list. List all
information you can find out about your
family car or a neighbor's car. Include
make, model, year, special features, etc.
 Notebook signed.

Lesson **23**

Research

LEAD-IN
Teacher introduces the Research Project:
Topic and Focus: Choosing resources/Automobiles or _____
Resource: Magazines, almanacs, encyclopedias, nonfiction books, or _____

RESEARCH PROJECT
Using the lists made in the previous lesson, choose one subtopic about automobiles to research. Select one of the available resources to locate information related to the topic. (Example: History of automobiles–Encyclopedia.) Work with a partner or team of three to four. Name the resource you selected, and write notes of main ideas you located.

SHARING
Share and compare information found with other teams or whole group, and evaluations of the resources used. Was the choice of resource a wise one? Why or why not?
   Papers are dated and filed.

Recreational Reading

For approximately 30 minutes, all students read books.

CONVERSATIONS
During the last ten minutes, the teacher may move to students' desks to ask about what they are reading. The teacher may ask several students to give a short book talk about their books for closure.

CLIPBOARD NOTES
Teacher notes who has difficulty reading for 30 minutes, and/or _____.

READ-ALOUD BOOK
Continue current selection or _____.

Writing

MINI-LESSON
Business letters or _____. Students brainstorm reasons to write a business letter to an automobile organization. Teacher shows a business letter format.
   Proofreading: Proper business letter form including sender's address, an inside address, greeting, body, and closing. Proper address form presented.

COMPOSING
Write a letter to an automotive related organization, or to any business for a reason you think is important. Or write about your ideas for "A World Without Cars," or "Future Cars," or _____.

SHARING
Read your letter or other writing to a partner and discuss the reasons for writing, check for complete sentences, and inclusion of business letter parts, if appropriate.
   Papers are dated and filed.

Word Study

CHART DEVELOPMENT
Spelling Emphasis: *ce* or _____
Other Emphasis: Businesses/careers (related to automobiles) or _____
Resource: Telephone books, newspapers, automobile brochures, or business directories, or _____

WRITING
Write associations with chart focus. Student choice

SPELLING
List words to spell in Word Study notebook. Exchange notebooks with a partner for a written team test. Check and file in folder.
   Papers are dated and filed.

HOMEWORK
Team test words on spelling list.
   Notebook signed.

Lesson 24

Research

LEAD-IN
Teacher introduces the Research Project:
Topic and Focus: Choosing
resources/Automobiles or _____
Resource: Newspapers, social studies
and science texts, or _____

RESEARCH PROJECT
Read in any material chosen to locate
facts about your subtopic or automobiles.
Read in more than one resource if time
allows. Write the main facts located.
Write the name of the resource.

SHARING
Share your facts with another team and
evaluate the resources used.
 Papers are dated and filed.

Recreational Reading

For approximately 30 minutes, all students read books.

CONVERSATIONS
Teacher moves among students having
two to three minute conversations with as
many students as possible. If appropriate,
ask students to tell why the title of their
book is appropriate (or suggest a different
one), and/or decoding skills for unfamiliar
words.

CLIPBOARD NOTES
Teacher notes who has difficulty reading
for 30 minutes, and/or _____.

READ-ALOUD BOOK
Continue current selection or _____.

Writing

MINI-LESSON
Business letters or _____. Teacher
presents stationery options available for
business letters.
 Proofreading: Correct business letter
form, including punctuation.

COMPOSING
Choose one writing from folder to revise
and edit, or write a final draft of your
business letter, or _____.

SHARING
With a partner, read your paper or letter,
discuss any questions or suggestions for
revision. Proofread for correct spellings.
Begin rewriting. Turn in letters for
teacher editing.
 Papers are dated and filed.

Word Study

CHART DEVELOPMENT

Spelling Emphasis: *sp* or _____
Other Emphasis: Safety or

_____
Resource: Newspapers, safety
brochures from Highway Dept., or

_____

WRITING
Write associations with chart focus. Student choice

SPELLING
List words to spell in Word Study notebook. Exchange notebooks with a partner
for a written team test. Check and file in
folder.
 Papers are dated and filed.

HOMEWORK
Team test words on spelling list. Discuss
and write home rules for safety with a
parent.
 Notebook signed.

Lesson 25

Research

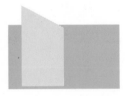

LEAD-IN
Teacher introduces the Research Project:
Topic and Focus: Choosing resources/Automobiles or _____
Resource: All available materials

RESEARCH PROJECT
Student teams read and discuss information they found in different resources related to automobiles. Design two or three "Where could you find it?" questions. Make a statement of information your team found, then ask, "Where could you find it?" to see if students can name

a possible resource. Example: "In 1989, more _____ cars were sold in the US than any other make. Where could you find this kind of information?"

SHARING
Each group presents their fact statements and asks "Where could you find it?" to another group or to the whole class. Some questions will have more than one correct response. Ask groups to share their most interesting facts.
 Papers are dated and filed.

Recreational Reading

For approximately 30 minutes, all students read books.

CONVERSATIONS
Teacher moves among students having two to three minute conversations with as many students as possible. If appropriate, ask students to tell why the title of their book is appropriate (or suggest a different one), and/or decoding skills for unfamiliar words.

CLIPBOARD NOTES
Teacher notes who has difficulty reading for 30 minutes, and/or _____.

READ-ALOUD BOOK
Continue current selection or _____.

Writing

MINI-LESSON
Sharing Day: Set time for all completed writings to be ready for sharing. Or

_____.

 Proofreading: Clear complete sentences, correct business letter form, correct address form.

COMPOSING
Final proofreading of your paper before sharing. Make any corrections needed. Teacher returns edited letters during this time. Address envelopes.

SHARING
In groups of six to eight students, or with the whole class, read your paper or letter.
 Papers are dated and filed.

Word Study

CHART DEVELOPMENT
Spelling Emphasis: *ng* or Chart Review Test
Other Emphasis: Parts and features of automobiles or _____
Resource: Student research information, brochures, newspapers, or

_____

WRITING
Write associations with chart focus. Student choice

SPELLING
List words to spell in Word Study notebook. Exchange notebooks with a partner for a written team test. Check and file in folder.
 Papers are dated and filed.

HOMEWORK
Team test words on spelling list.
 Notebook signed.

Lesson 26

Research

LEAD-IN
Teacher introduces the Research Project:
Topic and Focus: Native Americans
(North America)/Topic Selection or
_____

Resource: Social Studies textbook,
Word Study chart or _____

RESEARCH PROJECT
Whole class brainstorms subtopics to research. Form research teams for each
tribe. Make notetaking booklets of stapled together sheets. Write a subtopic

(Homes, Family Life) at the top of each
sheet. Collect resources. Begin taking
notes.

SHARING
Group members share and compare
resources and notes.
  Papers are dated and filed.

Recreational Reading

For approximately 30 minutes, all students read books.

CONVERSATIONS
Teacher moves among students having
two to three minute conversations with as
many students as possible. If appropriate,
ask students to tell why the title of their
book is appropriate (or suggest a different
one), and/or decoding skills for unfamiliar
words.

CLIPBOARD NOTES
Teacher notes who compares books by author, topics, or _____.

READ-ALOUD BOOK
Sign of the Beaver by Elizabeth George
Speare, *Indian in the Cupboard* by Lynne
Reid Banks, or _____

Writing

MINI-LESSON
Comparing and Contrasting: Fruits or
_____. Students volunteer words or
phrases to compare two different fruits (or
other items). Include words to describe
sensory images (taste/sweeter).
  Proofreading: Use of *er* or *est* endings to
show comparisons.

COMPOSING
Write about any items to show how they
are alike or different, or _____.

SHARING
Discuss comparisons and proofread for
words ending in *er* or *est*.
  Papers are dated and filed.

Word Study

CHART DEVELOPMENT
Spelling Emphasis: *qu* or
_____

Other Emphasis: Native Americans
of North America: tribes or _____
Resource: Social studies textbooks or
_____

WRITING
Write associations with chart focus. Student choice

SPELLING
List words to spell in Word Study notebook. Exchange notebooks to take a written team test. Check and file test papers
in folder.
  Papers are dated and filed.

HOMEWORK
Team test words on spelling list.
  Notebook signed.

Lesson 27

Research

LEAD-IN
Teacher introduces the Research Project:
Topic and Focus: Native Americans
(North America)/Collecting data or
_____

Resource: Encyclopedias, Social
studies textbook, or _____

RESEARCH PROJECT
Read to locate information on chosen Native American tribe. Take notes. Write a question(s) and answer(s) to share with the group.

SHARING
Groups meet to ask questions and share the information located. Add any new information discussed to notes, if desired.
Papers are dated and filed.

Recreational Reading

For approximately 30 minutes, all students read books.

CONVERSATIONS
For approximately 20 minutes, everyone, including the teacher, reads for pleasure. During the last ten minutes, the teacher may choose to talk with some individuals about what they have read. Or
_____.

CLIPBOARD NOTES
Teacher notes who compares books by author, topics, or _____.

READ-ALOUD BOOK
Continue current selection or _____.

Writing

MINI-LESSON
Comparing: A New School (House, Class) or _____. Include feelings about this new thing.
Proofreading: Adjectives with _er_ and _est_ endings to show comparison.

COMPOSING
List some new or changed things to compare with the older version. Choose one to write a comparison. Or _____.

SHARING
Discuss comparison with a partner.
Proofread for _er_ or _est_ endings and words that show feelings.
Papers are dated and filed.

Word Study

CHART DEVELOPMENT
Spelling Emphasis: _er_ or _____
Other Emphasis: Native American homes or _____
Resource: Library books, social studies textbooks, or _____

WRITING
Write associations with chart focus. Student choice

SPELLING
List words to spell in Word Study notebook. Exchange notebooks to take a written team test. Check and file test papers in folder.
Papers are dated and filed.

HOMEWORK
Team test words on spelling list.
Notebook signed.

Research

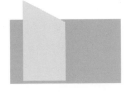

LEAD-IN
Teacher introduces the Research Project:
Topic and Focus: Native Americans/Map data or _____
Resource: Maps and all available resources collected on Native Americans or _____

RESEARCH PROJECT
Read to locate information on tribes, including map-related facts. Continue taking notes. Write question(s) to share.

SHARING
Group members share notes and ask questions. Add any notes from the group discussion.
    Papers are dated and filed.

Recreational Reading

For approximately 30 minutes, all students read books.

CONVERSATIONS
During the last ten to fifteen minutes, small groups discuss books/stories they are reading. Groups may be organized by topic, author, genre, or other. Or _____.

CLIPBOARD NOTES
Teacher notes who compares books by author, topic, or _____.

READ-ALOUD BOOK
Continue current selection, or _____.

Writing

MINI-LESSON
Comparisons of more than two items: three to four candy pieces, several pieces of art, school subjects, or _____.
    Proofreading: Correct use of comparative and superlative forms.

COMPOSING
Choose any items to write a comparison, or _____.

SHARING
Read and discuss comparison with a partner. Note the use of the ending *est* to show superlative form.
    Papers are dated and filed.

Word Study

CHART DEVELOPMENT
Spelling Emphasis: *is* or _____
Other Emphasis: Native American foods or _____
Resource: Encyclopedias, library books, or _____

WRITING
Write associations with chart focus. Student choice

SPELLING
List words.to spell in Word Study notebook. Exchange notebooks to take a written team test. Check and file test papers in folder.
    Papers are dated and filed.

HOMEWORK
Team test words on spelling list.
    Notebook signed.

Lesson **29**

Research

LEAD-IN
Teacher introduces the Research Project:
Topic and Focus: Native Americans/Notetaking or _____
Resource: Library books, filmstrips, all available resources, or _____

RESEARCH PROJECT
Continue notetaking, including facts about Native American customs and beliefs. Write notes and question(s).

SHARING
Read and discuss notes and ask questions.
Papers are dated and filed.

Recreational Reading

For approximately 30 minutes, all students read books.

CONVERSATIONS
Teacher holds seven to ten minute conversations with three to four students (individually) about comparing themselves with a story character, using context clues for word meanings, and/or _____ .

CLIPBOARD NOTES
Teacher notes who asks for help decoding words or _____ .

READ-ALOUD BOOK
Continue current selection or _____ .

Writing

MINI-LESSON
Compare different books or _____ .
Students volunteer comparative statements.
  Proofreading: Support opinion statements to explain likes or dislikes.

COMPOSING
Compare two different books (or movies, TV shows, etc.) or _____ .

SHARING
Share in writing groups. Did writers include support for opinions?
  Papers are dated and filed.

Word Study

CHART DEVELOPMENT
Spelling Emphasis: *ur* or _____
Other Emphasis: Customs and beliefs or _____
Resource: Encyclopedias, social studies books, or _____

WRITING
Write associations with chart focus. Student choice

SPELLING
List words to spell in Word Study notebook. Exchange notebooks to take a written team test. Check and file test papers in folder.
  Papers are dated and filed.

HOMEWORK
Team test words on spelling list.
  Notebook signed.

Lesson **30**

Research

LEAD-IN
Teacher introduces the Research Project:
Topic and Focus: Native Americans/Collecting data or _____
Resource: Library books, encyclopedias, textbooks, or _____

RESEARCH PROJECT
Continue collecting information about a tribe, including information about the roles of men and women. Write notes and questions to ask group members.

SHARING
Group meets to share and discuss information and ask questions. (On what subtopics does the group need to find more information?)
Papers are dated and filed.

Recreational Reading

For approximately 30 minutes, all students read books.

CONVERSATIONS
Teacher holds seven to ten minute conversations with three to four students (individually) about comparing themselves with a story character, using context clues for word meanings, and/or
_____.

CLIPBOARD NOTES
Teacher notes who asks for help decoding words or _____.

READ-ALOUD BOOK
Continue current selection or _____.

Writing

MINI-LESSON
Comparing: You and a book character or _____

Proofreading: Use *and, but,* and *or* with a comma to join sentences.

COMPOSING
Write a comparison of yourself and a character from a book, including likenesses and differences. Change paragraphs if needed. Or _____.

SHARING
Read with a partner to discuss points of comparison and check for correct use of *and, but,* and *or* to join sentences.
Papers are dated and filed.

Word Study

CHART DEVELOPMENT
Spelling Emphasis: *rr* or Chart Review Day
Other Emphasis: Weapons and tools or _____
Resource: Newspapers, encyclopedias, or _____

WRITING
Write associations with chart focus. Student choice

SPELLING
List words to spell in Word Study notebook. Exchange notebooks to take a written team test. Check and file test papers in folder.
Papers are dated and filed.

HOMEWORK
Team test words on spelling list.
Notebook signed.

Lesson **31**

Research

LEAD-IN
Teacher introduces the Research Project:
Topic and Focus: Native Americans/Organizing data or _____
Resource: All available resources, student notes, or _____

RESEARCH PROJECT
Groups meet to share information and make an outline of topics to be presented. How will collected information be shared? Write the steps of the presentation and list materials needed.

SHARING
Group members discuss ideas for their part in the presentation.
  Papers are dated and filed.

Recreational Reading

For approximately 30 minutes, all students read books.

CONVERSATIONS
Teacher holds seven to ten minute conversations with three to four students (individually) about comparing themselves with a story character, using context clues for word meanings, and/or
_____.

CLIPBOARD NOTES
Teacher notes who asks for help decoding words or _____.

READ-ALOUD BOOK
Save Queen of Sheba by Louise Moeri, *People of the Breaking Day* by Marcia Sewall, or _____

Writing

MINI-LESSON
Comparing opinions: Discuss topics about which students have different opinions, such as favorite TV shows, musical groups, or subjects. Students volunteer opinion statements. Or _____.
  Proofreading: Join sentences with *and, but,* and *or* and a comma.

COMPOSING
Meet with a partner to discuss opinions about a chosen topic. Write a comparison of views expressed (yours and another student's.) Or _____.

SHARING
Read papers to each other to make sure views are accurately recorded.
  Check correct use of *and, but,* and *or* with a comma to join sentences.
  Papers are dated and filed.

Word Study

CHART DEVELOPMENT
Spelling Emphasis: *ss* or _____
Other Emphasis: Games or
_____

Resource: Library books, dictionaries, encyclopedias, or _____

WRITING
Write associations with chart focus. Student choice

SPELLING
List words to spell in Word Study notebook. Exchange notebooks to take a written team test. Check and file test papers in folder.
  Papers are dated and filed.

HOMEWORK
Team test words on spelling list.
  Notebook signed.

Lesson **32**

Research

LEAD-IN
Teacher introduces the Research Project:
Topic and Focus: Native Americans/Summarizing or _____
Resource: All student notes and drawings, all available resources, or

_____

RESEARCH PROJECT
Summarize main facts. Prepare presentation materials.

SHARING
Group members review the plan for presentation.
Papers are dated and filed.

Recreational Reading

For approximately 30 minutes, all students read books.

CONVERSATIONS
Teacher holds seven to ten minute conversations with three to four students (individually) about comparing themselves with a story character, using context clues for word meanings, and/or

_____.

CLIPBOARD NOTES
Teacher notes where students choose to read or _____.

READ-ALOUD BOOK
Continue current selection or _____.

Writing

MINI-LESSON
Compare life now and the life of a young Native American during the early days of America. Students volunteer comparing statements. Or _____.
Proofreading: Support opinion statements with details and examples.

COMPOSING
Write a comparison of the your life with life in another time. Or _____.

SHARING
Read, respond, and proofread with a partner.
Papers are dated and filed.

Word Study

CHART DEVELOPMENT
Spelling Emphasis: *wa* or

_____

Other Emphasis: Leaders or

_____

Resource: Encyclopedias, library books, or _____

WRITING
Write associations with the chart focus. Student choice

SPELLING
List words to spell in Word Study notebook. Exchange notebooks to take a written team test. Check and file test papers in folder.
Papers are dated and filed.

HOMEWORK
Team test words on spelling list.
Notebook signed.

Lesson **33**

Research

LEAD-IN
Teacher introduces the Research Project:
Topic and Focus: Native Americans/Main ideas or _____
Resource: Student notes and materials or _____

RESEARCH PROJECT
Group writes main idea questions to present to the class before presentations. Practice reading aloud. Complete graphics.

SHARING
Proofread presentation materials with a partner or group. Review presentation plans.
Papers are dated and filed.

Recreational Reading

For approximately 30 minutes, all students read books.

CONVERSATIONS
Teacher holds seven to ten minute conversations with three to four students (individually) about comparing themselves with a story character, using context clues for word meanings, and/or _____.

CLIPBOARD NOTES
Teacher notes where students choose to read or _____.

READ-ALOUD BOOK
Continue current selection or _____.

Writing

MINI-LESSON
Acrostic poems: Native American or _____. Write an acrostics poem using a tribe name, famous Native American, or any chosen name.
Proofreading: Capitalize the first word in each line of a poem.

COMPOSING
List some possible topics, Native American or other, for poems, or write acrostic poems, or _____.

SHARING
Discuss poems in writing groups of three to five students.
Papers are dated and filed.

Word Study

CHART DEVELOPMENT
Spelling Emphasis: *br* or _____
Other Emphasis: Clothing or _____

Resource: Magazines, newspapers, or _____

WRITING
Write associations with the chart focus. Student choice

SPELLING
List the words to spell in your notebook. Exchange notebooks to take a written team test. Check and file test papers in folder.
Papers are dated and filed.

HOMEWORK
Team test words on spelling list.
Notebook signed.

Lesson **34**

Research

LEAD-IN
Teacher introduces the Research Project:
Topic and Focus: Native Americans/Project Presentations or _____
Resource: Student projects or _____

RESEARCH PROJECT
Students read or display main idea questions relating to the presentation. Students present research projects. (Two days)

SHARING
After each presentation, students respond either in writing or orally to questions and make comments on strengths and areas to improve.
Papers are dated and filed.

Recreational Reading

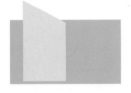

For approximately 30 minutes, all students read books.

CONVERSATIONS
Teacher holds seven to ten minute conversations with three to four students (individually) about comparing themselves with a story character, using context clues for word meanings, and/or _____.

CLIPBOARD NOTES
Teacher notes where students choose to read, or _____.

READ-ALOUD BOOK
Continue current selection or _____.

Writing

MINI-LESSON
Revision and editing conferences or _____

Proofreading: Final draft checklist and proofreading skills review.

COMPOSING
Choose a piece to revise, edit and rewrite. Or _____.

SHARING
Read, respond, and final editing.
Papers are dated and filed.

Word Study

CHART DEVELOPMENT
Spelling Emphasis: *gl* or _____
Other Emphasis: Communication or _____

Resource: Newspapers, any textbook, or _____

WRITING
Write associations with the chart focus. Student choice

SPELLING
List words to spell in Word Study notebook. Exchange notebooks to take a written team test. Check and file test papers in folder.
Papers are dated and filed.

HOMEWORK
Team test words on spelling list.
Notebook signed.

Lesson 35

Research

LEAD-IN
Teacher introduces the Research Project:
Topic and Focus: Native Americans/Project Presentations, continued, or _____

Resource: Student research projects or _____

RESEARCH PROJECT
Students read or display main idea questions relating to the presentation. Students present research projects.

SHARING
After each presentation, students respond either in writing or orally to questions and make comments on strengths and areas to improve.
   Papers are dated and filed.

Recreational Reading

For approximately 30 minutes, all students read books.

CONVERSATIONS
Teacher holds seven to ten minute conversations with three to four students (individually) about comparing themselves with a story character, using context clues for word meanings, and/or _____.

CLIPBOARD NOTES
Teacher notes titles being read or _____.

READ-ALOUD BOOK
Continue current selection or _____.

Writing

MINI-LESSON
Share Day or _____. Writing groups of three to four. Writers read their paper silently, then pass it around the group. They read a paper, then write responses to the paper. They continue passing until all papers are read.
   Proofreading: Proofread own paper for corrections before passing.

COMPOSING
After reading each paper, write your reaction to the writing.

SHARING
After read-around is completed, share notes about each paper.
   Papers are dated and filed.

Word Study

CHART DEVELOPMENT
Spelling Emphasis: _di_ or Chart Review Day
Other Emphasis: Native Americans or _____
Resource: All charts and material displayed in the classroom or _____

WRITING
Write associations with the chart focus. Student choice

SPELLING
List words to spell in Word Study notebook. Exchange notebooks to take a written team test. Check and file test papers in folder.
   Papers are dated and filed.

HOMEWORK
Team test words on spelling list.
   Notebook signed.

Research

LEAD-IN
Teacher introduces the Research Project:
Topic and Focus: Authors/Notetaking
or _____
Resource: All recreational reading
materials, and/or book covers, or

_____

RESEARCH PROJECT
Choose one book you have read that includes information about the author.
Read about the author. With a partner or
individually, make notes of main information given about the author on index
cards.

SHARING
Share the information written with another team or person. What is the most
interesting fact you found?
  Papers are dated and filed.

Recreational Reading

For approximately 30 minutes, all students read books.

CONVERSATIONS
Teacher holds seven to ten minute conversations with individual students discussing favorite authors and locating
information about authors on their current book, if appropriate, and/or

_____.

CLIPBOARD NOTES
Teacher notes titles being read and/or

_____.

READ-ALOUD BOOK
A Girl from Yamhill by Beverly Cleary;
Bill Peet, An Autobiography by Bill Peet,
Homesick: My Own Story by Jean Fritz,
or _____

Writing

MINI-LESSON
Book Reviews or _____. What's in a
book review? Read a review. Ask students
to identify kinds of information given.
  Proofreading: Reviews may include
summarizing statements and opinions.

COMPOSING
Write a book review, including statements about the plot of the book, as well
as your opinion of the book. Or write
about how you feel about reading. Or

_____.

SHARING
Share your ideas about a book with a
partner. Identify plot-summarizing statements and an opinion statement. Discuss
the best thing about the book with your
partner.
  Papers are dated and filed.

Word Study

CHART DEVELOPMENT
Spelling Emphasis: *pe* or _____
Other Emphasis: Reading, books, or

_____

Resource: Library books or

_____

WRITING
Write associations to the chart focus. Student choice

SPELLING
List words to spell in Word Study notebook. Exchange notebook with a partner
for a written team test. Check and file in
folder.
  Papers are dated and filed.

HOMEWORK
Team test words on spelling list.
  Notebook signed.

139

Lesson 37

Research

LEAD-IN
Teacher introduces the research project:
Topic and Focus:
Authors/Notetaking or _____
Resource: Reference materials about authors, encyclopedias, biographies, or

_____

RESEARCH PROJECT
Locate information about the same author from the previous lesson, or about a different author. Read to find new information. Write data gathered that does not repeat previous facts. Or write why you like the author chosen. Or

_____ .

SHARING
Share facts with another person or whole class. What different kinds of basic information have you found? Suggest headings, such as early life, books written, personal life, etc.
   Papers are dated and filed.

Recreational Reading

For approximately 30 minutes, all students read books.

CONVERSATIONS
Teacher holds seven to ten minute conversations with individual students discussing favorite authors and locating information about authors of their current book, if appropriate, and/or

_____ .

CLIPBOARD NOTES
Teacher notes titles being read and/or

_____ .

READ-ALOUD BOOK
Continue current selection or _____ .

Writing

MINI-LESSON
Fact and Opinion Statements, or
_____ . Ask students to volunteer statements about the current read-aloud selection. Classify them as factual statements or opinion statements. Ask students to support their opinions.
   Proofreading: Include fact statements and opinion statements. Give support for opinions.

COMPOSING
Write a review of a different book, or continue writing from the previous lesson, or

_____ .

SHARING
Read, respond, and proofread for both plot summary statements and supported opinion statements.
   Papers are dated and filed.

Word Study

CHART DEVELOPMENT
Spelling Emphasis: *ar* or _____
Other Emphasis: Characters and/or plot or _____
Resource: Current read-aloud selection, library books, or _____

WRITING
Write associations to the chart focus. Student choice

SPELLING
List words to spell in Word Study notebook. Exchange notebook with a partner for a written team test. Check and file in folder.
   Papers are dated and filed.

HOMEWORK
Team test words on spelling list. Tell someone about our read-aloud book. Tell about the plot and how you like it.
   Notebook signed.

Lesson 38

Research

LEAD-IN
Teacher introduces the research project:
Topic and Focus: Authors/Organizing information or _____
Resource: Reference materials about authors, class and library books, or

_____

RESEARCH PROJECT
Each team will read information collected to classify facts into headings to be used in organizing facts for an Authors File for classroom. Write suggestions for basic

headings for an information outline sheet to be part of an Authors File.

SHARING
Each group presents suggestions for an organizational outline for the Authors File. Teachers write the basic format on a chart or overhead projector transparency when the plan is final.
   Papers are dated and filed.

Recreational Reading

For approximately 30 minutes, all students read books.

CONVERSATIONS
Teacher holds seven to ten minute conversations with individual students discussing favorite authors and locating information about authors of their current book, if appropriate, and/or

_____ .

CLIPBOARD NOTES
Teacher notes students who stay seated, and/or _____ .

READ-ALOUD BOOK
Continue current selection or _____ .

Writing

MINI-LESSON
Class discusses how to share book reviews. (A Classroom Book Review File, a hall or library bulletin board, a video-tape or tape recording for the library, book jackets, etc.) Class decides on the format and makes an outline of basic information to include. Or _____ .
   Proofreading: Underline book titles in paragraphs, and change paragraphs to show different kinds of information.

COMPOSING
Select a book review to revise for the class project, or _____ .

SHARING
Read and respond with a partner to decide if your review includes required information. Are paragraph changes needed?
   Papers are dated and filed.

Word Study

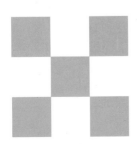

CHART DEVELOPMENT
Spelling Emphasis: *or* or _____
Other Emphasis: Authors or

_____

Resource: All class and library books or _____

WRITING
Write associations to the chart focus. Student choice

SPELLING
List words to spell in Word Study notebook. Exchange notebook with a partner for a written team test. Check and file in folder.
   Papers are dated and filed.

HOMEWORK
Team test words on spelling list. Ask at least five other people who is their favorite author. List names and choices.
   Notebook signed.

Lesson **39**

Research

LEAD-IN
Teacher introduces the research project:
Topic and Focus: Authors/Organizing information or _____
Resource: All author-reference materials available or _____

RESEARCH PROJECT
Read notes collected with a partner and decide how they best fit into the outline. Copies of the outline should be available. Write collected data on the outline in the correct space.

SHARING
Share outline sketches of authors with groups. Evaluate the outline form. Should any changes be made? File completed forms in file folders marked in alphabetical order. Store in the class.
    Papers are dated and filed.

Recreational Reading

For approximately 30 minutes, all students read books.

CONVERSATIONS
Teacher holds seven to ten minute conversations with individual students discussing favorite authors and locating information about authors of their current book, if appropriate, and/or _____.

CLIPBOARD NOTES
Teacher notes students who stay seated, and/or _____.

READ-ALOUD BOOK
Continue current selection or _____.

Writing

MINI-LESSON
Present materials for completed book reviews and for illustrations, if included. Review project outline. Or _____.
    Proofreading: Correct use of verbs *don't* and *doesn't* in sentences.

COMPOSING
Complete revision of book reviews, using the format agreed upon by the class. Or review an illustrator for the project. Or _____.

SHARING
Read and discuss book reviews in groups of six to eight. Ask some students to volunteer to read their review to the whole class. Respond to well-supported opinion statements.
    Papers are dated and filed.

Word Study

CHART DEVELOPMENT
Spelling Emphasis: *ti* or _____
Other Emphasis: Illustrations/Illustrators or _____
Resource: Class and library books, reference books, or _____

WRITING
Write associations to the chart focus. Student choice

SPELLING
List words to spell in Word Study notebook. Exchange notebook with a partner for a written team test. Check and file in folder.
    Papers are dated and filed.

HOMEWORK
Team test words on spelling list. Write about some part of the book you are now reading and draw an illustration of the scene.
    Notebook signed.

142

S u c c e s **S** u c c e s **S** u c c e s **S** u c c e s **S** u c c e s **S** u c c e s **S** u c c e s **S** u c c e s **S**

Lesson **40**

Research

LEAD-IN
Teacher introduces the research project:
Topic and Focus: Authors/Locating information or _____
Resource: Reference books about books, authors, library and class books, or _____

RESEARCH PROJECT
Read to locate addresses for authors. If no address is given, locate the publishers' address on a book by that author. Write clear complete addresses for contacting authors. Include this information on a data sheet for the author and file the sheet in Authors File.

SHARING
Share names of authors you could find addresses for and list those not found for future searches.
  Papers are dated and filed.

Recreational Reading

For approximately 30 minutes, all students read books.

CONVERSATIONS
Teacher holds seven to ten minute conversations with individual students discussing favorite authors and locating information about authors of their current book, if appropriate, and/or _____.

CLIPBOARD NOTES
Teacher notes who needs to be prompted to share, and/or _____.

READ-ALOUD BOOK
Continue current selection or _____.

Writing

MINI-LESSON
Letters to Authors or _____. What questions do you have about authors, books, or writing? Students suggest sentences or questions for authors.
  Proofreading: The basic structure of a friendly letter, including address, greeting, body, and closing.

COMPOSING
Write a letter to an author of a book you have read, or write a list of authors you might like to write and tell why, or _____.

SHARING
Read and discuss your letter with a partner.
  Check for basic letter form.
  Papers are dated and filed.

Word Study

CHART DEVELOPMENT
Spelling Emphasis: *ct* or Chart Review Day
Other Emphasis: Different kinds of books (genre) or _____
Resource: All class, library, and textbooks or _____

WRITING
Write associations to the chart focus. Student choice

SPELLING
List words to spell in Word Study notebook. Exchange notebook with a partner for a written team test. Check and file in folder.
  Papers are dated and filed.

HOMEWORK
Team test words on spelling list. Interview someone at home about how they feel about reading and their favorite kinds of books. Write their responses.
  Notebook signed.

Lesson 41

Research

LEAD-IN
Teacher introduces the research project:
Topic and Focus: Skeletons and Bones/Locating facts or _____
Resource: Health and/or science textbooks or _____

RESEARCH PROJECT
Read to locate facts about skeletons and bones with a partner or teams of three to four students. Write facts in question/answer mode.

SHARING
Share questions and answers with another team.
  Papers are dated and filed.

Recreational Reading

For approximately 30 minutes, all students read books.

CONVERSATIONS
Teacher holds seven to ten minute conversations with individual students discussing favorite authors and locating information about authors of their current book, if appropriate, and/or
_____.

CLIPBOARD NOTES
Teacher notes who needs to be prompted to share, and/or _____.

READ-ALOUD BOOK
Dear Mr. Henshaw by Beverly Cleary, *Short and Shivery: Thirty Chilling Tales* retold by Robert D. San Souci, *The Haunting* by Margaret Mahy, or
_____

Writing

MINI-LESSON
Brainstorm people to whom students might write letters other than authors. Why write to them?
  Proofreading: Correct punctuation and friendly letter form.

COMPOSING
Make a list of possibilities for letter writing. Beside each name, add some words or phrases to tell why you might choose to write to them. (Grandmother: to thank her for birthday gift) Or arrange a pen pal class to correspond with your class. Or _____.

SHARING
Read and discuss possible letters with a partner. Choose at least one to begin writing a rough draft.
  Check for correct letter form.
  Papers are dated and filed.

Word Study

CHART DEVELOPMENT
Spelling Emphasis: *te* or _____
Other Emphasis: Family titles or
_____

Resource: Newspapers or _____

WRITING
Write associations to the chart focus. Student choice

SPELLING
List words to spell in Word Study notebook. Exchange notebook with a partner for a written team test. Check and file in folder.
  Papers are dated and filed.

HOMEWORK
Team test words on spelling list. List the titles of all family members at your house.
  Notebook signed.

Lesson 42

Research

LEAD-IN
Teacher introduces the research project:
Topic and Focus: Skeletons and Bones/Locating Facts or _____
Resource: Nonfiction library books, encyclopedias, textbooks, or _____

RESEARCH PROJECT
Read to locate facts about skeletons and bones. Write facts in question/answer mode. Discuss the idea of creating fact booklets in the shape of bones or making a bulletin board display of facts written on bone shapes.

SHARING
Share facts with another team.
  Papers are dated and filed.

Recreational Reading

For approximately 30 minutes, all students read books.

CONVERSATIONS
Teacher holds seven to ten minute conversations with individual students discussing favorite authors and locating information about authors of their current book, if appropriate, and/or _____.

CLIPBOARD NOTES
Teacher notes who needs to be prompted to share, and/or _____.

READ-ALOUD BOOK
Continue current selection or _____.

Writing

MINI-LESSON
Continue discussing possible letters students might wish to write. Why do people write "fan" letters? To whom might you write a fan letter? What would you include?
  Proofreading: Correct use of commas in addresses, dates, and after greeting and closing.

COMPOSING
Write a rough draft of a fan letter. Or continue writing the letter from the previous lesson. Or _____.

SHARING
Meet with a partner to share ideas and rough drafts of letters.
  Proofread for correct form and use of commas.
  Papers are dated and filed.

Word Study

CHART DEVELOPMENT
Spelling Emphasis: *tt* or _____
Other Emphasis: Kinds of letters or
  _____
Resource: Magazines, newspapers, or
  _____

WRITING
Write associations to the chart focus. Student choice

SPELLING
List words to spell in Word Study notebook. Exchange notebook with a partner for a written team test. Check and file in folder.
  Papers are dated and filed.

HOMEWORK
Team test words on spelling list.
  Notebook signed.

145

Lesson 43

Research

LEAD-IN
Teacher introduces the research project:
Topic and Focus: Skeletons and Bones/Locating Facts or _____
Resource: Science and health magazines, nonfiction books, or _____

RESEARCH PROJECT
Read to locate new information related to skeletons and bones. Write new facts in question/answer format.

SHARING
Share questions/answers with another team. Discuss resources.
Papers are dated and filed.

Recreational Reading

For approximately 30 minutes, all students read books.

CONVERSATIONS
Teacher moves among students having two to three minute conversations with as many individuals as possible. If appropriate, discuss different genres of books, what genre is being read, and/or _____

CLIPBOARD NOTES
Teacher notes genres students prefer, or
_____.

READ-ALOUD BOOK
Book Talk: Books that use letters as part of the main plot.
Continue current selection or
_____.

Writing

MINI-LESSON
Discuss letters to complain or compliment. Who might you write to complain, or to tell how much you like something? Or read entries from *Stringbean's Trip to the Shining Sea,* and discuss postcard format.
Proofreading: Review business letter format if choice is to write in a business tone to a company.

COMPOSING
Write a letter to either complain or praise a product. Or write and design a postcard. Or write a letter of your choice.

SHARING
Read your letter to a partner to see if it fits your purpose. Respond to your partner's letter.
Proofread for correct letter form and punctuation.
Papers are dated and filed.

Word Study

CHART DEVELOPMENT
Spelling Emphasis: *gh* or
_____

Other Emphasis: Candy, Halloween, or _____
Resource: Newspapers and/or magazines or _____

WRITING
Write associations to the chart focus. Student choice

SPELLING
List words to spell in Word Study notebook. Exchange notebook with a partner for a written team test. Check and file in folder.
Papers are dated and filed.

HOMEWORK
Team test words on spelling list. Survey favorite candies at your house. List each person and favorites.
Notebook signed.

Lesson 44

Research

LEAD-IN
Teacher introduces the research project:
Topic and Focus: Skeletons and Bones/Organizing Facts or _____
Resource: All student notes, any available materials, or _____

RESEARCH PROJECT
Read notes and choose form of reporting information and materials needed. (Suggestions: fact booklets in bone shape, fact cards for a bulletin board display, questions and answers on bone shapes for a game) Write plan for final form of facts collected. Begin project.

SHARING
Group members collaborate to make final project decisions.
  Papers are dated and filed.

Recreational Reading

For approximately 30 minutes, all students read books.

CONVERSATIONS
Teacher moves among students having two to three minute conversations with as many individuals as possible. If appropriate, discuss different genres of books, what genre is being read, and/or
_____.

CLIPBOARD NOTES
Teacher notes genres students prefer, or
_____.

READ-ALOUD BOOK
Continue current selection or _____.

Writing

MINI-LESSON
Students choose one letter to revise, rewrite, and mail by the end of tomorrow's writing module. Teachers provide stationery materials and envelopes. Or
_____.
  Proofreading: Correct address form for envelopes.

COMPOSING
Confer with an editor, revise, and rewrite your letter. Or draw postcard illustrations, if appropriate. Or _____.

SHARING
Meet as needed to make additions and changes in your letter with a partner. Check spellings with dictionaries. Check correct address form.
  Papers are dated and filed.

Word Study

CHART DEVELOPMENT
Spelling Emphasis: *wr* or
_____

Other Emphasis: Skeletons and bones or _____
Resource: Health textbooks or
_____

WRITING
Write associations to the chart focus. Student choice

SPELLING
List words to spell in Word Study notebook. Exchange notebook with a partner for a written team test. Check and file in folder.
  Papers are dated and filed.

HOMEWORK
Team test words on spelling list. List any *wr* words you can find in a source at home.
  Notebook signed.

Lesson 45

Research

LEAD-IN
Teacher introduces the research project:
Topic and Focus: Skeletons and Bones/Reporting Information or

_____
Resource: Student prepared projects
or _____

RESEARCH PROJECT
Read facts collected for project. Complete project using collected facts. Write evaluation statements about your project.

SHARING
Present projects to the whole class. Evaluate projects as learning tools.
    Papers are dated and filed.

Recreational Reading

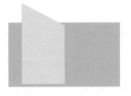

For approximately 30 minutes, all students read books.

CONVERSATIONS
Teacher meets with individual students to tape record oral reading selections from their book, discuss passage read, and/or any word attack skills indicated, and/or _____.

CLIPBOARD NOTES
Teacher notes genres students prefer, or _____.

READ-ALOUD BOOK
Continue current selection or _____.

Writing

MINI-LESSON
Share Day or _____. Letters and envelopes are completed.
    Proofreading: Final draft format for letters, correct spelling, and legible handwriting.

COMPOSING
Final drafts of letters and envelopes. Final proofreading. Or _____.

SHARING
Writing groups share letters. Groups may be based on types of letters on any appropriate method.
    Papers are dated and filed.

Word Study

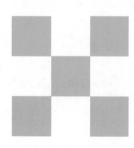

CHART DEVELOPMENT
Spelling Emphasis: *th* or _____
Other Emphasis: City, state, or

_____
Resource: Maps or _____

WRITING
Write associations to the chart focus. Student choice

SPELLING
List words to spell in Word Study notebook. Exchange notebook with a partner for a written team test. Check and file in folder.
    Papers are dated and filed.

HOMEWORK
Team test words on spelling list.
    Notebook signed.

Lesson 46

Research

LEAD-IN
Teacher introduces the research project:
Topic and Focus: Exploration/
Explorers/*Who, What, When, Where, Why*
or _____
Resource: Social Studies textbooks,
maps, globes, or _____

RESEARCH PROJECT
Read to locate information about exploration. Brainstorm explorers with the class
and form research groups. Discuss five
W's to answer. Begin taking notes individually to answer *Where* and *When*.

Write any other main facts located on the
explorer.

SHARING
Group members compare *When* and
Where information and discuss any other
facts.
    Papers are dated and filed.

Recreational Reading

For approximately 30 minutes, all students read books.

CONVERSATIONS
Teacher meets with individual students
to tape record oral reading selections
from their book, discuss passage read,
and/or any word attack skills indicated,
and/or _____.

CLIPBOARD NOTES
Teacher notes who seeks recommendations from others, and/or _____.

READ-ALOUD BOOK
Chocolate Fever by Robert Kimmel Smith,
Where Do You Think You Are Going,
Christopher Columbus? by Jean Fritz, or
_____

Writing

MINI-LESSON
Writing descriptions or _____. Discuss favorite foods. Read from *Chocolate*
Fever by Robert Kimmel Smith. Students
volunteer food "fever" (pizza) or teacher
reads *O Sliver of Liver* by Myra Cohn
Livingston to discuss food dislikes.
    Proofreading: Adjectives can describe
senses of taste, smell, touch, and sound as
well as creating visual images. Expand
the list on the board by adding adjectives
(thick, spicy, pepperoni pizza).

COMPOSING
Write about your favorite food, or write
about another "fever." Or _____.

SHARING
Share your papers. Locate the best
descriptions for your foods. Did you include words that relate to the different
senses?
    Papers are dated and filed.

Word Study

CHART DEVELOPMENT
Spelling Emphasis: *le* or _____
Other Emphasis: Foods or
_____
Resource: Newspapers, advertising
supplements, or _____

WRITING
Write associations to the chart focus. Student choice

SPELLING
List words to spell in Word Study notebook. Exchange notebook with a partner
for a written team test. Check and file in
folder.
    Papers are dated and filed.

HOMEWORK
Team test words on spelling list.
    Notebook signed.

Lesson 47

Research

LEAD-IN
Teacher introduces the research project:
Topic and Focus: Explorers/Locating Information or _____
Resource: Social Studies textbooks, encyclopedias, or _____

RESEARCH PROJECT
Read to locate *Why* information about exploration. Write information located, and add interesting facts.

SHARING
Group members share all information, adding to notes.
    Papers are dated and filed.

Recreational Reading

For approximately 30 minutes, all students read books.

CONVERSATIONS
Teacher meets with individual students to tape record oral reading selections from their book, discuss passage read, and/or any word attack skills indicated, and/or _____.

CLIPBOARD NOTES
Teacher notes who seeks recommendations from others, and/or _____.

READ-ALOUD BOOK
Continue current selection or _____.

Writing

MINI-LESSON
Describe "A Special Place" or _____.
Students list their own special places, telling why. Teacher elicits some describing words that help us picture the place.
    Proofreading: Use of describing words to create moods and scenes.

COMPOSING
Think about some place you particularly like and why, or when. Write about this special place, giving a picture and a mood. Or continue writing in progress. Or _____.

SHARING
Read your paper with a partner and select the words that create the picture or mood of your special place. Or volunteers read their pieces and students recall most effective adjectives used.
    Papers are dated and filed.

Word Study

CHART DEVELOPMENT
Spelling Emphasis: *ic* or _____
Other Emphasis: Places or _____

Resource: Magazines, newspapers, or _____

WRITING
Write associations to the chart focus. Student choice

SPELLING
List words to spell in Word Study notebook. Exchange notebook with a partner for a written team test. Check and file in folder.
    Papers are dated and filed.

HOMEWORK
Team test words on spelling list.
    Notebook signed.

Research

LEAD-IN
Teacher introduces the research project:
Topic and Focus: Explorers/Locating Details or _____
Resource: Nonfiction library books, all other resources available, or _____

RESEARCH PROJECT
Read to expand *Who* and *What* information, locating details about the exploration trip and the explorer. Write details that add interest, drama, or action to the facts. Discuss presentations that are dramatized: Role-playing, "You Are There" skits, TV Interviews or a talk show with the explorer, etc. Or present material in wall chart summary (Five W's) or as a news story with headline.

SHARING
Compile all information and discuss presentation ideas, dramatization, or other. Agree on roles or responsibilities.
 Papers are dated and filed.

Recreational Reading

For approximately 30 minutes, all students read books.

CONVERSATIONS
Teacher meets with individual students to tape record oral reading selections from their book, discuss passage read, and/or any word attack skills indicated, and/or _____.

CLIPBOARD NOTES
Teacher notes who seeks recommendations from others, and/or _____.

READ-ALOUD BOOK
Continue current selection or _____.

Writing

MINI-LESSON
"A Special Someone" or _____. Students name some people who are very special to them. List responses.
 Proofreading: Use of specific adjectives to make clear descriptions.

COMPOSING
Write a list of special people, adding some notes to tell why they are special. After conferring with a partner, begin a rough draft to tell about your special someone. Or continue a writing in progress. Or _____.

SHARING
Meet with a partner to talk about special people and decide which one you will write about today.
 Papers are dated and filed.

Word Study

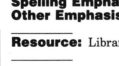

CHART DEVELOPMENT
Spelling Emphasis: *gy* or _____
Other Emphasis: Describing words or _____

Resource: Library books or _____

WRITING
Write associations to the chart focus. Student choice

SPELLING
List words to spell in Word Study notebook. Exchange notebook with a partner for a written team test. Check and file in folder.
 Papers are dated and filed.

HOMEWORK
Team test words on spelling list.
 Notebook signed.

Lesson 49

Research

LEAD-IN
Teacher introduces the research project:
Topic and Focus: Explorers/Organizing
Information or _____
Resource: All student notes and available resources or _____

RESEARCH PROJECT
Read and organize notes for project ideas/presentations. Outline a project plan and list materials needed.

SHARING
Discuss main ideas of presentation. Practice project plan and help members with parts. (Depending on projects, extend to two days)
Papers are dated and filed.

Recreational Reading

For approximately 30 minutes, all students read books.

CONVERSATIONS
Teacher meets with individual students to tape record oral reading selections from their book, discuss passage read, and/or any word attack skills indicated, and/or _____.

CLIPBOARD NOTES
Teacher notes who uses pictures for word and content clues, and/or _____.

READ-ALOUD BOOK
Continue current selection or _____.

Writing

MINI-LESSON
Review or _____. Discuss topics of the last three lessons (special people, places, things) and how adjectives help share your ideas and feelings with others. Review revision and editing steps. Discuss publication ideas.
Proofreading: Effective use of describing words.

COMPOSING
Choose a paper to revise for a Favorite Things publication or _____.

SHARING
Read and discuss your description with a response group (four to six students). Respond to effective adjective use in papers or any content that helps you know how the author thinks or feels.
Papers are dated and filed.

Word Study

CHART DEVELOPMENT
Spelling Emphasis: *lo* or _____
Other Emphasis: Exploration or
_____
Resource: Social Studies textbook, newspapers, or _____

WRITING
Write associations to the chart focus. Student choice

SPELLING
List words to spell in Word Study notebook. Exchange notebook with a partner for a written team test. Check and file in folder.
Papers are dated and filed.

HOMEWORK
Team test words on spelling list.
Notebook signed.

Lesson **50**

Research

LEAD-IN
Teacher introduces the research project:
Topic and Focus: Explorers/Presentations or _____
Resource: Student-designed presentations of collected data.

RESEARCH PROJECT
Groups write two or three main idea questions on chart for class to answer after presentations. Display the questions before presentations. Present projects.

SHARING
After each presentation, students respond to questions and comment on main ideas of presentation.
Papers are dated and filed.

Recreational Reading

For approximately 30 minutes, all students read books.

CONVERSATIONS
Teacher meets with individual students to tape record oral reading selections from their book, discuss passage read, and/or any word attack skills indicated, and/or _____.

CLIPBOARD NOTES
Teacher notes who uses pictures for word and content clues and/or _____.

READ-ALOUD BOOK
Continue current selection or _____.

Writing

MINI-LESSON
Share Day or _____. Option: Compile a class booklet, "Special Things" or "Favorites" with illustrations, etc. Set time for sharing.
Proofreading: Effective use of adjectives to describe subject.

COMPOSING
Proofread final draft. Edit for spelling and punctuation. Or _____.

SHARING
Read and discuss writing with the class or group (four to six students). Respond to effective adjective use in papers, or any content that helps you know how the author thinks or feels.
Papers are dated and filed.

Word Study

CHART DEVELOPMENT
Spelling Emphasis: *tl* or Chart Review Day
Other Emphasis: Drama or
_____
Resource: Newspapers, plays in books, or _____

WRITING
Write associations to the chart focus. Student choice

SPELLING
List words to spell in Word Study notebook. Exchange notebook with a partner for a written team test. Check and file in folder.
Papers are dated and filed.

HOMEWORK
Team test words on spelling list.
Notebook signed.

Lesson **51**

Research

LEAD-IN
Teacher introduces the Research Project:
Topic and Focus: Fairy
Tales/Headlines or _____
Resource: Newspapers or _____

RESEARCH PROJECT
With a partner, locate and discuss headlines. Choose a fairy tale and write a
headline for the story. Write several
headlines that relate to one or more fairy
tales.

SHARING
Students read their headlines to another
pair, share with the class, or display
them on a bulletin board in bold letters.
   Papers are dated and filed.

Recreational Reading

For approximately 30 minutes, all students read books.

CONVERSATIONS
Teacher moves among students having
two to three minute conversations with as
many individuals as possible. If appropriate, discuss how their book compares with
a fairy tale, and/or _____.

CLIPBOARD NOTES
Teacher notes students who move their
fingers along the words as they read, or
_____.

READ-ALOUD BOOK
Sleeping Ugly by Jane Yolen, *The White
Cat* retold by Robert San Souci, or
_____

Writing

MINI-LESSON
What makes a fairy tale a "fairy tale"?
Students brainstorm and list elements of
a fairy tale.
   Proofreading: Correct use of quotation
marks.

COMPOSING
Write about a favorite fairy tale, or list
examples of elements of fairy tales from a
specific tale, or _____.

SHARING
Read and respond with a partner, compar-
ing fairy tale choices.
   Check correctly used quotation marks.
   Papers are dated and filed.

Word Study

CHART DEVELOPMENT
Spelling Emphasis: *ai* or _____
Other Emphasis: Fairy tales: titles
or _____
Resource: Library books, classroom
books, or _____

WRITING
Write associations to the chart focus. Student choice

SPELLING
List words to spell in Word Study notebook. Exchange notebook with a partner
for a written team test. Check and file in
folder.
   Papers are dated and filed.

HOMEWORK
Team test words on spelling list. Summa-
rize a fairy tale in three to five sentences.
Share your summary.
   Notebook signed.

Lesson **52**

Research

LEAD-IN
Teacher introduces the Research Project:
Topic and Focus: Fairy Tales/Survey
or _____
Resource: Word Study chart (Fairy Tale Titles) or _____

RESEARCH PROJECT
Class Survey: Favorite Fairy Tale. Write survey results on a chart. Groups of three or four plan to survey a class or grade level. Design survey topic and how to conduct your survey. (Students choose topic)

SHARING
Teams share survey plans with the class. Papers are dated and filed.

Recreational Reading

For approximately 30 minutes, all students read books.

CONVERSATIONS
Teacher moves among students having two to three minute conversations with as many individuals as possible. If appropriate, discuss how their book compares with a fairy tale, and/or _____.

CLIPBOARD NOTES
Teacher notes students who move their fingers along the words as they read, or _____.

READ-ALOUD BOOK
The True Story of the 3 Little Pigs! by Jon Scieszka, *Beauty, A Retelling of the Story of Beauty and the Beast* by Robin McKinley, or _____.

Writing

MINI-LESSON
Put yourself in a fairy tale. Tell your side, or point of view. Or _____.
  Proofreading: Use the pronoun *I* for first person narrator point of view.

COMPOSING
Be a character and rewrite a fairy tale from your point of view. Or write a fairy tale in news story mode. Or _____.

SHARING
Read stories in small writing groups (three or four), discussing how the story is changed. Check for consistent point of view, and the use of *I*.
  Papers are dated and filed.

Word Study

CHART DEVELOPMENT
Spelling Emphasis: *oa* or _____
Other Emphasis: Fairy tale characters or _____
Resource: Library books, classroom books, or _____

WRITING
Write associations to the chart focus. Student choice

SPELLING
List words to spell in Word Study notebook. Exchange notebook with a partner for a written team test. Check and file in folder.
  Papers are dated and filed.

HOMEWORK
Team test words on spelling list.
  Notebook signed.

Lesson 53

Research

LEAD-IN
Teacher introduces the Research Project:
Topic and Focus: Charts, tables, and graphs/Survey or _____
Resource: Social Studies or Science textbooks or _____

RESEARCH PROJECT
Locate examples of charts or graphs. Teams plan how survey results can be shown as graphs. Collect survey data.

SHARING
Teams discuss and compile collected survey data.
　Papers are dated and filed.

Recreational Reading

For approximately 30 minutes, all students read books.

CONVERSATIONS
Teacher moves among students having two to three minute conversations with as many individuals as possible. If appropriate, discuss how their book compares with a fairy tale, and/or _____.

CLIPBOARD NOTES
Teacher notes students who move their fingers along the words as they read, or _____.

READ-ALOUD BOOK
Tattercoats by Flora Steele, *The Snow Queen* retold by Naomi Lewis, or _____

Writing

MINI-LESSON
Discuss setting as time and place. Identify some settings in fairy tales. Or _____.

　Proofreading: Correct use of quotation marks.

COMPOSING
Rewrite a fairy tale changing the setting to modern times, or _____

SHARING
Share papers with partners.
　Check correct use of quotation marks.
　Papers are dated and filed.

Word Study

CHART DEVELOPMENT
Spelling Emphasis: *ca* or _____
Other Emphasis: Fairy tales: settings or _____
Resource: Any fairy tale selections or _____

WRITING
Write associations to the chart focus. Student choice

SPELLING
List words to spell in Word Study notebook. Exchange notebook with a partner for a written team test. Check and file in folder.
　Papers are dated and filed.

HOMEWORK
Team test words on spelling list.
　Notebook signed.

Research

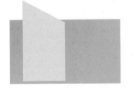

LEAD-IN
Teacher introduces the Research Project:
Topic and Focus: Charts and graphs/Survey Results or _____
Resource: Math and other textbooks or _____

RESEARCH PROJECT
In teams, locate examples of charts and graphs. Tabulate data and make charts or graphs to show survey results.

SHARING
Share survey results with the whole class.
Papers are dated and filed.

Recreational Reading

For approximately 30 minutes, all students read books.

CONVERSATIONS
Teacher holds seven to ten minute conversations with three or four students (individually) discussing point of view in their book, noting use of dialogue, and/or _____.

CLIPBOARD NOTES
Teacher notes student conference responses, demonstrated skills, or _____.

READ-ALOUD BOOK
Princess Furball retold by Charlotte Huck, *Lon Po Po* by Ed Young, or _____.

Writing

MINI-LESSON
Revising and editing conference tips.
Proofreading: Use dictionaries to check spelling, review quotation marks, capitalize *I*, and change of paragraphs.

COMPOSING
Choose a paper to revise. Confer, edit, and write final draft. Or _____.

SHARING
Conference with a partner for editing final revisions.
Papers are dated and filed.

Word Study

CHART DEVELOPMENT
Spelling Emphasis: *ma* or _____

Other Emphasis: Magic or _____

Resource: Poems ("Magic" by Shel Silverstein), library books, or _____

WRITING
Write associations to the chart focus. Student choice

SPELLING
List words to spell in spelling notebook. Exchange notebook with a partner for a written team test. Check and file test paper in folder.
Papers are dated and filed.

HOMEWORK
Team test words on spelling list. Look around your house to find an object to give magic powers. Describe what it would do or cause.
Notebook signed.

Lesson 55

Research

LEAD-IN
Teacher introduces the Research Project:
Topic and Focus: Fairy tales/Picture associations or _____
Resource: Magazines or _____

RESEARCH PROJECT
Locate magazine pictures that can be associated with fairy tales with a partner or group of three to four. Group and mount pictures on chart paper. Write words or phrases to tell how they relate to fairy tales.

SHARING
Present charts to the class.
  Papers are dated and filed.

Recreational Reading

For approximately 30 minutes, all students read books.

CONVERSATIONS
Teacher holds seven to ten minute conversations with three or four students (individually) discussing point of view in their book, noting use of dialogue, and/or _____.

CLIPBOARD NOTES
Teacher notes student conference responses, demonstrated skills, or _____.

READ-ALOUD BOOK
Vasilisa the Beautiful by Thomas Whitney, *The Twelve Dancing Princesses* by Jacob and Wilhelm Grimm (Illus. by Warwick Hutton) or _____.

Writing

MINI-LESSON
Share Day or _____. Form writing response groups (four to six) for sharing final drafts.
  Proofreading: Final draft proofreading, capitalize the title.

COMPOSING
Complete final draft (Illustration optional), or _____.

SHARING
Writing response groups share and discuss pieces about fairy tales.
  Papers are dated and filed.

Word Study

CHART DEVELOPMENT
Spelling Emphasis: *my* or Chart Review Day
Other Emphasis: Words or phrases related to fairy tales or _____
Resource: Magazines, newspapers, or _____

WRITING
Write associations to the chart focus. Student choice

SPELLING
List words to spell in Word Study notebook. Exchange notebook with a partner for a written team test. Check and file in folder.
  Papers are dated and filed.

HOMEWORK
Team test words on spelling list.
  Notebook signed.

Research

LEAD-IN
Teacher introduces the Research Project:
Topic and Focus: American Colonies
(10 day project)/Topic Selection or
_____

Resource: Social Studies textbooks or
_____

RESEARCH PROJECT
Locate information on American colonies.
Brainstorm a list of topics for research.
Form research teams and choose topics.
Locate resources. Begin reading and tak-
ing notes.

SHARING
Compare resources for research. Share
any notes taken.
  Papers are dated and filed.

Recreational Reading

For approximately 30 minutes, all students read books.

CONVERSATIONS
Teacher holds seven to ten minute conversations with three to four students (individually) discussing point of view in
their book, noting use of dialogue, and/or
_____.

CLIPBOARD NOTES
Teacher notes student conference
responses, skills, or _____.

READ-ALOUD BOOK
And Then What Happened, Paul Revere?,
or *Can't You Make Them Behave, King
George?* both by Jean Fritz or _____

Writing

MINI-LESSON
Brainstorm student ideas for a class
newspaper. Students select topics or
"jobs," or _____.
  Proofreading: Include *Who, What,
Where, Why,* and *When* information.

COMPOSING
Work individually or with partners to discuss ideas for newspaper assignment. Begin rough drafts of articles. Or
_____.

SHARING
Partners read and respond to articles.
Check Five W's.
  Papers are dated and filed.

Word Study

CHART DEVELOPMENT
Spelling Emphasis: *nn* or
_____

Other Emphasis: American colonies
or _____
Resource: Social Studies textbook or
_____

WRITING
Write associations to the chart focus. Student choice

SPELLING
List words to spell in Word Study notebook. Exchange notebook with a partner
for a written team test. Check and file in
folder.
  Papers are dated and filed.

HOMEWORK
Team test words on spelling list. Practice
naming and spelling the original thirteen
colonies with a partner.
  Notebook signed.

Lesson 57

Research

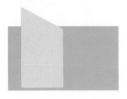

LEAD-IN
Teacher introduces the Research Project:
Topic and Focus: American Colonies/Main ideas or _____
Resource: Encyclopedias, textbooks, or _____

RESEARCH PROJECT
Read to locate *When* and *Where* information, if appropriate. Write main ideas. Write at least one question and answer.

SHARING
Share question(s) with a partner or with team members.
  Papers are dated and filed.

Recreational Reading

For approximately 30 minutes, all students read books.

CONVERSATIONS
Teacher holds seven to ten minute conversations with three to four students (individually) discussing point of view in their book, noting use of dialogue, and/or _____.

CLIPBOARD NOTES
Teacher notes student conference responses, skills, or _____.

READ-ALOUD BOOK
Continue current selection or Book Talk selections related to colonial days, fiction and nonfiction, or _____.

Writing

MINI-LESSON
Brief discussion of deadlines for articles, ways to include artwork, photographs, interview schedule, etc. Class chooses newspaper masthead and name. Or _____.
  Proofreading: Use quotation marks to signal direct quotes.

COMPOSING
Continue newspaper assignment or _____.

SHARING
Read completed rough draft to co-editor or other writers to check for five W's and punctuation of quotes, if used.
  Papers are dated and filed.

Word Study

CHART DEVELOPMENT
Spelling Emphasis: *ia* or _____
Other Emphasis: American colonial leaders or _____
Resource: Encyclopedias and/or library books or _____

WRITING
Write associations to the chart focus. Student choice

SPELLING
List words to spell in Word Study notebook. Exchange notebook with a partner for a written team test. Check and file in folder.
  Papers are dated and filed.

HOMEWORK
Team test words on spelling list. Name and arrange the thirteen colonies (or colonial leaders) in alphabetical order.
  Notebook signed.

Lesson **58**

Research

LEAD-IN
Teacher introduces the Research Project:
Topic and Focus: American Colonies/Main ideas or _____
Resource: Nonfiction library books or _____

RESEARCH PROJECT
Read to locating *How* or *Why* facts. Write question(s) and answer(s) based on information located.

SHARING
Share notes and question with team members.
  Papers are dated and filed.

Recreational Reading

For approximately 30 minutes, all students read books.

CONVERSATIONS
Teacher holds seven to ten minute conversations with three to four students (individually) discussing point of view in their book, noting use of dialogue, and/or _____.

CLIPBOARD NOTES
Teacher notes student conference responses, skills, or _____.

READ-ALOUD BOOK
Where Was Patrick Henry on the 29th of May? by Jean Fritz, *Why Don't You Get a Horse, SAM ADAMS?* (Fritz), or _____.

Writing

MINI-LESSON
Students discuss roles of proofreaders. Teacher presents printing options. Articles complete by tomorrow. Or

_____.

  Proofreading: Correct spelling and punctuation, headings or headlines correctly capitalized.

COMPOSING
Complete revision of articles, adding graphics, or _____

SHARING
Meet with co-editors or teacher to discuss final format. Revise with a partner and proofread.
  Papers are dated and filed.

Word Study

CHART DEVELOPMENT
Spelling Emphasis: *ew* or

_____

Other Emphasis: Newspaper (sections, jobs, etc.) or _____
Resource: Newspaper or _____

WRITING
Write associations to the chart focus. Student choice

SPELLING
List words to spell in Word Study notebook. Exchange notebook with a partner for a written team test. Check and file in folder.
  Papers are dated and filed.

HOMEWORK
Team test words on spelling list. Locate and list *ew* words in any source.
  Notebook signed.

Lesson 59

Research

LEAD-IN
Teacher introduces the Research Project:
Topic and Focus: American Colonies/Picture information or _____
Resource: Film strips, study prints, all available resources, or _____

RESEARCH PROJECT
Locate picture information related to topic. Write notes and question(s).

SHARING
Share pictures located and information gathered. Ask questions.
   Papers are dated and filed.

Recreational Reading

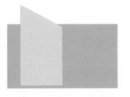

For approximately 30 minutes, all students read books.

CONVERSATIONS
Teacher hold seven to ten minute conversations with three to four students (individually) discussing point of view in their book, noting use of dialogue, and/or _____.

CLIPBOARD NOTES
Teacher notes student conference responses, skills, or _____.

READ-ALOUD BOOK
Continue current selection or _____.

Writing

MINI-LESSON
Final newspaper articles deadline. Students add captions for photos and artwork. Or _____.
   Proofreading: Review and complete all proofreading skills.

COMPOSING
Rewrite articles and headlines. Final copies submitted. Or _____.

SHARING
Exchange articles with another writing team for final proofreading.
   Papers are dated and filed.

Word Study

CHART DEVELOPMENT
Spelling Emphasis: *ou* or _____

Other Emphasis: Occupations or _____

Resource: Newspapers or _____

WRITING
Write associations to the chart focus. Student choice

SPELLING
List words to spell in Word Study notebook. Exchange notebook with a partner for a written team test. Check and file in folder.
   Papers are dated and filed.

HOMEWORK
Team test words on spelling list. Write about two or three different occupations you would like to have. List occupations of family members.
   Notebook signed.

Lesson **60**

Research

LEAD-IN
Teacher introduces the Research Project:
Topic and Focus: American Colonies/Map Information or _____
Resource: All available research material, maps, or _____

RESEARCH PROJECT
Locate a map related to topic. Write statements or question(s) and answer(s) based on map information.

SHARING
Team members share map and other information. Share questions. Discuss what other information needs to be researched for the project.
  Papers are dated and filed.

Recreational Reading

For approximately 30 minutes, all students read books.

CONVERSATIONS
Teacher holds seven to ten minute conversations with three to four students (individually) discussing point of view in their book, noting use of dialogue, and/or _____.

CLIPBOARD NOTES
Teacher notes students who are eager to share, or _____.

READ-ALOUD BOOK
Sarah, Plain and Tall by Patricia MacLachlan or *John Billington, Friend of Squanto* by Clyde Robert Bulla or _____

Writing

MINI-LESSON
Share Day: Class Newspaper. Or _____. Share newspaper articles in peer sharing groups or whole class.
  Proofreading: All proofreading skills.

COMPOSING
Read class newspaper and write comments and suggestions for improvement, or _____.

SHARING
Writers read articles, and hear student responses to each article. Share newspaper with parents, other classes, school administrators.
  Papers are dated and filed.

Word Study

CHART DEVELOPMENT
Spelling Emphasis: *mn* or Chart Review Day
Other Emphasis: Seasonal words or _____

Resource: Magazines, class newspaper, or _____

WRITING
Write associations to the chart focus. Student choice

SPELLING
List words to spell in Word Study notebook. Exchange notebook with a partner for a written team test. Check and file in folder.
  Papers are dated and filed.

HOMEWORK
Team test words on spelling list.
  Notebook signed.

Lesson **61**

Research

LEAD-IN
Teacher introduces the Research Project:
Topic and Focus: American Colonies/Interpreting Charts and Graphs or _____

Resource: All available research materials or _____

RESEARCH PROJECT
Continue notetaking. Locate charts, graphs, and tables associated with the topic for information. Write final notes and/or questions.

SHARING
New information and questions shared in the team.
  Papers are dated and filed.

Recreational Reading

For approximately 30 minutes, all students read books.

CONVERSATIONS
For 20 minutes everyone, including the teacher, reads for pleasure. During the last ten minutes, the teacher may choose to talk with some individuals about what they have read. Or _____.

CLIPBOARD NOTES
Teacher notes students who are eager to share, or _____.

READ-ALOUD BOOK
Selections from *Hey World, Here I Am* by Jean Little or Book Talk books of poetry or _____

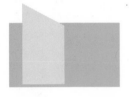

Writing

MINI-LESSON
Read and identify alliterative phrases and rhythm in poems. Or read examples of alliteration in *Animalia* by Graeme Base. Or _____.
  Proofreading: Alliteration and rhythm in poetry.

COMPOSING
List possible poem topics and words associated with the topic. Or write examples of alliteration in poems or descriptive phrases. Or _____.

SHARING
Read list of poetry topics or alliteration with a partner.
  Papers are dated and filed.

Word Study

CHART DEVELOPMENT
Spelling Emphasis: *oe* or _____
Other Emphasis: Poetry or
_____

Resource: Poetry collections, language textbooks, basal readers, or _____

WRITING
Write associations to the chart focus. Student choice

SPELLING
List words to spell in Word Study notebook. Exchange notebook with a partner for a written team test. Check and file in folder.
  Papers are dated and filed.

HOMEWORK
Team test words on spelling list. Read a poem you like to someone at home.
  Notebook signed.

Research

LEAD-IN
Teacher introduces the Research Project:
Topic and Focus: American Colonies/Classifying or _____
Resource: All research information collected by team members or _____

RESEARCH PROJECT
Read and group information into categories for an outline. Write an outline of the topics to be presented in the order to be presented. Write a presentation plan.

SHARING
Review presentation plan and responsibilities. Who will do what?
 Papers are dated and filed.

Recreational Reading

For approximately 30 minutes, all students read books.

CONVERSATIONS
During the last ten to fifteen minutes small groups discuss books/stories group members have read. Groups may be organized by topic, author, same book, or other. Or _____.

CLIPBOARD NOTES
Teacher notes students who are eager to share, or _____.

READ-ALOUD BOOK
Continue current selection or _____.

Writing

MINI-LESSON
Teacher introduces the *clustering* technique to help students generate words associated to topics for poems. Or illustrate onomatopoeia in poems. Or _____.
 Proofreading: Include sound words in poems. Capitalize each line.

COMPOSING
Choose a topic to cluster or brainstorm for five minutes, then begin writing first draft of a poem. Or write a poem using onomatopoeia. Or _____.

SHARING
Share your word list or cluster with a partner and then show your poem.
 Check capital letters to begin lines. Underline any onomatopoeia.
 Papers are dated and filed.

Word Study

CHART DEVELOPMENT
Spelling Emphasis: *oo* or _____
Other Emphasis: Sound words or _____

Resource: Newspapers and magazines or _____

WRITING
Write associations to the chart focus. Student choice

SPELLING
List words to spell in Word Study notebook. Exchange notebook with a partner for a written team test. Check and file in folder.
 Papers are dated and filed.

HOMEWORK
Team test words on spelling list.
 Notebook signed.

Lesson **63**

Research

LEAD-IN
Teacher introduces the Research Project:
Topic and Focus: American Colonies/Presentation Planning or _____
Resource: Team notes and outline of research or _____

RESEARCH PROJECT
Review all notes and information to be presented. Discuss responsibilities and prepare presentation visuals. Write main idea questions for the audience to answer after presentation.

SHARING
Team members practice and finalize presentation plans.
   Papers are dated and filed.

Recreational Reading

For approximately 30 minutes, all students read books.

CONVERSATIONS
Teacher moves among students having two to three minute conversations with as many students as possible. If appropriate, discuss poetry selections being read, or ask students to describe a major event in their book, and/or _____.

CLIPBOARD NOTES
Teacher notes who chooses to read poetry or _____.

READ-ALOUD BOOK
Continue current selection or poetry (including many haiku selections) from *O Sliver of Liver* by Myra Cohn Livingston or _____.

Writing

MINI-LESSON
Teacher reads and writes haiku with the class. (The boy John composes haiku in the book *Tracker* by Gary Paulsen. Teacher reads one aloud for a model.) Or

_____.
   Proofreading: Check the correct number of syllables in each line.

COMPOSING
Write a haiku or any poem. Or

_____.

SHARING
Share poem(s) and check haiku form, if appropriate.
   Papers are dated and filed.

Word Study

CHART DEVELOPMENT
Spelling Emphasis: *dr* or _____
Other Emphasis: Weather words or ·
_____

Resource: Newspapers, science books, or _____

WRITING
Write associations to the chart focus. Student choice

SPELLING
List words to spell in Word Study notebook. Exchange notebook with a partner for a written team test. Check and file in folder.
   Papers are dated and filed.

HOMEWORK
Team test words on spelling list.
   Notebook signed.

Research

LEAD-IN
Teacher introduces the Research Project:
Topic and Focus: American Colonies/Presentations and evaluations or
_____

Resource: Student team research materials or _____

RESEARCH PROJECT
Display the questions your presentation will answer. Present information to the class. Respond to questions.

SHARING
After presentation, share questions, answers, and evaluative comments on the presentation.
Papers are dated and filed.

Recreational Reading

For approximately 30 minutes, all students read books.

CONVERSATIONS
Teacher moves among students having two to three minute conversations with as many students as possible. If appropriate, discuss poetry selections being read or ask students to describe a major event in their book, and/or _____.

CLIPBOARD NOTES
Teacher notes which students choose to read poetry, or _____.

READ-ALOUD BOOK
Poetry from *4-Way Stop and Other Poems* by Myra Cohn Livingston, *Max Makes a Million* by Maira Kalman, or _____.

Writing

MINI-LESSON
Teacher introduces and writes a cinquain with class. Students suggest topics. Or _____.
 Proofreading: Check for proper form of cinquain poems.

COMPOSING
Write a cinquain or other poem. Or _____.

SHARING
Share cinquains with writing groups or whole class. Check form.
Papers are dated and filed.

Word Study

CHART DEVELOPMENT
Spelling Emphasis: *ck* or _____
Other Emphasis: Poets or _____

Resource: Library books, classroom poetry books, or _____

WRITING
Write associations to the chart focus. Student choice

SPELLING
List words to spell in Word Study notebook. Exchange notebook with a partner for a written team test. Check and file in folder.
Papers are dated and filed.

HOMEWORK
Team test words on spelling list.
Notebook signed.

Lesson **65**

Research

LEAD-IN
Teacher introduces the Research Project:
Topic and Focus: American Colonies/Presentations, continued, or
_____

Resource: Student team research materials or _____

RESEARCH PROJECT
Display the questions your presentation will answer. Present information to the class. Respond to questions.

SHARING
After presentation, share questions, answers, and evaluative comments on the presentation.
Papers are dated and filed.

Recreational Reading

For approximately 30 minutes, all students read books.

CONVERSATIONS
Teacher moves among students having two to three minute conversations with as many students as possible. If appropriate, discuss poetry selections being read, or ask students to describe a major event in their book, and/or _____.

CLIPBOARD NOTES
Teacher notes which students choose to read poetry or _____.

READ-ALOUD BOOK
Hailstones and Halibut Bones by Mary O'Neill, other poetry selections, or _____.

Writing

MINI-LESSON
Teacher reads a poem that does not rhyme. Class writes a poem about a color. Or teacher reads poem from _Hailstones and Halibut Bones_ by Mary O'Neill as a poem pattern.
Proofreading: Include words of feelings and moods.

COMPOSING
Choose a color to write a poem about using free verse or other form. Or _____.

SHARING
Read color poems with a partner or group. Check words of feeling and/or mood.
Papers are dated and filed.

Word Study

CHART DEVELOPMENT
Spelling Emphasis: _ow_ or _____

Other Emphasis: Colors or _____

Resource: Newspapers, magazines, or _____

WRITING
Write associations to the chart focus. Student choice

SPELLING
List words to spell in Word Study notebook. Exchange notebook with a partner for a written team test. Check and file in folder.
Papers are dated and filed.

HOMEWORK
Team test words on spelling list.
Notebook signed.

Lesson **66**

Research

LEAD-IN
Teacher introduces the Research Project:
Topic and Focus: Nutrition/Reading labels or _____
Resource: Collected food labels (Cereal boxes, frozen foods, etc.) or _____

RESEARCH PROJECT
Read nutritional information charts. List products and write statements related to nutrition.

SHARING
Share findings with other groups or whole class.
 Papers are dated and filed.

Recreational Reading

For approximately 30 minutes, all students read books.

CONVERSATIONS
Teacher holds seven to ten minute conversations with three to four students (individually) discussing qualities of main characters, action words describing the main character, and/or _____.

CLIPBOARD NOTES
Teacher notes student responses in conversations or _____.

READ-ALOUD BOOK
Poetry from *Where the Sidewalk Ends* or *A Light in the Attic,* both by Shel Silverstein, or *Out in the Dark and Daylight* by Aileen Fisher, or _____.

Writing

MINI-LESSON
Rhyming couplets: animals. Or share poems from *Zoo Doings,* Jack Prelutsky. Or _____.
 Proofreading: Check rhyming words. Use of punctuation in poetry.

COMPOSING
Write rhyming couplets about an animal or use another poem form. Or _____.

SHARING
Share poems aloud, respond, and proofread with a partner.
 Papers are dated and filed.

Word Study

CHART DEVELOPMENT
Spelling Emphasis: *ate* or _____

Other Emphasis: Nutrition or _____

Resource: Health and/or Science textbooks or _____

WRITING
Write associations to the chart focus. Student choice

SPELLING
List words to spell in Word Study notebook. Exchange notebook with a partner for a written team test. Check and file in folder.
 Papers are dated and filed.

HOMEWORK
Team test words on spelling list.
 Notebook signed.

Lesson 67

Research

LEAD-IN
Teacher introduces the Research Project:
Topic and Focus: Nutrition/Main
ideas or _____
Resource: Newspapers, magazines, or
_____

RESEARCH PROJECT
Locate articles related to nutrition. Write
main ideas.

SHARING
Present facts to class or another team.
  Papers are dated and filed.

Recreational Reading

For approximately 30 minutes, all students read books.

CONVERSATIONS
Teacher holds seven to ten minute conversations with three to four students (individually) discussing qualities of main
characters, action words describing the
main character, and/or _____.

CLIPBOARD NOTES
Teacher notes student responses in conversations or _____.

READ-ALOUD BOOK
Poetry from *Custard and Company* by Og-
den Nash, *The Random House Book of
Poetry for Children* selected by Jack
Prelutsky, or _____.

Writing

MINI-LESSON
Concrete poems: "Rattlesnake!" Or
_____. Students suggest topics for
concrete poems or write a poem together
in the shape of a rattlesnake.
  Proofreading: Proofread for rhythm, me-
ter, or beat in the poem.

COMPOSING
Write a poem that might be effective in a
concrete shape. Or read poems in books,
and choose one to write about. Or
_____.

SHARING
Share first draft of poem, listening for
rhythm.
  Papers are dated and filed.

Word Study

CHART DEVELOPMENT
Spelling Emphasis: *tle* or
_____

Other Emphasis: Vegetables or
_____

Resource: Food labels and packages or
_____

WRITING
Write associations to the chart focus. Student choice

SPELLING
List words to spell in Word Study notebook. Exchange notebook with a partner
for a written team test. Check and file in
folder.
  Papers are dated and filed.

HOMEWORK
Team test words on spelling list.
  Notebook signed.

Lesson 68

Research

LEAD-IN
Teacher introduces the Research Project:
Topic and Focus: Nutrition/Comparing or _____
Resource: Collected food labels and packages or _____

RESEARCH PROJECT
Read lists of percentage of U.S. RDA of vitamins on packages. Make charts or write statements comparing vitamin percentages.

SHARING
Share data with the class.
  Papers are dated and filed.

Recreational Reading

For approximately 30 minutes, all students read books.

CONVERSATIONS
Teacher holds seven to ten minute conversations with three to four students (individually) discussing qualities of main characters, action words describing the main character, and/or _____.

CLIPBOARD NOTES
Teacher notes student responses in conversations or _____.

READ-ALOUD BOOK
Oh, the Places You'll Go! by Dr. Seuss, *The Giving Tree* by Shel Silverstein, or _____.

Writing

MINI-LESSON
Class chooses how to share and publish poetry (make poetry booklets, tape record poems, or invite classes to poetry readings). Or _____.
  Proofreading: Proofread poems for rhythm, rhyme, mood, and capitalizations.

COMPOSING
Select poems to be revised for presentation. Begin revisions. Or _____.

SHARING
Conference with a partner. Read, respond, and proofread.
  Papers are dated and filed.

Word Study

CHART DEVELOPMENT
Spelling Emphasis: *ter* or
_____

Other Emphasis: Dairy products or
_____

Resource: Newspapers, magazines or
_____

WRITING
Write associations to the chart focus. Student choice

SPELLING
List words to spell in Word Study notebook. Exchange notebook with a partner for a written team test. Check and file in folder.
  Papers are dated and filed.

HOMEWORK
Team test words on spelling list.
  Notebook signed.

Lesson 69

Research

LEAD-IN
Teacher introduces the Research Project:
Topic and Focus: Nutrition/Making charts or _____
Resource: Health textbooks, encyclopedias, or _____

RESEARCH PROJECT
Read to locate information about vitamins to make a chart to show their sources or other facts. Or summarize nutritional facts to present to the class.

SHARING
Compare and share findings with other groups or whole class.
Papers are dated and filed.

Recreational Reading

For approximately 30 minutes, all students read books.

CONVERSATIONS
Teacher holds seven to ten minute conversations with three to four students (individually) discussing qualities of main characters, action words describing the main character, and/or _____.

CLIPBOARD NOTES
Teacher notes student responses in conversations or _____.

READ-ALOUD BOOK
The Cabin Faced West by Jean Fritz, poetry from *A Book of Americans* by Rosemary and Stephen Vincent Benet, or

_____

Writing

MINI-LESSON
Poetry: Illustrations. Or _____.
Teacher shows examples of illustrated poetry.
Proofreading: Make a checklist of proofreading points for poems.

COMPOSING
Final revision and editing. Prepare final copy and illustration. Or _____.

SHARING
Read aloud poems for final editing. Share any problems in groups.
Papers are dated and filed.

Word Study

CHART DEVELOPMENT
Spelling Emphasis: *ure* or

_____

Other Emphasis: Health or

_____

Resource: Magazines or _____

WRITING
Write associations to the chart focus. Student choice

SPELLING
List words to spell in Word Study notebook. Exchange notebook with a partner for a written team test. Check and file in folder.
Papers are dated and filed.

HOMEWORK
Team test words on spelling list.
Notebook signed.

Lesson **70**

Research

LEAD-IN
Teacher introduces the Research Project:
Topic and Focus: Nutrition/
Presentations or _____
Resource: Food labels and packages,
student facts, or _____

RESEARCH PROJECT
Write questions about nutritional value
of products, or present summarized information to the class.

SHARING
Present questions or facts to whole class.
Papers are dated and filed.

Recreational Reading

For approximately 30 minutes, all students read books.

CONVERSATIONS
Teacher holds seven to ten minute conversations with three to four students (individually) discussing qualities of main
characters, action words describing the
main character, and/or _____.

CLIPBOARD NOTES
Teacher notes student responses in conversations or _____.

READ-ALOUD BOOK
Continue current selection, any poetry
selections, or _____.

Writing

MINI-LESSON
Share Day or _____. Read poems in
groups, whole class, or present to other
groups.
  Proofreading: All proofreading skills for
poems.

COMPOSING
After listening to poems, write your feelings about poetry. Or _____.

SHARING
Poetry readings, discussions, and
responses.
  Papers are dated and filed.

Word Study

CHART DEVELOPMENT
Spelling Emphasis: *thr* or Chart Re-
view Day
Other Emphasis: Mood words or

_____
Resource: Newspapers or _____

WRITING
Write associations to the chart focus. Student choice

SPELLING
List words to spell in Word Study notebook. Exchange notebook with a partner
for a written team test. Check and file in
folder.
  Papers are dated and filed.

HOMEWORK
Team test words on spelling list.
  Notebook signed.

Lesson 71

Research

LEAD-IN
Teacher introduces the Research Project:
Topic and Focus: War/Topic selection or _____
Resource: Social Studies textbooks or _____

RESEARCH PROJECT
Read to locate names of wars. Student teams choose a war for research. Class lists topics related to wars or questions to answer about wars. (Who fought? When? Where? Why?) Make a list of questions to answer. Collect resources.

SHARING
Share questions or topics to be researched, and resources.
Papers are dated and filed.

Recreational Reading

For approximately 30 minutes, all students read books.

CONVERSATIONS
Teacher holds seven to ten minute conversations with three to four students (individually) discussing qualities of main characters, action words describing the main character, and/or _____.

CLIPBOARD NOTES
Teacher notes student responses in conversations or _____.

READ-ALOUD BOOK
From Anna by Jean Little, *The Endless Steppe: A Girl in Exile* by Ester Hautzig, or _____.

Writing

MINI-LESSON
Brainstorm reasons for writing invitations, announcements, posters, and greeting cards. Or _____.
Proofreading: Include necessary information (dates, addresses, time).

COMPOSING
Design an invitation to your next birthday party, or design a poster to promote a book or school cause. Or _____.

SHARING
Read, respond, and proofread with a partner. Choose a project.
Papers are dated and filed.

Word Study

CHART DEVELOPMENT
Spelling Emphasis: *igh* or _____

Other Emphasis: War or _____
Resource: Social Studies textbook or _____

WRITING
Write associations to the chart focus. Student choice

SPELLING
List words to spell in Word Study notebook. Exchange notebook with a partner for a written team test. Check and file in folder.
Papers are dated and filed.

HOMEWORK
Team test words on spelling list.
Notebook signed.

Lesson **72**

Research

LEAD-IN
Teacher introduces the Research Project:
Topic and Focus: War/Collecting data or _____
Resource: Library books, encyclopedias, histories, or _____

RESEARCH PROJECT
Locate information to answer questions. Write answers to questions, and write any new question from information that is important.

SHARING
Share answers to questions, and discuss new questions and answers.
 Papers are dated and filed.

Recreational Reading

For approximately 30 minutes, all students read books.

CONVERSATIONS
Teacher holds seven to ten minute conversations with three to four students (individually) discussing qualities of main characters, action words describing the main character, and/or _____.

CLIPBOARD NOTES
Teacher notes student responses in conversations, or _____.

READ-ALOUD BOOK
Continue current selection, Book Talk selections relating to the war theme, or _____.

Writing

MINI-LESSON
List needed information for posters, announcements, and invitations. Ask students to share ideas for projects. Or _____.

 Proofreading: Correctly written time, and titles, if needed.

COMPOSING
Write rough draft of project chosen, or _____.

SHARING
Read, respond, and proofread with a partner or group.
 Papers are dated and filed.

Word Study

CHART DEVELOPMENT
Spelling Emphasis: *tch* or _____

Other Emphasis: Military or _____

Resource: Newspapers, magazines, or _____

WRITING
Write associations to the chart focus. Student choice

SPELLING
List words to spell in Word Study notebook. Exchange notebook with a partner for a written team test. Check and file in folder.
 Papers are dated and filed.

HOMEWORK
Team test words on spelling list.
 Notebook signed.

Lesson **73**

Research

LEAD-IN
Teacher introduces the Research Project:
Topic and Focus: War/Collecting
data or _____
Resource: All collected resources,
speakers, videos, or _____

RESEARCH PROJECT
Write questions and answers related to
the topic.

SHARING
Share information with group.
  Papers are dated and filed.

Recreational Reading

For approximately 30 minutes, all students read books.

CONVERSATIONS
Teacher moves among students having
two to three minute conversations with as
many individuals as possible. If appropriate, discuss conflict in stories, how
characters deal with conflict, and/or
_____.

CLIPBOARD NOTES
Teacher notes students who move their
lips or show eye regressions as they read.
Or _____.

READ-ALOUD BOOK
Continue current selection or _____.

Writing

MINI-LESSON
Present materials available for completed
projects. Consider purpose and audience.
Or _____.
  Proofreading: Correct use of commas in
dates, addresses, and words in a series.

COMPOSING
Design an invitation you would like to receive. Or begin revision of project. Or
_____.

SHARING
Read, respond, and proofread with a
partner.
  Papers are dated and filed.

Word Study

CHART DEVELOPMENT
Spelling Emphasis: *gle* or
_____

Other Emphasis: Weapons or
_____

Resource: Newspapers, library books,
encyclopedias, or _____

WRITING
Write associations to the chart focus. Student choice

SPELLING
List words to spell in Word Study notebook. Exchange notebook with a partner
for a written team test. Check and file in
folder.
  Papers are dated and filed.

HOMEWORK
Team test words on spelling list.
  Notebook signed.

Research

LEAD-IN
Teacher introduces the Research Project:
Topic and Focus: War/Collecting
data or _____
Resource: All collected resource
materials, newspapers, magazines, filmstrips, or _____

RESEARCH PROJECT
Read to locate information about war.
Write answers to questions, and write
new questions of interest.

SHARING
Discuss information collected with team.
  Papers are dated and filed.

Recreational Reading

For approximately 30 minutes, all students read books.

CONVERSATIONS
Teacher moves among students having
two to three minute conversations with as
many individuals as possible. If appropriate, discuss conflict in stories, how
characters deal with conflict, and/or
_____.

CLIPBOARD NOTES
Teacher notes students who move their
lips or show eye regressions as they read.
Or _____.

READ-ALOUD BOOK
Continue current selection or _____.

Writing

MINI-LESSON
Review purpose of the project, and examine qualities of some effective posters, invitations, etc.
  Proofreading: Correct use of commas,
capitals, and colons.

COMPOSING
Revise a writing. Construct illustrations
or designs. Or _____.

SHARING
Read, respond, and proofread with a
partner.
  Papers are dated and filed.

Word Study

CHART DEVELOPMENT
Spelling Emphasis: *spl* or
_____

Other Emphasis: Peace or
_____

Resource: Newspapers or _____

WRITING
Write associations to the chart focus. Student choice

SPELLING
List words to spell in Word Study notebook. Exchange notebook with a partner
for a written team test. Check and file in
folder.
  Papers are dated and filed.

HOMEWORK
Team test words on spelling list.
  Notebook signed.

Lesson 75

Research

LEAD-IN
Teacher introduces the Research Project:
Topic and Focus: War/Collecting data or _____
Resource: Question/Answer information books (If You Lived at the Time of . . . type books), any project ideas, or _____

RESEARCH PROJECT
List ideas for projects. (Project suggestion: Form Question/Answer booklets of main ideas.) Teams meet to plan final research. Write answers to final questions.

SHARING
Share information and discuss how to form information booklets.
Papers are dated and filed.

Recreational Reading

For approximately 30 minutes, all students read books.

CONVERSATIONS
Teacher moves among students having two to three minute conversations with as many individuals as possible. If appropriate, discuss conflict in stories, how characters deal with conflict, and/or _____.

CLIPBOARD NOTES
Teacher notes students who move their lips, or show eye regressions as they read. Or _____.

READ-ALOUD BOOK
Continue current selection or _____.

Writing

MINI-LESSON
Response groups or _____. Select writing project to share.
Proofreading: Necessary information included, spelling and capitalization.

COMPOSING
Write evaluative comments about project or writing progress. Or _____.

SHARING
Read and respond to projects in groups of five to six students.
Papers are dated and filed.

Word Study

CHART DEVELOPMENT
Spelling Emphasis: *tho* or Chart Review Day
Other Emphasis: Music or _____
Resource: TV Guides, entertainment guides, or _____

WRITING
Write associations to the chart focus. Student choice

SPELLING
List words to spell in Word Study notebook. Exchange notebook with a partner for a written team test. Check and file in folder.
Papers are dated and filed.

HOMEWORK
Team test words on spelling list. List the favorite songs of at least three people.
Notebook signed.

Research

LEAD-IN
Teacher introduces the Research Project:
Topic and Focus: War/Organizing data or _____
Resource: All student collected data or _____

RESEARCH PROJECT
Teams work together to review information and arrange in order for project. Write an outline (introduction, questions, conclusion, for example).

SHARING
Discuss and assign responsibilities for research project. (Each team member prepares a portion of information for a team booklet.)
Papers are dated and filed.

Recreational Reading

For approximately 30 minutes, all students read books.

CONVERSATIONS
For approximately 20 minutes everyone, including the teacher, reads for pleasure. During the last ten minutes the teacher may choose to talk with some individuals about what they have read.

CLIPBOARD NOTES
Teacher notes students who read slowly, reread pages, or _____.

READ-ALOUD BOOK
Number the Stars by Lois Lowery, *Snow Treasure* by Marie McSwigan, or _____.

Writing

MINI-LESSON
Writing directions: Teacher demonstrates a simple procedure. Students observe, then tell what they observed in order. Or _____.

Proofreading: Use of time order words such as first, next, then, and last.

COMPOSING
Write clear, sequential directions for a game or other activity. Or _____.

SHARING
Read, respond, and proofread for clear orders in directions.
Papers are dated and filed.

Word Study

CHART DEVELOPMENT
Spelling Emphasis: *tion* or _____

Other Emphasis: Dance or _____

Resource: TV Guides, Newspapers, or _____

WRITING
Write associations to the chart focus. Student choice

SPELLING
List words to spell in Word Study notebook. Exchange notebook with a partner for a written team test. Check and file in folder.
Papers are dated and filed.

HOMEWORK
Team test words on spelling list.
Notebook signed.

Lesson 77

Research

LEAD-IN
Teacher introduces the Research Project:
Topic and Focus: War/Organizing
data or _____
Resource: All student data, outline for
booklet, or _____

RESEARCH PROJECT
Team members write information in question/answer format, or other project idea.
Add drawings, diagrams, maps.

SHARING
Share and compare booklet pages being completed, and make suggestions and/or revisions.
Papers are dated and filed.

Recreational Reading

For approximately 30 minutes, all students read books.

CONVERSATIONS
During the last ten to fifteen minutes small groups discuss books or stories group members have read. Groups may be organized by topic, author, same book, or other criterion.

CLIPBOARD NOTES
Teacher notes students who read slowly, reread pages, or _____.

READ-ALOUD BOOK
Continue current selection or _____.

Writing

MINI-LESSON
Writing directions: Emergencies or
_____. How would you direct a Rescue Service to your house?
Proofreading: Capitalize street names.
Use of commas in complex sentences.

COMPOSING
Write clear directions to your house, or
_____.

SHARING
Read, respond, and proofread with a partner. Make corrections.
Papers are dated and filed.

Word Study

CHART DEVELOPMENT
Spelling Emphasis: *tious* or
_____

Other Emphasis: Emergency agencies or _____
Resource: Telephone books, agency leaflets, brochures, or _____

WRITING
Write associations to the chart focus. Student choice

SPELLING
List words to spell in Word Study notebook. Exchange notebook with a partner for a written team test. Check and file in folder.
Papers are dated and filed.

HOMEWORK
Team test words on spelling list.
Notebook signed.

Research

LEAD-IN
Teacher introduces the Research Project:
Topic and Focus: War/Presentation materials or _____
Resource: All student collected data and resources, booklet drafts, or

_____

RESEARCH PROJECT
Proofread and compile information for final copies. Write questions, answers, and draw graphics for completed booklet.

SHARING
Group members share fact booklet sheets. Organize booklet.
Papers are dated and filed.

Recreational Reading

For approximately 30 minutes, all students read books.

CONVERSATIONS
Teacher holds seven to ten minute conversations with three to four students (individually) discussing sequence of events in their book, what will happen next, and/or _____.

CLIPBOARD NOTES
Teacher notes responses in conversations, or _____.

READ-ALOUD BOOK
Continue current selection, *Be a Perfect Person in Just Three Days* by Stephen Manes, or _____.

Writing

MINI-LESSON
Writing "How To" instructions: Students suggest topics (How to catch a slippery pig, How to be an "A" student, etc.). Or read Shel Silverstein's, "Recipe for a Hippopotamus Sandwich." Or _____.
Proofreading: Include time order words for sequence, if needed.

COMPOSING
Write a list of possible "How To" titles. Choose one to begin first draft. Or write a "recipe for a _____." Or

_____.

SHARING
Work together to read, respond, select a title, and write.
Papers are dated and filed.

Word Study

CHART DEVELOPMENT
Spelling Emphasis: *sion* or

_____

Other Emphasis: Snack foods or

_____

Resource: Grocery coupons, advertising supplements, or _____

WRITING
Write associations to the chart focus. Student choice

SPELLING
List words to spell in Word Study notebook. Exchange notebook with a partner for a written team test. Check and file in folder.
Papers are dated and filed.

HOMEWORK
Team test words on spelling list.
Notebook signed.

Lesson 79

Research

LEAD-IN
Teacher introduces the Research Project:
Topic and Focus: War/Making Conclusions or _____
Resource: Compiled research booklets or _____

RESEARCH PROJECT
Teams discuss conclusions of research. Write final drafts of introduction and conclusion for fact booklet or other project.

SHARING
Share final project with group members, and discuss strengths and weaknesses.
  Papers are dated and filed.

Recreational Reading

For approximately 30 minutes, all students read books.

CONVERSATIONS
Teacher holds seven to ten minute conversations with three to four students (individually) discussing sequence of events in their book, what will happen next, and/or _____.

CLIPBOARD NOTES
Teacher notes responses in conversations or _____.

READ-ALOUD BOOK
Continue current selection or _____.

Writing

MINI-LESSON
Students volunteer "How To" titles for a class manual, or _____.
  Proofreading: Use imperative sentences for instructions.

COMPOSING
Continue writing "How To" instructions. Revise as needed. Or _____.

SHARING
Read, respond, and proofread with a partner, or other team.
  Papers are dated and filed.

Word Study

CHART DEVELOPMENT
Spelling Emphasis: _cious_ or _____

Other Emphasis: Recipe words and phrases or _____
Resource: Magazines, cookbooks, or _____

WRITING
Write associations to the chart focus. Student choice

SPELLING
List words to spell in Word Study notebook. Exchange notebook with a partner for a written team test. Check and file in folder.
  Papers are dated and filed.

HOMEWORK
Team test words on spelling list.
  Notebook signed.

Lesson 80

Research

LEAD-IN
Teacher introduces the Research Project:
Topic and Focus: War/Presentations
or _____
Resource: Student-compiled fact book-lets, charts, or other projects, or
_____

RESEARCH PROJECT
Groups present booklets or other projects. Present main idea questions for the class to answer.

SHARING
Students respond to questions and conclu-sions of projects.
 Papers are dated and filed.

Recreational Reading

For approximately 30 minutes, all stu-dents read books.

CONVERSATIONS
Teacher holds seven to ten minute con-versations with three to four students (in-dividually) discussing sequence of events in their book, what will happen next, and/or _____.

CLIPBOARD NOTES
Teacher notes responses in conversations, or _____.

READ-ALOUD BOOK
Continue current selection or _____.

Writing

MINI-LESSON
Compile class "How To" manuals. Volun-teers make covers. Or _____.
 Proofreading: Proofread for clear se-quential order.

COMPOSING
Final copies of "How To" instructions, or
_____.

SHARING
Students read and respond to writings in groups or whole class.
 Papers are dated and filed.

Word Study

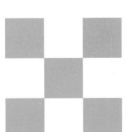

CHART DEVELOPMENT
Spelling Emphasis: *por* or Chart Re-view Day
Other Emphasis: Transportation or
_____
Resource: Travel brochures, phone-books, magazines, or _____

WRITING
Write associations to the chart focus. Stu-dent choice

SPELLING
List words to spell in Word Study note-book. Exchange notebook with a partner for a written team test. Check and file in folder.
 Papers are dated and filed.

HOMEWORK
Team test words on spelling list.
 Notebook signed.

Lesson 81

Research

LEAD-IN
Teacher introduces the Research Project:
Topic and Focus: Summarizing/
Listening Skills or _____
Resource: Any taped (or read-aloud)
material or _____

RESEARCH PROJECT
Class discusses elements of a summary.
Listen carefully to taped or read-aloud
material. Make notes. Work with a partner to write a short summary.

SHARING
Compare and discuss summaries with
others. Read some aloud and discuss effective summaries.
   Papers are dated and filed.

Recreational Reading

For approximately 30 minutes, all students read books.

CONVERSATIONS
Teacher holds seven to ten minute conversations with three to four students (individually) discussing sequence of events
in their book, what will happen next,
and/or _____.

CLIPBOARD NOTES
Teacher notes responses in conversations,
or _____.

READ-ALOUD BOOK
Where the Red Fern Grows by Wilson
Rawls, *Roll of Thunder, Hear My Cry* by
Mildred Taylor, or _____

Writing

MINI-LESSON
Story writing/Realism: (five to seven
days) Teacher and students give examples
from stories and books. Or _____.
   Proofreading: Characters and plot idea
are realistic.

COMPOSING
List story ideas which show realism.
Choose one to write about. Or
_____.

SHARING
Discuss and respond to story plot ideas.
Check for realism.
   Papers are dated and filed.

Word Study

CHART DEVELOPMENT
Spelling Emphasis: *ent* or
_____

Other Emphasis: Holidays or
_____

Resource: Newspapers, magazines, or
_____

WRITING
Write associations to the chart focus. Student choice

SPELLING
List words to spell in Word Study notebook. Exchange notebook with a partner
for a written team test. Check and file in
folder.
   Papers are dated and filed.

HOMEWORK
Team test words on spelling list.
   Notebook signed.

Lesson **82**

Research

LEAD-IN
Teacher introduces the Research Project:
Topic and Focus: Summarizing/Any fiction topic or _____
Resource: Current read-aloud selection, student's book choice, or _____

RESEARCH PROJECT
Listen to read-aloud, or read one chapter (or for ten minutes) with a partner or individually. Write a summary individually or with a partner.

SHARING
Discuss summaries to delete details or add main ideas. Read summaries to the class or in small groups.
Papers are dated and filed.

Recreational Reading

For approximately 30 minutes, all students read books.

CONVERSATIONS
Teacher holds seven to ten minute conversations with three to four students (individually) discussing sequence of events in their book, what will happen next, and/or _____.

CLIPBOARD NOTES
Teacher notes responses in conversations, or _____.

READ-ALOUD BOOK
Continue current selection or _____.

Writing

MINI-LESSON
Realism: Setting descriptions. Or _____.
Proofreading: Include vivid adjectives.

COMPOSING
Describe setting in your realistic story or _____.

SHARING
Read, respond, and proofread with a partner.
Papers are dated and filed.

Word Study

CHART DEVELOPMENT
Spelling Emphasis: *ity* or _____
Other Emphasis: Settings or _____
Resource: Library and classroom books or _____

WRITING
Write associations to the chart focus. Student choice

SPELLING
List words to spell in Word Study notebook. Exchange notebook with a partner for a written team test. Check and file in folder.
Papers are dated and filed.

HOMEWORK
Team test words on spelling list.
Notebook signed.

Lesson 83

Research

LEAD-IN
Teacher introduces the Research Project:
Topic and Focus: Summarizing/Any nonfiction topic or _____
Resource: Any textbook, encyclopedia, nonfiction taped material, or _____

RESEARCH PROJECT
Read or listen to nonfiction material. Write short summary of important facts with a partner, using your own words.

SHARING
Share summaries to compare facts included, delete unimportant details, add main data agreed upon. Read aloud to the class.
 Papers are dated and filed.

Recreational Reading

For approximately 30 minutes, all students read books.

CONVERSATIONS
Teacher holds seven to ten minute conversations with three to four students (individually) discussing sequence of events in their book, what will happen next, and/or _____.

CLIPBOARD NOTES
Teacher notes responses in conversations, or _____.

READ-ALOUD BOOK
Continue current selection or _____.

Writing

MINI-LESSON
Realism: Character descriptions. Teacher reads examples of character descriptions (physical, nonphysical traits, and actions). Or _____.
 Proofreading: Include actions to "show" a character.

COMPOSING
Expand character descriptions, or continue story development. Or _____.

SHARING
Read, discuss, and proofread for actions that reveal character.
 Papers are dated and filed.

Word Study

CHART DEVELOPMENT
Spelling Emphasis: *ble* or _____

Other Emphasis: Character traits or _____

Resource: Newspapers, magazines, current reading selections, or _____

WRITING
Write associations to the chart focus. Student choice

SPELLING
List words to spell in Word Study notebook. Exchange notebook with a partner for a written team test. Check and file in folder.
 Papers are dated and filed.

HOMEWORK
Team test words on spelling list.
 Notebook signed.

Research

LEAD-IN
Teacher introduces the Research Project:
Topic and Focus: Summarizing/
Student-chosen topic or _____
Resource: Any student selected material, story collection, textbook, or

_____

RESEARCH PROJECT
Work with a partner to select material. After one partner reads aloud for five minutes, both partners summarize orally, then switch readers. Summarize and collaborate to write a summary.

SHARING
Share summaries with another team or the class.
  Papers are dated and filed.

Recreational Reading

For approximately 30 minutes, all students read books.

CONVERSATIONS
Teacher holds seven to ten minute conversations with three to four students (individually) discussing sequence of events in their book, what will happen next, and/or _____.

CLIPBOARD NOTES
Teacher notes responses in conversations, or _____.

READ-ALOUD BOOK
Continue current selection or _____.

Writing

MINI-LESSON
Story Parts: Students identify beginning, middle, and end of familiar stories. Identify main problem or conflict in stories. Or _____.
  Proofreading: Include adverbs to tell how, when, or where.

COMPOSING
Continue writing story, conferring and revising as needed. Or _____.

SHARING
Read, respond, and proofread. Identify beginning, middle, and end.
  Papers are dated and filed.

Word Study

CHART DEVELOPMENT
Spelling Emphasis: *ley* or *ly* or
_____

Other Emphasis: "How" words or phrases or _____
Resource: Magazines, newspapers, or

_____

WRITING
Write associations to the chart focus. Student choice

SPELLING
List words to spell in Word Study notebook. Exchange notebook with a partner for a written team test. Check and file in folder.
  Papers are dated and filed.

HOMEWORK
Team test words on spelling list.
  Notebook signed.

Lesson 85

Research

LEAD-IN
Teacher introduces the Research Project:
Topic and Focus: Summarizing/Visual information or _____
Resource: Any visual presentation, video, filmstrip, film, teacher demonstration, or _____

RESEARCH PROJECT
Observe visual presentation. Write a summary of observation.

SHARING
Share summaries with whole class or in groups to note similarities and differences. Reduce or add to summaries, if needed.
 Papers are dated and filed.

Recreational Reading

For approximately 30 minutes, all students read books.

CONVERSATIONS
Teacher moves among students having two to three minute conversations with as many individuals as possible. If appropriate, identify settings in books being read, locate dialogue in books, and/or _____.

CLIPBOARD NOTES
Teacher notes which students do not complete books before returning them, or _____.

READ-ALOUD BOOK
Continue current selection or _____.

Writing

MINI-LESSON
Story leads: Teacher reads examples of effective leads. Or _____.
 Proofreading: Correct use of quotation marks.

COMPOSING
Experiment with different ideas for leads in your story. Confer as needed for revision. Complete rough drafts. Or _____.

SHARING
Read, respond, revise, and proofread with partner or writing group.
 Papers are dated and filed.

Word Study

CHART DEVELOPMENT
Spelling Emphasis: *bly* or _____

Other Emphasis: Movies or _____

Resource: Newspapers, magazines, or _____

WRITING
Write associations to the chart focus. Student choice

SPELLING
List words to spell in Word Study notebook. Exchange notebook with a partner for a written team test. Check and file in folder.
 Papers are dated and filed.

HOMEWORK
Team test words on spelling list.
 Notebook signed.

Lesson 86

Research

LEAD-IN
Teacher introduces the Research Project:
Topic and Focus: Time line/American History or _____
Resource: Social Studies textbooks or _____

RESEARCH PROJECT
Skim chapters to outline time or date range (from _____ to _____) for an American history time line. Form research teams. Student teams choose a time period to locate events and dates they feel should be included on a time line. List dates and events for time line.

SHARING
Teams discuss events selected for the time line.
  Papers are dated and filed.

Recreational Reading

For approximately 30 minutes, all students read books.

CONVERSATIONS
Teacher moves among students having two to three minute conversations with as many individuals as possible. If appropriate, identify settings in books being read, locate dialogue in books, and/or _____.

CLIPBOARD NOTES
Teacher notes which students do not complete books before returning them, or _____.

READ-ALOUD BOOK
Hatchet by Gary Paulsen, *Bridge to Terabithia* by Katherine Paterson, or _____.

Writing

MINI-LESSON
Discuss title page or cover format and illustrations for stories. Review final revision and proofreading checklist. Or _____.

  Proofreading: All proofreading criteria, including paragraph structure, spelling, punctuation, and quotation marks.

COMPOSING
Complete revision, proofreading, and final draft. Illustrate. Or _____.

SHARING
Read revised drafts, respond, final editing and proofreading.
  Papers are dated and filed.

Word Study

CHART DEVELOPMENT
Spelling Emphasis: *ple* or _____

Other Emphasis: Magazines or _____

Resource: Newspapers, magazines, or _____

WRITING
Write associations to the chart focus. Student choice

SPELLING
List words to spell in Word Study notebook. Exchange notebook with a partner for a written team test. Check and file in folder.
  Papers are dated and filed.

HOMEWORK
Team test words on spelling list.
  Notebook signed.

Lesson 87

Research

LEAD-IN
Teacher introduces the Research Project:
Topic and Focus: Time line/American History or _____
Resource: Encyclopedias, textbooks, library books, or _____

RESEARCH PROJECT
Continue reading to select events and dates for the time line. Write selected events and dates on tagboard or strips, adding graphics, if desired.

SHARING
Present time line events and attach to wall area in proper sequence.
  Papers are dated and filed.

Recreational Reading

For approximately 30 minutes, all students read books.

CONVERSATIONS
Teacher moves among students having two to three minute conversations with as many individuals as possible. If appropriate, identify settings in books being read, locate dialogue in books, and/or _____.

CLIPBOARD NOTES
Teacher notes which students do not complete books before returning them, or _____.

READ-ALOUD BOOK
Continue current selection or _____.

Writing

MINI-LESSON
Share Day or _____. Review tips for group sharing.
  Proofreading: Proofread for elements of realism.

COMPOSING
Proofread title page and final draft. Or _____.

SHARING
Small groups meet to read and respond to stories.
  Papers are dated and filed.

Word Study

CHART DEVELOPMENT
Spelling Emphasis: *dge* or _____

Other Emphasis: Computers or _____

Resource: Science books, newspapers, or _____

WRITING
Write associations to the chart focus. Student choice

SPELLING
List words to spell in Word Study notebook. Exchange notebook with a partner for a written team test. Check and file in folder.
  Papers are dated and filed.

HOMEWORK
Team test words on spelling list.
  Notebook signed.

Lesson 88

Research

LEAD-IN
Teacher introduces the Research Project:
Topic and Focus: Time line/American History or _____
Resource: Textbooks, encyclopedias, completed wall time line in the classroom, or _____

RESEARCH PROJECT
Complete adding events to the time line. Read events and dates. Make summarizing and/or opinion statements based on time line.

SHARING
Whole class discusses summarizing statements.
Papers are dated and filed.

Recreational Reading

For approximately 30 minutes, all students read books.

CONVERSATIONS
For approximately 20 minutes, everyone, including the teacher, reads for pleasure. During the last ten minutes, the teacher may choose to talk with some individuals about what they have read, or
_____.

CLIPBOARD NOTES
Teacher notes students who appear to be sleepy or read with their heads down, or
_____.

READ-ALOUD BOOK
Continue current selection or _____.

Writing

MINI-LESSON
Persuasive writing: Advertisements. Or
_____.
Proofreading: Proofread for persuasive words.

COMPOSING
Write an advertisement to persuade buyers. Or locate and write persuasive words and phrases in magazines. Or
_____.

SHARING
Read, respond, and check words that persuade someone to buy.
Papers are dated and filed.

Word Study

CHART DEVELOPMENT
Spelling Emphasis: *ial* or
_____
Other Emphasis: Advertisements or
_____
Resource: Magazines, newspapers, or
_____

WRITING
Write associations to the chart focus. Student choice

SPELLING
List words to spell in Word Study notebook. Exchange notebook with a partner for a written team test. Check and file in folder.
Papers are dated and filed.

HOMEWORK
Team test words on spelling list.
Notebook signed.

Lesson **89**

Research

LEAD-IN
Teacher introduces the Research Project:
Topic and Focus: Time line/Your Life or _____
Resource: Classroom time line, any time line in any resource, or _____

RESEARCH PROJECT
Whole class brainstorms important events in the lives of students (time range: birth to now). Make a list of important events in your life, giving dates. Work individually or in pairs.

SHARING
Share events and dates with a partner. List events without exact dates to complete for homework with parent information.
  Papers are dated and filed.

Recreational Reading

For approximately 30 minutes, all students read books.

CONVERSATIONS
Everyone reads for 20 minutes. During the last ten to fifteen minutes, small groups discuss books/stories group members have read. Groups may be organized by topic, author, genre, or same book, or _____.

CLIPBOARD NOTES
Teacher notes students who appear to be sleepy or read with their heads down, or _____.

READ-ALOUD BOOK
Continue current selection or _____.

Writing

MINI-LESSON
Persuasive writing/Supporting opinions. (Examples: I think kids should/should not be able to wear hats in school; I think women should/should not be in the army.) Or _____.
  Proofreading: Show at least two supporting reasons for opinions.

COMPOSING
Write opinion statements and supporting reasons. Or _____.

SHARING
Read, discuss, and choose a topic opinion sentence to support.
  Papers are dated and filed.

Word Study

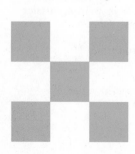

CHART DEVELOPMENT
Spelling Emphasis: *ance* or _____

Other Emphasis: Persuasive words and phrases or _____
Resource: Advertising supplements, coupons, labels, or _____

WRITING
Write associations to the chart focus. Student choice

SPELLING
List words to spell in Word Study notebook. Exchange notebook with a partner for a written team test. Check and file in folder.
  Papers are dated and filed.

HOMEWORK
Team test words on spelling list.
  Notebook signed.

Lesson **90**

Research

LEAD-IN
Teacher introduces the Research Project:
Topic and Focus: Time line/Your Life or _____
Resource: Student time line information or _____

RESEARCH PROJECT
Read collected data for personal time line. Select events to include on your time line. Write events on time line. Draw graphics.

SHARING
Share and compare time lines and why you included or excluded items.
 Papers are dated and filed.

Recreational Reading

For approximately 30 minutes, all students read books.

CONVERSATIONS
Teacher holds seven to ten minute conversations with three to four students (individually) discussing the lead or introduction in their story, oral reading of a chosen passage, or _____.

CLIPBOARD NOTES
Teacher notes students who appear to be sleepy or read with their heads down, or
_____.

READ-ALOUD BOOK
Continue current selection or _____.

Writing

MINI-LESSON
Discuss the role of audience and purpose of persuasive writing. (Persuasive writing includes an opinion statement, supporting details, and a concluding sentence.) Or

_____.
 Proofreading: Arrange supporting details in clear and logical order.

COMPOSING
Choose an opinion from your list and write to persuade others. Or _____.

SHARING
Read, respond, and proofread for at least two supporting details.
 Papers are dated and filed.

Word Study

CHART DEVELOPMENT
Spelling Emphasis: *tro* or Chart Review Day
Other Emphasis: Time line events or _____
Resource: Research papers, student information, or _____

WRITING
Write associations to the chart focus. Student choice

SPELLING
List words to spell in Word Study notebook. Exchange notebook with a partner for a written team test. Check and file in folder.
 Papers are dated and filed.

HOMEWORK
Team test words on spelling list.
 Notebook signed.

Lesson 91

Research

LEAD-IN
Teacher introduces the Research Project:
Topic and Focus: Scientists/Selecting Topics or _____
Resource: Health and/or Science text-books or _____

RESEARCH PROJECT
Read to list names of scientists and/or subtopics to research. Form teams and choose topics. Staple together notetaking sheets, and locate resources. Write any facts already known.

SHARING
Discuss any information already known by group members. Share lists of resources and ideas for further research.
 Papers are dated and filed.

Recreational Reading

For approximately 30 minutes, all students read books.

CONVERSATIONS
Teacher holds seven to ten minute conversations with three to four students (individually) discussing the lead or introduction in their story, oral reading of a chosen passage, or _____.

CLIPBOARD NOTES
Teacher notes oral reading fluency, or _____.

READ-ALOUD BOOK
Einstein by Nigel Hunter, *Einstein Anderson, Science Sleuth* by Seymore Simon, or _____

Writing

MINI-LESSON
Writer's technique: Conversations. Or _____. Staple together sheets to keep in Writing folder as a sourcebook to practice writing techniques.
 Proofreading: Dialogue adds action, feelings, and thoughts.

COMPOSING
Write conversations between two people, an animal and a person, or between an animal and a plant. Or _____.

SHARING
Read, respond, and proofread for natural dialogue and punctuation.
 Papers are dated and filed.

Word Study

CHART DEVELOPMENT
Spelling Emphasis: Words with prefixes *un, im,* or _____
Other Emphasis: Research or _____

Resource: Spelling and/or language textbooks, or _____

WRITING
Write associations to the chart focus. Student choice

SPELLING
List words to spell in Word Study notebook. Exchange notebook with a partner for a written team test. Check and file in folder.
 Papers are dated and filed.

HOMEWORK
Team test words on spelling list.
 Notebook signed.

Lesson **92**

Research

LEAD-IN
Teacher introduces the Research Project:
Topic and Focus: Scientists/
Notetaking or _____
Resource: Encyclopedias, science texts, reference books, or _____

RESEARCH PROJECT
Read to locate information about a scientist. List main contribution(s) and other notes of interest in notetaking booklet. Or _____.

SHARING
Compare findings with group members and add to notes. Share main contribution statements with the class.
    Papers are dated and filed.

Recreational Reading

For approximately 30 minutes, all students read books.

CONVERSATIONS
Teacher holds seven to ten minute conversations with three to four students (individually) discussing the lead or introduction in their story, oral reading of a chosen passage, or _____.

CLIPBOARD NOTES
Teacher notes oral reading fluency, or _____.

READ-ALOUD BOOK
Continue current selection or _____.

Writing

MINI-LESSON
Writer's technique: Time. Or _____.
Experiment with changing time by changing verb tenses.
    Proofreading: Consistent verb tense to show time in writing.

COMPOSING
Write about a trip, first in the past and then rewrite it in the future tense. Or _____.

SHARING
Read, respond, and proofread for consistent verb tense to show time.
    Papers are dated and filed.

Word Study

CHART DEVELOPMENT
Spelling Emphasis: Words with prefixes *dis, in,* or _____
Other Emphasis: Scientists or _____
Resource: Health and/or science textbooks, or _____

WRITING
Write associations to the chart focus. Student choice

SPELLING
List words to spell in Word Study notebook. Exchange notebook with a partner for a written team test. Check and file in folder.
    Papers are dated and filed.

HOMEWORK
Team test words on spelling list.
    Notebook signed.

Lesson 93

Research

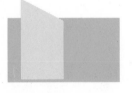

LEAD-IN
Teacher introduces the Research Project:
Topic and Focus: Scientists/
Notetaking or _____
Resource: Library books, filmstrips,
videos, or _____

RESEARCH PROJECT
Read to locate information about a scientist. *When* and *where* information. Write data on notetaking sheets. Write other interesting facts.

SHARING
Compare findings with other group members. Add to notes. Share *When* and *Where* information with the class.
  Papers are dated and filed.

Recreational Reading

For approximately 30 minutes, all students read books.

CONVERSATIONS
Teacher holds seven to ten minute conversations with three to four students (individually) discussing the lead or introduction in their story, oral reading of a chosen passage, or _____.

CLIPBOARD NOTES
Teacher notes oral reading fluency, or
_____.

READ-ALOUD BOOK
Continue current selection or _____.

Writing

MINI-LESSON
Writer's technique: Point of View. Or
_____. Illustrate point of view in books (*Ben and Me* by Robert Lawson or *Two Bad Ants* by Chris Van Allsburg).
  Proofreading: Punctuation of sentences beginning with *when, if,* and *because.*

COMPOSING
Be an ant on the kitchen counter, and write what you see and do. Or
_____.

SHARING
Read, respond, and proofread with a partner.
  Papers are dated and filed.

Word Study

CHART DEVELOPMENT
Spelling Emphasis: Words with prefixes *pre, re,* or _____
Other Emphasis: Diseases or
_____

Resource: Newspapers, health books, or _____

WRITING
Write associations to the chart focus. Student choice

SPELLING
List words to spell in Word Study notebook. Exchange notebook with a partner for a written team test. Check and file in folder.
  Papers are dated and filed.

HOMEWORK
Team test words on spelling list.
  Notebook signed.

Research

LEAD-IN
Teacher introduces the Research Project:
Topic and Focus: Scientists/Cause and Effect or _____
Resource: Newspapers, magazines, textbooks, or _____

RESEARCH PROJECT
Read to locate effects of the work of the scientist. Write cause-and-effect statements based on your information.

SHARING
Compare and compile cause and effect statements.
   Papers are dated and filed.

Recreational Reading

For approximately 30 minutes, all students read books.

CONVERSATIONS
Teacher holds seven to ten minute conversations with three to four students (individually) discussing the lead or introduction in their story, oral reading of a chosen passage, or _____.

CLIPBOARD NOTES
Teacher notes oral reading fluency, or _____.

READ-ALOUD BOOK
Continue current selection or _____.

Writing

MINI-LESSON
Writer's technique: Clustering (Blue). Or _____. Class volunteers words related to *blue*. Use clustering as a prewriting technique in your sourcebook.
   Proofreading: Correct use of *there, they're,* and *their*

COMPOSING
Cluster a word in your sourcebook (*fright, dark, fuzzy*) and write using words in the cluster as a focus. Or _____.

SHARING
Read, respond, and proofread with a partner.
   Papers are dated and filed.

Word Study

CHART DEVELOPMENT
Spelling Emphasis: Words with prefixes *ex, en, non,* or _____
Other Emphasis: Current events or _____

Resource: Newspapers, magazines, or _____

WRITING
Write associations to the chart focus. Student choice

SPELLING
List words to spell in Word Study notebook. Exchange notebook with a partner for a written team test. Check and file in folder.
   Papers are dated and filed.

HOMEWORK
Team test words on spelling list.
   Notebook signed.

Lesson **95**

Research

LEAD-IN
Teacher introduces the Research Project:
Topic and Focus: Scientists/
Presentations or _____
Resource: All student notes or _____

RESEARCH PROJECT
Read all notes in groups to evaluate most important information. Write most interesting/important data on charts or posters to present to the class. Or _____.

SHARING
Share posters or charts with class. (This may be a two-day lesson). Evaluate presentations.
   Papers are dated and filed.

Recreational Reading

For approximately 30 minutes, all students read books.

CONVERSATIONS
Teacher holds seven to ten minute conversations with three to four students (individually) discussing the lead or introduction in their story, oral reading of a chosen passage, or _____.

CLIPBOARD NOTES
Teacher notes oral reading fluency, or _____.

READ-ALOUD BOOK
Continue current selection or _____.

Writing

MINI-LESSON
Writer's technique: Metaphors. Or _____. (*The Search for Delicious* by Natalie Babbitt or *Two Bad Ants* by Chris Van Allsburg or poems) Give examples.
   Proofreading: Include a metaphor, if appropriate.

COMPOSING
Create metaphors in poems or lists. (Delicious is _____; Some days I am a _____) Or _____.

SHARING
Read, respond, and proofread.
   Papers are dated and filed.

Word Study

CHART DEVELOPMENT
Spelling Emphasis: Words with prefixes *il, ir, mis,* or _____. Or Chart Review Day.
Other Emphasis: Law or _____
Resource: Newspapers, magazines, or _____

WRITING
Write associations to the chart focus. Student choice

SPELLING
List words to spell in Word Study notebook. Exchange notebook with a partner for a written team test. Check and file in folder.
   Papers are dated and filed.

HOMEWORK
Team test words on spelling list.
   Notebook signed.

Lesson **96**

Research

LEAD-IN
Teacher introduces the Research Project:
Topic and Focus: Map reading/Kinds of maps or _____
Resource: Social Studies textbooks, house magazines, any maps, or _____

RESEARCH PROJECT
Locate and list different kinds of maps. Work with partners or groups.

SHARING
Discuss different kinds of maps to choose one to make. Discuss ideas for the map.
Papers are dated and filed.

Recreational Reading

For approximately 30 minutes, all students read books.

CONVERSATIONS
Teacher holds seven to ten minute conversations with three to four students (individually) discussing the lead or introduction in their story, oral reading of a chosen passage, or _____.

CLIPBOARD NOTES
Teacher notes oral reading fluency, or _____.

READ-ALOUD BOOK
The Search for Delicious by Natalie Babbitt, *Two Bad Ants* by Chris Van Allsburg, or _____.

Writing

MINI-LESSON
Writer's technique: Similes. Or _____. Find examples in poems or stories. Create similes with students.
Proofreading: Include a simile.

COMPOSING
Write a poem or description of a blizzard. Or create a list of similes in your sourcebook. Or _____.

SHARING
Read, respond, and proofread for a simile.
Papers are dated and filed.

Word Study

CHART DEVELOPMENT
Spelling Emphasis: Words with suffixes *ment, sion,* or _____
Other Emphasis: Maps or

_____
Resource: Social Studies textbooks, maps, or _____

WRITING
Write associations to the chart focus. Student choice

SPELLING
List words to spell in Word Study notebook. Exchange notebook with a partner for a written team test. Check and file in folder.
Papers are dated and filed.

HOMEWORK
Team test words on spelling list.
Notebook signed.

Lesson 97

Research

LEAD-IN
Teacher introduces the Research Project:
Topic and Focus: Map making/Symbols and map parts or _____
Resource: Library books, floor plans, atlases, gazetteers, or _____.

RESEARCH PROJECT
Read to locate different map views, symbols, and parts of maps. List map parts. With a partner, list ideas for a map you will create. (A treasure map, a map of the school, any student ideas.)

SHARING
Teams share and evaluate map ideas.
  Papers are dated and filed.

Recreational Reading

For approximately 30 minutes, all students read books.

CONVERSATIONS
Teacher moves among students having two to three minute conversations with as many individuals as possible. If appropriate, have students predict what might happen next, call attention to words with affixes, or _____.

CLIPBOARD NOTES
Teacher notes titles being read, or _____.

READ-ALOUD BOOK
Continue current selection or _____.

Writing

MINI-LESSON
Writer's technique: Descriptive phrases.
Or _____. Students volunteer descriptive phrases and words about a picture.
  Proofreading: Include specific action and color words.

COMPOSING
Choose a piece of art to observe, list descriptive words and phrases, and then write a poem or description. Or _____.

SHARING
Read, respond with a partner or groups, proofread.
  Papers are dated and filed.

Word Study

CHART DEVELOPMENT
Spelling Emphasis: Words with suffixes *tion, ful,* or _____
Other Emphasis: Art or _____
Resource: Newspapers, magazines, or _____

WRITING
Write associations to the chart focus. Student choice

SPELLING
List words to spell in Word Study notebook. Exchange notebook with a partner for a written team test. Check and file in folder.
  Papers are dated and filed.

HOMEWORK
Team test words on spelling list.
  Notebook signed.

Lesson **98**

Research

LEAD-IN
Teacher introduces the Research Project:
Topic and Focus: Map making/Map symbols or _____
Resource: Any maps or _____

RESEARCH PROJECT
Continue reading and looking at maps to plan map design. Write and/or draw a sketch of the map. Discuss additional features needed and materials for design.

SHARING
Share your map plan with another team to explain symbols and plan.
   Papers are dated and filed.

Recreational Reading

For approximately 30 minutes, all students read books.

CONVERSATIONS
Teacher moves among students having two to three minute conversations with as many individuals as possible. If appropriate, have students predict what might happen next, call attention to words with affixes, or _____.

CLIPBOARD NOTES
Teacher notes titles being read, or
_____.

READ-ALOUD BOOK
Continue current selection or _____.

Writing

MINI-LESSON
Writer's technique: "Show, not tell." Or _____. Model examples in books, or write a sentence, such as, "Mom was furious." Students suggest ways to *show,* not tell.
   Proofreading: Include adverbs to show *How.*

COMPOSING
Write a *telling* statement, then list behaviors or actions that *show.* Or
_____.

SHARING
Read, respond, and proofread with a partner or group.
   Papers are dated and filed.

Word Study

CHART DEVELOPMENT
Spelling Emphasis: Words with suffixes *ness, ing,* or _____
Other Emphasis: Our town or
_____
Resource: Chamber of Commerce info, newspapers, or _____.

WRITING
Write associations to the chart focus. Student choice

SPELLING
List words to spell in Word Study notebook. Exchange notebook with a partner for a written team test. Check and file in folder.
   Papers are dated and filed.

HOMEWORK
Team test words on spelling list.
   Notebook signed.

Lesson 99

Research

LEAD-IN
Teacher introduces the Research Project:
Topic and Focus: Map Making/Map description or _____
Resource: Student information, any maps, or _____

RESEARCH PROJECT
Complete drawing final map. Complete legend and title of the map. Write a description of the area.

SHARING
Discuss final design and description with another team.
  Papers are dated and filed.

Recreational Reading

For approximately 30 minutes, all students read books.

CONVERSATIONS
Teacher moves among students having two to three minute conversations with as many individuals as possible. If appropriate, have students predict what might happen next, call attention to words with affixes, or _____.

CLIPBOARD NOTES
Teacher notes titles being read, or _____.

READ-ALOUD BOOK
Continue current selection or _____.

Writing

MINI-LESSON
Writer's technique: Thesaurus. Or _____. List different words to replace overused words, such as *said,* or *went.*
  Proofreading: Identify and replace overused words with specific words.

COMPOSING
Choose a sourcebook entry to revise, and share in writing group. List words to replace overused words (*said, went, pretty, good, nice*). Or _____.

SHARING
Read, respond, and proofread.
  Papers are dated and filed.

Word Study

CHART DEVELOPMENT
Spelling Emphasis: Words with suffixes *ly, less,* or _____
Other Emphasis: Geography: land forms or _____
Resource: Maps, Social Studies textbooks, or _____

WRITING
Write associations to the chart focus. Student choice

SPELLING
List words to spell in Word Study notebook. Exchange notebook with a partner for a written team test. Check and file in folder.
  Papers are dated and filed.

HOMEWORK
Team test words on spelling list.
  Notebook signed.

Lesson **100**

Research

LEAD-IN
Teacher introduces the Research Project:
Topic and Focus: Map making/
Presentations or _____
Resource: Student-created maps or
_____

RESEARCH PROJECT
Class suggests points for evaluation of
map presentations. Partners present completed maps to the class. Write responses
to map design and information. Or
_____.

SHARING
Share comments on presentations and
projects.
Papers are dated and filed.

Recreational Reading

For approximately 30 minutes, all students read books.

CONVERSATIONS
For approximately 20 minutes, everyone,
including the teacher, reads for pleasure.
During the last ten minutes, the teacher
may choose to talk with some individuals
about what they have read, or
_____.

CLIPBOARD NOTES
Teacher notes students who reread the
same books, or _____.

READ-ALOUD BOOK
Continue current selection or _____.

Writing

MINI-LESSON
Writer's technique: Combining sentences.
Or _____.
Proofreading: Combine short repetitive
sentences.

COMPOSING
Final revision of a sourcebook entry. Or
_____.

SHARING
Read and respond to completed pieces in
writing groups.
Papers are dated and filed.

Word Study

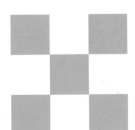

CHART DEVELOPMENT
Spelling Emphasis: Words with
suffixes *or, er,* or Chart Review Day
Other Emphasis: Geography: water
forms or _____
Resource: Newspapers, magazines, or
_____

WRITING
Write associations to the chart focus. Student choice

SPELLING
List words to spell in Word Study notebook. Exchange notebook with a partner
for a written team test. Check and file in
folder.
Papers are dated and filed.

HOMEWORK
Team test words on spelling list.
Notebook signed.

Lesson **101**

Research

LEAD-IN
Teacher introduces the Research Project:
Topic and Focus: Environment/Main idea or _____
Resource: Newspapers, science textbooks or _____

RESEARCH PROJECT
Read to locate information about an environmental issue. With a partner, discuss and write the main idea of the article/information. Or _____.

SHARING
Share main ideas with other partners or with whole class.
    Papers are dated and filed.

Recreational Reading

For approximately 30 minutes, all students read books.

CONVERSATIONS
During the last ten to fifteen minutes, small groups form to discuss books/stories group members are presently reading, using summarizing statements, or

_____.

CLIPBOARD NOTES
Teacher notes students who have difficulty summarizing, or _____.

READ-ALOUD BOOK
The Wump World by Bill Peet, *The Lorax* by Dr. Seuss, Book Talk fantasy selections (*The Dark Is Rising* Sequence by Susan Cooper, *Prydain Chronicles* by Lloyd Alexander, *The Owlstone Crown* by X. J. Kennedy), or _____

Writing

MINI-LESSON
Story Writing: Fantasy and/or Science Fiction. (Ten days) Or _____. List some elements of both.
    Proofreading: Correct use of apostrophe in contractions and possessives.

COMPOSING
List ideas for fantasy and/or science fiction stories. Or _____.

SHARING
Read, respond, and proofread with a partner.
    Papers are dated and filed.

Word Study

CHART DEVELOPMENT
Spelling Emphasis: Contractions or _____

Other Emphasis: Pollution or _____

Resource: Newspapers, magazines, or _____

WRITING
Write associations to the chart focus. Student choice

SPELLING
List words to spell in Word Study notebook. Exchange notebook with a partner for a written team test. Check and file in folder.
    Papers are dated and filed.

HOMEWORK
Team test words on spelling list. Read in a library book for five minutes, and list any contractions.
    Notebook signed.

Lesson 102

Research

LEAD-IN
Teacher introduces the Research Project:
Topic and Focus: Environment/
Cause and Effect or _____
Resource: Social Studies textbooks,
magazines, or _____

RESEARCH PROJECT
Partners read to locate information
related to environmental issues. Write
cause-and-effect statements based on reading. Or _____.

SHARING
Partners compare statements, or share
with the whole class.
  Papers are dated and filed.

Recreational Reading

For approximately 30 minutes, all students read books.

CONVERSATIONS
Teacher holds seven to ten minute conversations with three to four students (individually), discussing and locating
examples of actions that "show" characters in their books, or _____.

CLIPBOARD NOTES
Teacher notes student responses in conversations, or _____.

READ-ALOUD BOOK
Continue current selection or *Mrs. Frisby
and the Rats of NIMH* by Robert O'Brien,
The Iron Giant by Ted Hughes, or
_____

Writing

MINI-LESSON
Fantasy or science fiction: Setting. Or
_____.

  Proofreading: Include mood words, or
adverbs to create suspense or tension,
such as *suddenly, creepily,* or *silently.*

COMPOSING
Begin writing a fantasy story, describing
the setting. Or write descriptions of possible settings. Or _____.

SHARING
Read, respond, and proofread with a
partner.
  Papers are dated and filed.

Word Study

CHART DEVELOPMENT
Spelling Emphasis: Contractions or
_____

Other Emphasis: Air or _____
Resource: Science textbooks, magazines, Language textbooks, or _____

WRITING
Write associations to the chart focus. Student choice

SPELLING
List words to spell in Word Study notebook. Exchange notebook with a partner
for a written team test. Check and file in
folder.
  Papers are dated and filed.

HOMEWORK
Team test words on spelling list.
  Notebook signed.

Lesson **103**

Research

LEAD-IN
Teacher introduces the Research Project:
Topic and Focus: Environment/Problem Solving or _____
Resource: Newspapers, printed information from environmental groups, textbooks, library books, or _____

RESEARCH PROJECT
Read to locate solutions for environmental problems. List or make a chart to show problem, cause, possible solutions. Work with a partner or small group. Or _____.

SHARING
Share information with another team, combine into one main chart.
  Papers are dated and filed.

Recreational Reading

For approximately 30 minutes, all students read books.

CONVERSATIONS
Teacher holds seven to ten minute conversations with three to four students (individually), discussing and locating examples of actions that "show" characters in their books, or _____.

CLIPBOARD NOTES
Teacher notes student responses in conversations, or _____.

READ-ALOUD BOOK
Continue current selection or _____.

Writing

MINI-LESSON
Fantasy or science fiction: Characters. Or _____.
  Proofreading: Join sentences with conjunctions and a comma.

COMPOSING
Write a description of a fantasy or science fiction character. Or continue writing in progress. Or _____.

SHARING
Read, respond, and proofread with a partner.
  Papers are dated and filed.

Word Study

CHART DEVELOPMENT
Spelling Emphasis: Compound words or _____
Other Emphasis: Water or _____

Resource: Health and Science textbooks, encyclopedias, or _____

WRITING
Write associations to the chart focus. Student choice

SPELLING
List words to spell in Word Study notebook. Exchange notebook with a partner for a written team test. Check and file in folder.
  Papers are dated and filed.

HOMEWORK
Team test words on spelling list.
  Notebook signed.

Lesson **104**

Research

LEAD-IN
Teacher introduces the Research Project:
Topic and Focus: Environment/Main Ideas or _____
Resource: Local newspaper, environmental speaker, news broadcast or video, or _____

RESEARCH PROJECT
Read to investigate a local environmental issue. Write about the two (or more) sides of the issue. Or write an editorial about the issue. Or _____.

SHARING
Discuss the issue with another team and take sides based on facts.
    Papers are dated and filed.

Recreational Reading

For approximately 30 minutes, all students read books.

CONVERSATIONS
Teacher holds seven to ten minute conversations with three to four students (individually), discussing and locating examples of actions that "show" characters in their books, or _____.

CLIPBOARD NOTES
Teacher notes student responses in conversations, or _____.

READ-ALOUD BOOK
Continue current selection or _____.

Writing

MINI-LESSON
Fantasy: "Metamorphosis." Or _____. List things you might "change" into.
    Proofreading: Include feelings from the changed point of view.

COMPOSING
"One morning I looked in my mirror, and saw that I had changed into a _____." Or continue writing in progress. Or _____.

SHARING
Read, respond, and proofread with a partner.
    Papers are dated and filed.

Word Study

CHART DEVELOPMENT
Spelling Emphasis: Compound words or _____
Other Emphasis: Chemicals or _____

Resource: Newspapers, Science textbooks, or _____

WRITING
Write associations to the chart focus. Student choice

SPELLING
List words to spell in Word Study notebook. Exchange notebook with a partner for a written team test. Check and file in folder.
    Papers are dated and filed.

HOMEWORK
Team test words on spelling list.
    Notebook signed.

Lesson 105

Research

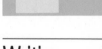

LEAD-IN
Teacher introduces the Research Project:
Topic and Focus: Environment/
Presentations or _____
Resource: Bumper stickers, buttons, slogans, leaflets about the environment, or _____ .

RESEARCH PROJECT
Read the materials and discuss what they mean. Design a poster, bumper sticker, or button that makes your views known on an issue. Or choose a slogan to explain in writing. Or _____ .

SHARING
Share with the class. Explain why you feel as you do about the environmental issue.
   Papers are dated and filed.

Recreational Reading

For approximately 30 minutes, all students read books.

CONVERSATIONS
Teacher holds seven to ten minute conversations with three to four students (individually), discussing and locating examples of actions that "show" characters in their books, or _____ .

CLIPBOARD NOTES
Teacher notes student responses in conversations, or _____ .

READ-ALOUD BOOK
Continue current selection or _____ .

Writing

MINI-LESSON
Science fiction: Robots or Aliens. Or
_____ .
   Proofreading: Review dialogue and dialect.

COMPOSING
Write a conversation between an alien and a human. Or continue writing in progress. Or _____ .

SHARING
Read aloud dialogues, giving speech intonation and/or dialect.
   Papers are dated and filed.

Word Study

CHART DEVELOPMENT
Spelling Emphasis: Possessive nouns or Chart Review Day
Other Emphasis: Fantasy or science fiction or _____
Resource: Library books, newspapers, or _____ .

WRITING
Write associations to the chart focus. Student choice

SPELLING
List words to spell in Word Study notebook. Exchange notebook with a partner for a written team test. Check and file in folder.
   Papers are dated and filed.

HOMEWORK
Team test words on spelling list.
   Notebook signed.

Lesson 106

Research

LEAD-IN
Teacher introduces the Research Project:
Topic and Focus: Super-heroes/Charting Information or _____

Resource: Comic books, cartoons, magazines, library books, videos, or _____

RESEARCH PROJECT
Work in groups or with a partner to select a superhero/heroine to read about. List "super" qualities and information about the character. Or _____.

SHARING
Read list of qualities to the class, and suggest chart headings for the information. (Name, secret identity, powers, special body features, etc.)
   Papers are dated and filed.

Recreational Reading

For approximately 30 minutes, all students read books.

CONVERSATIONS
Teacher holds seven to ten minute conversations with three to four students (individually), discussing and locating examples of actions that "show" characters in their books, or _____.

CLIPBOARD NOTES
Teacher notes student responses in conversations, or _____.

READ-ALOUD BOOK
A Wrinkle in Time by Madeline L'Engle, _The Trolley to Yesterday_ by John Bellairs, _Tuck Everlasting_ by Natalie Babbitt, or
_____

Writing

MINI-LESSON
Fantasy: Time travel. Or _____.
   Proofreading: Correct use of possessive forms in sentences.

COMPOSING
Write about a time travel experience you would like to have. Or continue writing in progress. Or _____.

SHARING
Read, respond, and proofread with a partner.
   Papers are dated and filed.

Word Study

CHART DEVELOPMENT
Spelling Emphasis: Possessive nouns or _____
Other Emphasis: Superheroes or _____

Resource: Comic books, cartoons, comic strips, or _____

WRITING
Write associations to the chart focus. Student choice

SPELLING
List words to spell in Word Study notebook. Exchange notebook with a partner for a written team test. Check and file in folder.
   Papers are dated and filed.

HOMEWORK
Team test words on spelling list.
   Notebook signed.

Lesson **107**

Research

LEAD-IN
Teacher introduces the Research Project:
Topic and Focus: Super-heroes/Charting Information or
_____

Resource: Newspapers, library books, comic books, or _____

RESEARCH PROJECT
Read to locate information about special equipment or tools of superheroes, heroines, or other qualities. Make chart, add headings, and fill in information. Or _____.

SHARING
Share chart information with another pair or whole class.
　Papers are dated and filed.

Recreational Reading

For approximately 30 minutes, all students read books.

CONVERSATIONS
Teacher holds seven to ten minute conversations with three to four students (individually), discussing and locating examples of actions that "show" characters in their books, or _____.

CLIPBOARD NOTES
Teacher notes student responses in conversations, or _____.

READ-ALOUD BOOK
Continue current selection or _____.

Writing

MINI-LESSON
Fantasy: Creatures. Or _____. (Set date for sharing Fantasy writings: Lesson 110.)
　Proofreading: Correct use of *was* and *were* in sentences.

COMPOSING
Write about a fantasy creature, or create a new one. Or continue writing in progress. Or _____.

SHARING
Read, respond, and proofread with a partner.
　Papers are dated and filed.

Word Study

CHART DEVELOPMENT
Spelling Emphasis: Possessive forms or _____
Other Emphasis: Cartoon characters or _____
Resource: TV guides, newspapers, entertainment guides, or _____

WRITING
Write associations to the chart focus. Student choice

SPELLING
List words to spell in Word Study notebook. Exchange notebook with a partner for a written team test. Check and file in folder.
　Papers are dated and filed.

HOMEWORK
Team test words on spelling list.
　Notebook signed.

Research

LEAD-IN
Teacher introduces the Research Project:
Topic and Focus: Super-heroes/Charting Information or
_____

Resource: All available materials or
_____

RESEARCH PROJECT
Read about a superhero/heroine to locate information about how the hero helps others, or other facts. List facts in chart columns. Or _____.

SHARING
Compare chart information with other teams.
    Papers are dated and filed.

Recreational Reading

For approximately 30 minutes, all students read books.

CONVERSATIONS
Teacher holds seven to ten minute conversations with three to four students (individually), discussing and locating examples of actions that "show" characters in their books, or _____.

CLIPBOARD NOTES
Teacher notes student responses in conversations, or _____.

READ-ALOUD BOOK
Continue current selection or _____.

Writing

MINI-LESSON
Fantasy, science fiction: Plot Sequence. Or _____. Fantasy and science fiction need enough reality to make them believable.
    Proofreading: Clear logical transitions in plot.

COMPOSING
Choose a fantasy writing to complete and revise. Or _____.

SHARING
Read, respond, and proofread with a partner.
    Papers are dated and filed.

Word Study

CHART DEVELOPMENT
Spelling Emphasis: Past tense verbs or _____
Other Emphasis: Ancient times or civilizations, or _____
Resource: Social Studies textbooks, encyclopedias, or _____

WRITING
Write associations to the chart focus. Student choice

SPELLING
List words to spell in Word Study notebook. Exchange notebook with a partner for a written team test. Check and file in folder.
    Papers are dated and filed.

HOMEWORK
Team test words on spelling list.
    Notebook signed.

Lesson **109**

Research

LEAD-IN
Teacher introduces the Research Project:
Topic and Focus: Super-heroes/Charting Information or
_____

Resource: Student designed charts or
_____

RESEARCH PROJECT
Read charts to make final chart additions. Create a new superhero/heroine, listing information on the chart. Or
_____.

SHARING
Tell about new superhero to another team, using chart information.
Papers are dated and filed.

Recreational Reading

For approximately 30 minutes, all students read books.

CONVERSATIONS
Teacher moves among students having two to three minute conversations with as many individuals as possible. If appropriate, discuss inferences, and/or _____.

CLIPBOARD NOTES
Teacher notes who might benefit from assisted reading, or _____.

READ-ALOUD BOOK
Continue current selection or _____.

Writing

MINI-LESSON
Revision and illustration of fantasy or science fiction piece. Or _____. Students design sharing mode.
Proofreading: Check for run-on sentences, correct use of subjunctive *were*.

COMPOSING
Write final copy of piece; illustrate. Or write about a future time. Or _____.

SHARING
Read, respond, and proofread with a partner. Classify piece as fantasy, science fiction, or other.
Papers are dated and filed.

Word Study

CHART DEVELOPMENT
Spelling Emphasis: Future tense verbs or _____
Other Emphasis: Future or
_____

Resource: Newspapers, library books, magazines, or _____

WRITING
Write associations to the chart focus. Student choice

SPELLING
List words to spell in Word Study notebook. Exchange notebook with a partner for a written team test. Check and file in folder.
Papers are dated and filed.

HOMEWORK
Team test words on spelling list.
Notebook signed.

Research

LEAD-IN
Teacher introduces the Research Project:
Topic and Focus: Super-heroes/Presentations or _____
Resource: Completed student charts or _____

RESEARCH PROJECT
Complete charts, headings, and new heroes. Or write a short adventure for your superhero. Or _____.

SHARING
Present your new hero to the class, displaying chart information. Or read aloud your new superhero's adventure.
   Papers are dated and filed.

Recreational Reading

For approximately 30 minutes, all students read books.

CONVERSATIONS
Teacher moves among students having two to three minute conversations with as many individuals as possible. If appropriate, discuss inferences, and/or _____.

CLIPBOARD NOTES
Teacher notes who might benefit from assisted reading, or _____.

READ-ALOUD BOOK
Continue current selection or _____.

Writing

MINI-LESSON
Share Day: Fantasy and science fiction stories. Or _____.
   Proofreading: Use of prepositional phrases in sentences.

COMPOSING
Final editing. Write evaluative comments about your paper. Or _____.

SHARING
Share stories in response groups or whole class. Or have a fantasy story contest: Select judges and winners.
   Papers are dated and filed.

Word Study

CHART DEVELOPMENT
Spelling Emphasis: Present tense verbs or Chart Review Day
Other Emphasis: Musicians, musical groups, or _____
Resource: Newspapers or _____

WRITING
Write associations to the chart focus. Student choice

SPELLING
List words to spell in Word Study notebook. Exchange notebook with a partner for a written team test. Check and file in folder.
   Papers are dated and filed.

HOMEWORK
Team test words on spelling list.
   Notebook signed.

Lesson 111

Research

LEAD-IN
Teacher introduces the research project:
Topic and Focus: Real heroes/heroines/Topic Selection or
_____

Resource: Library books, textbooks, encyclopedias, or _____

RESEARCH PROJECT
Choose a real hero/heroine. Work with a partner or individually to write what you know, what you want to find out, and how you will learn it. Or _____.

SHARING
Share WHY this person is a "hero/heroine" to you.
Papers are dated and filed.

Recreational Reading

For approximately 30 minutes, all students read books.

CONVERSATIONS
Teacher moves among students having two to three minute conversations with as many individuals as possible. If appropriate, discuss inferences, or _____.

CLIPBOARD NOTES
Teacher notes who asks about unfamiliar words in books, or _____.

READ-ALOUD BOOK
El Chino by Allen Say, _Shadow of a Bull_ by Maia Woiciechowska, or _____

Writing

MINI-LESSON
Factual Writing: Caterpillars. Or
_____.
Proofreading: Combining sentences to form compound sentences.

COMPOSING
Write what you know and/or how you feel about caterpillars. Or list topics for factual writing; choose one for composing. Or _____.

SHARING
Read, respond, and proofread with a partner.
Papers are dated and filed.

Word Study

CHART DEVELOPMENT
Spelling Emphasis: Plurals or
_____

Other Emphasis: Crawling things or
_____

Resource: Science books, encyclopedias, or _____

WRITING
Write associations to the chart focus. Student choice

SPELLING
List words to spell in Word Study notebook. Exchange notebook with a partner for a written team test. Check and file in folder.
Papers are dated and filed.

HOMEWORK
Team test words on spelling list.
Notebook signed.

Lesson 112

Research

LEAD-IN
Teacher introduces the research project:
Topic and Focus: Real heroes/Notetaking or _____
Resource: Library books, encyclopedias, textbooks, or _____

RESEARCH PROJECT
Read to locate information to support your topic as a hero. Take notes. Or _____.

SHARING
Share notes with a partner or another team.
Papers are dated and filed.

Recreational Reading

For approximately 30 minutes, all students read books.

CONVERSATIONS
For approximately 20 minutes, everyone, including the teacher, reads. During the last ten minutes, the teacher may choose to talk with some individuals about what they have read. Ask one or two students to tell about their book.

CLIPBOARD NOTES
Teacher notes who asks about unfamiliar words in books, or _____.

READ-ALOUD BOOK
Continue current selection or _____.

Writing

MINI-LESSON
Factual Writing: Stars. Or _____.
Proofreading: Correctly written plural forms.

COMPOSING
Write what you know and how you feel about stars or other topic. Or _____.

SHARING
Read, respond, and proofread with a partner.
Papers are dated and filed.

Word Study

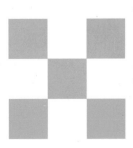

CHART DEVELOPMENT
Spelling Emphasis: Plurals or _____

Other Emphasis: Stars or _____
Resource: Science textbooks, newspapers, or _____

WRITING
Write associations to the chart focus. Student choice

SPELLING
List words to spell in Word Study notebook. Exchange notebook with a partner for a written team test. Check and file in folder.
Papers are dated and filed.

HOMEWORK
Team test words on spelling list.
Notebook signed.

Lesson 113

Research

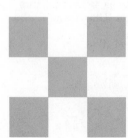

LEAD-IN
Teacher introduces the research project:
Topic and Focus: Heroes/Notetaking
or _____
Resource: Newspapers, magazines, library books, or _____

RESEARCH PROJECT
Continue reading to take notes about a real hero. Or _____.

SHARING
Discuss notes with a partner or another team.
   Papers are dated and filed.

Recreational Reading

For approximately 30 minutes, all students read books.

CONVERSATIONS
During the last ten to fifteen minutes small groups discuss books/stories group members have read. Groups may be organized by topic, author, or same book. Or _____.

CLIPBOARD NOTES
Teacher notes favorite authors or genres, or _____.

READ-ALOUD BOOK
Continue current selection or _____.

Writing

MINI-LESSON
Factual Writing: Music. Or _____.
   Proofreading: Correctly written plural forms.

COMPOSING
Write about music, including factual information. Or _____.

SHARING
Read, respond, and proofread with a partner.
   Papers are dated and filed.

Word Study

CHART DEVELOPMENT
Spelling Emphasis: Plurals (Words ending in *o, x, ch*) or _____
Other Emphasis: Musical instruments or _____
Resource: Dictionaries, newspapers, encyclopedias, or _____

WRITING
Write associations to the chart focus. Student choice

SPELLING
List words to spell in Word Study notebook. Exchange notebook with a partner for a written team test. Check and file in folder.
   Papers are dated and filed.

HOMEWORK
Team test words on spelling list.
   Notebook signed.

Research

LEAD-IN
Teacher introduces the research project:
Topic and Focus: Heroes/Organizing information or _____
Resource: Written notes, all resources used, or _____

RESEARCH PROJECT
Classify notes into outline headings. Write paragraphs. List resources. Or _____.

SHARING
Teams present one interesting fact to the whole class.
    Papers are dated and filed.

Recreational Reading

For approximately 30 minutes, all students read books.

CONVERSATIONS
Teacher holds seven to ten minute conversations with individual students discussing realism and fantasy, identifying author's intent, and/or _____.

CLIPBOARD NOTES
Teacher notes student responses in conversations, or _____.

READ-ALOUD BOOK
Continue current selection or _____.

Writing

MINI-LESSON
Factual Writing: Reports. Or _____.
Reports include introduction, main ideas, and conclusion.
    Proofreading: Indent to change paragraphs.

COMPOSING
Choose a factual writing to revise into report format. Or revise Hero (Research Project) report. Or _____.

SHARING
Read, respond, and proofread with a partner.
    Papers are dated and filed.

Word Study

CHART DEVELOPMENT
Spelling Emphasis: Abbreviations or _____

Other Emphasis: Addresses or _____

Resource: Telephone books, newspapers, mail, or _____

WRITING
Write associations to the chart focus. Student choice

SPELLING
List words to spell in Word Study notebook. Exchange notebook with a partner for a written team test. Check and file in folder.
    Papers are dated and filed.

HOMEWORK
Team test words on spelling list.
    Notebook signed.

Lesson 115

Research

LEAD-IN
Teacher introduces the research project:
Topic and Focus: Heroes/Written
Reports or _____
Resource: Student written reports or
_____

RESEARCH PROJECT
Complete writing report, including a bib-
liography. Or _____.

SHARING
Share reports in groups, whole class, or
"Our Heroes" bulletin board.
    Papers are dated and filed.

Recreational Reading

For approximately 30 minutes, all students read books.

CONVERSATIONS
Teacher holds seven to ten minute conversations with individual students discussing realism and fantasy, identifying
author's intent, and/or _____.

CLIPBOARD NOTES
Teacher notes student responses in conversations, or _____.

READ-ALOUD BOOK
Continue current selection or _____.

Writing

MINI-LESSON
Factual Writing: Share Day. Or
_____. Review revision and editing
points.
    Proofreading: Change paragraphs for in-
troduction, main ideas, conclusion.

COMPOSING
Complete revision and editing of factual
report. Or _____.

SHARING
Share revised writing in writing response
groups.
    Papers are dated and filed.

Word Study

CHART DEVELOPMENT
Spelling Emphasis: Abbreviations or
_____

Other Emphasis: Measurement or
_____

Resource: Catalogues, Math textbooks, or _____

WRITING
Write associations to the chart focus. Student choice

SPELLING
List words to spell in Word Study notebook. Exchange notebook with a partner
for a written team test. Check and file in
folder.
    Papers are dated and filed.

HOMEWORK
Team test words on spelling list.
    Notebook signed.

Lesson 116

Research

LEAD-IN
Teacher introduces the research project:
Topic and Focus: Measurement/
Classifying or _____
Resource: Math textbooks, catalogues,
or _____

RESEARCH PROJECT
Work in small groups. Skim resources to
locate terms of measurement. Write
words or phrases and classify into groups.
Or _____.

SHARING
Share classifications with the class or an-
other group.
   Papers are dated and filed.

Recreational Reading

For approximately 30 minutes, all students read books.

CONVERSATIONS
Teacher holds seven to ten minute conversations with individual students discussing realism and fantasy, identifying
author's intent, and/or _____.

CLIPBOARD NOTES
Teacher notes student responses in conversations, or _____.

READ-ALOUD BOOK
The Celery Stalks at Midnight by James
Howe, *Half Magic* by Howard Eager, or
_____

Writing

MINI-LESSON
Interviews. Or _____. Tips for writing questions for interviews.
   Proofreading: Correctly punctuated
questions.

COMPOSING
Write questions to interview a classmate.
Interview a partner and write responses.
Or _____.

SHARING
Read the most interesting question/re-
sponse to the class.
   Papers are dated and filed.

Word Study

CHART DEVELOPMENT
Spelling Emphasis: Synonyms or
_____

Other Emphasis: Slick or slimy
things or _____
Resource: Thesauruses, dictionaries,
magazines, or _____

WRITING
Write associations to the chart focus. Student choice

SPELLING
List words to spell in Word Study notebook. Exchange notebook with a partner
for a written team test. Check and file in
folder.
   Papers are dated and filed.

HOMEWORK
Team test words on spelling list.
   Notebook signed.

Lesson 117

Research

LEAD-IN
Teacher introduces the research project:
Topic and Focus: Measurement/
Forming Conclusions or _____
Resource: Food labels and packages,
food advertising coupons, or _____

RESEARCH PROJECT
Read measurement information to write
factual statements. Work in small groups.
Or _____.

SHARING
Share conclusions about products and
measurement with the class.
    Papers are dated and filed.

Recreational Reading

For approximately 30 minutes, all students read books.

CONVERSATIONS
Teacher holds seven to ten minute conversations with individual students discussing realism and fantasy, identifying
author's intent, and/or _____.

CLIPBOARD NOTES
Teacher notes student responses in
conversations.

READ-ALOUD BOOK
Continue current selection or *Eight Ate:
A Feast of Homonym Riddles* by Marvin
Terban, *The King Who Rained* by Fred
Gwynne, or _____.

Writing

MINI-LESSON
"If I could interview anyone, I'd choose
_____." Or _____.
    Proofreading: Use of commas in sen-
tences starting with *When, If, After, Until, Because,* and *Since.*

COMPOSING
Tell who you would interview and why.
Write questions you would ask. Or
_____.

SHARING
Read, respond, and proofread with a partner or with the class.
    Papers are dated and filed.

Word Study

CHART DEVELOPMENT
Spelling Emphasis: Homonyms
(Homophones) or _____
Other Emphasis: Shiny things or
_____
Resource: Newspapers, textbooks,
magazines, or _____

WRITING
Write associations to the chart focus. Student choice

SPELLING
List words to spell in Word Study notebook. Exchange notebook with a partner
for a written team test. Check and file in
folder.
    Papers are dated and filed.

HOMEWORK
Team test words on spelling list.
    Notebook signed.

Research

?

LEAD-IN

Teacher introduces the research project:
Topic and Focus: Measurement/
Notetaking or _____
Resource: Encyclopedias, library
books, textbooks, or _____

RESEARCH PROJECT

Locate, read, and take notes on information related to measurement systems,
terms, or other facts. Work with a partner or small groups. Or _____.

SHARING

Share information with another team or
whole class.
  Papers are dated and filed.

Recreational Reading

For approximately 30 minutes, all students read books.

CONVERSATIONS

Teacher holds seven to ten minute conversations with individual students discussing realism and fantasy, identifying
author's intent, and/or _____.

CLIPBOARD NOTES

Teacher notes student responses in conversations, or _____.

READ-ALOUD BOOK

Continue current selection or _____.

Writing

MINI-LESSON

Interview Projects. Or _____. List
ideas for interview projects and purposes
of the interview.
  Proofreading: Use commas to set apart
a noun of direct address.

COMPOSING

Select an interview project, and write
questions. Work with a partner or individually. Or write questions for a whole
class interview of a local VIP, or the prin-
cipal. Or _____.

SHARING

Read, respond, and proofread with a
partner.
  Papers are dated and filed.

Word Study

CHART DEVELOPMENT
Spelling Emphasis: Antonyms or

_____

Other Emphasis: Soft things or

_____

Resource: Magazines, textbooks,
newspapers, or _____

WRITING

Write associations to the chart focus. Student choice

SPELLING

List words to spell in Word Study notebook. Exchange notebook with a partner
for a written team test. Check and file in
folder.
  Papers are dated and filed.

HOMEWORK

Team test words on spelling list.
  Notebook signed.

Lesson 119

Research

LEAD-IN
Teacher introduces the research project:
Topic and Focus: Measurement/Expressions of equality or _____

Resource: Cookbooks, Math textbooks, dictionaries, or _____

RESEARCH PROJECT
Read to locate and list expressions of equalities of measurements, or any information related to measurement. Or _____.

SHARING
Select most interesting information to share with the class.
  Papers are dated and filed.

Recreational Reading

For approximately 30 minutes, all students read books.

CONVERSATIONS
Teacher holds seven to ten minute conversations with individual students discussing realism and fantasy, identifying author's intent, and/or _____.

CLIPBOARD NOTES
Teacher notes student responses in conversations, or _____.

READ-ALOUD BOOK
Continue current selection or _____.

Writing

MINI-LESSON
Fantasy Interviews: Cinderella. Or _____.
  Proofreading: Comma use after introductory words such as *Well, Yes, Oh.*

COMPOSING
Write questions to interview Cinderella, or another fictional character. Create responses to your questions. Or continue other interview project. Or _____.

SHARING
Read, respond, and proofread with a partner.
  Papers are dated and filed.

Word Study

CHART DEVELOPMENT
Spelling Emphasis: Homographs or _____

Other Emphasis: Sharp things or _____

Resource: Dictionaries, newspapers, catalogues, or _____

WRITING
Write associations to the chart focus. Student choice

SPELLING
List words to spell in Word Study notebook. Exchange notebook with a partner for a written team test. Check and file in folder.
  Papers are dated and filed.

HOMEWORK
Team test words on spelling list.
  Notebook signed.

Lesson **120**

Research

LEAD-IN
Teacher introduces the research project:
Topic and Focus: Measurement/Writing Problems or _____
Resource: Newspapers, catalogues, food labels, or _____

RESEARCH PROJECT
Locate information to write math problems related to measurement, or summarize information related to measurement for sharing. Work in small groups. Or _____.

SHARING
Exchange, solve, and discuss measurement problems with another group. Or share any measurement facts with the class.
   Papers are dated and filed.

Recreational Reading

For approximately 30 minutes, all students read books.

CONVERSATIONS
Teacher holds seven to ten minute conversations with individual students discussing realism and fantasy, identifying author's intent, and/or _____.

CLIPBOARD NOTES
Teacher notes student responses in conversations, or _____.

READ-ALOUD BOOK
A Chocolate Moose for Dinner by Fred Gwynne, *In a Pickle, and Other Funny Idioms* by Marvin Terban, or _____

Writing

MINI-LESSON
Interviews: Share Day. Or _____.
   Proofreading: Appropriate and correctly written questions.

COMPOSING
Choose an interview project to share. Or _____.

SHARING
Read, respond, and proofread with partner, response group, or class.
   Papers are dated and filed.

Word Study

CHART DEVELOPMENT
Spelling Emphasis: Idioms or _____

Other Emphasis: Fuzzy things or _____

Resource: Magazines, library books, textbooks, or _____

WRITING
Write associations to the chart focus. Student choice

SPELLING
List words to spell in Word Study notebook. Exchange notebook with a partner for a written team test. Check and file in folder.
   Papers are dated and filed.

HOMEWORK
Team test words on spelling list.
   Notebook signed.

Lesson 121

Research

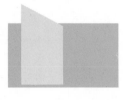

LEAD-IN
Teacher introduces the research project:
Topic and Focus: Inventions/Topic selection or _____
Resource: Science and/or social studies textbooks or _____

RESEARCH PROJECT
Skim resources to list inventions. Choose an invention for research. Work with a partner or small group. List possible resources. Or _____.

SHARING
Team discusses topic selection and ideas for resources.
Papers are dated and filed.

Recreational Reading

For approximately 30 minutes, all students read books.

CONVERSATIONS
Teacher holds seven to ten minute conversations with individual students discussing realism and fantasy, identifying author's intent, and/or _____.

CLIPBOARD NOTES
Teacher notes student responses in conversations, or _____.

READ-ALOUD BOOK
Book Talk selections related to the Research theme (*How To Be an Inventor* and *Machines and How They Work* both by Harvey Weiss, *Extraordinary Stories Behind the Invention of Ordinary Things* by Don L. Wulffson). Or _____.

Writing

MINI-LESSON
Critique: Television or a TV show. Or _____.

Proofreading: Support positive and/or negative comments with examples.

COMPOSING
Write a criticism of a current TV show or movie. Or _____.

SHARING
Read, respond, and proofread with a partner.
Papers are dated and filed.

Word Study

CHART DEVELOPMENT
Spelling Emphasis: Hyphenated words or _____
Other Emphasis: Inventions/Inventors or _____
Resource: Science or Social Studies texts, newspapers, or _____

WRITING
Write associations to the chart focus. Student choice

SPELLING
List words to spell in Word Study notebook. Exchange notebook with a partner for a written team test. Check and file in folder.
Papers are dated and filed.

HOMEWORK
Team test words on spelling list.
Notebook signed.

Lesson 122

Research

LEAD-IN
Teacher introduces the research project:
Topic and Focus: Inventions/
Background Information or _____
Resource: Textbooks, encyclopedias, library books, or _____

RESEARCH PROJECT
Read to locate background information about invention. Write main ideas. Or _____.

SHARING
Team members share information located and add to notes. Discuss resources located by team members.
  Papers are dated and filed.

Recreational Reading

For approximately 30 minutes, all students read books.

CONVERSATIONS
Teacher moves among students having two to three minute conversations with as many individuals as possible. If appropriate, discuss main parts of the plot, (beginning, middle, and end), or _____.

CLIPBOARD NOTES
Teacher notes who seeks recommendations from others, or _____.

READ-ALOUD BOOK
What's the Big Idea, Ben Franklin? by Jean Fritz, *Breakthroughs in Science* by Isaac Asimov, or _____

Writing

MINI-LESSON
Critique: "Good News, Bad News." Or _____.

  Proofreading: Correct use of *there, they're,* and *their.*

COMPOSING
Write about, "The good side of being older is. . . . The bad side is. . . ." (Other topics include my sister/brother, school, my dog.) Or _____.

SHARING
Read, respond, and proofread with a partner.
  Papers are dated and filed.

Word Study

CHART DEVELOPMENT
Spelling Emphasis: Acronyms or _____

Other Emphasis: Organizations or _____

Resource: Telephone book, Social Studies textbooks, or _____

WRITING
Write associations to the chart focus. Student choice

SPELLING
List words to spell in Word Study notebook. Exchange notebook with a partner for a written team test. Check and file in folder.
  Papers are dated and filed.

HOMEWORK
Team test words on spelling list.
  Notebook signed.

Lesson 123

Research

LEAD-IN
Teacher introduces the research project:
Topic and Focus: Inventions/Critical Thinking or _____
Resource: Textbooks, newspapers, encyclopedias, library books, or _____

RESEARCH PROJECT
Read about an invention to compare how life has been changed by this invention. List positive and negative results of the invention. Or _____.

SHARING
Teams discuss lists and if the invention is more helpful or harmful.
Papers are dated and filed.

Recreational Reading

For approximately 30 minutes, all students read books.

CONVERSATIONS
Teacher moves among students having two to three minute conversations with as many individuals as possible. If appropriate, discuss main parts of the plot (beginning, middle, and end), or _____.

CLIPBOARD NOTES
Teacher notes who seeks recommendations from others, or _____.

READ-ALOUD BOOK
The Whipping Boy by Sid Fleischman, *When I Was Young in the Mountains* by Cynthia Rylant, or _____

Writing

MINI-LESSON
Critique: "Then and Now." Or _____. Discuss the positive and negative sides of the modern life (televisions, computers, fast foods).
Proofreading: Correct use of *this, that, these,* and *those.*

COMPOSING
Write about the pros and cons of being a young person now instead of some other time. Or _____.

SHARING
Read, respond, and proofread with a partner.
Papers are dated and filed.

Word Study

CHART DEVELOPMENT
Spelling Emphasis: Words with multiple meanings or _____
Other Emphasis: Brand names or _____
Resource: Advertising inserts, coupons, magazines, or _____

WRITING
Write associations to the chart focus. Student choice

SPELLING
List words to spell in Word Study notebook. Exchange notebook with a partner for a written team test. Check and file in folder.
Papers are dated and filed.

HOMEWORK
Team test words on spelling list.
Notebook signed.

226

Research

LEAD-IN
Teacher introduces the research project:
Topic and Focus: Inventions/Diagrams or _____
Resource: Library books, science encyclopedias, or _____

RESEARCH PROJECT
Skim resources to locate a picture or diagram of your invention. Team members choose a picture/diagram to draw and label main parts or explain how it works. Use chart paper. Or use the diagram to "act out" what the invention does. Or _____.

SHARING
Plan how to present your invention to the class tomorrow.
   Papers are dated and filed.

Recreational Reading

For approximately 30 minutes, all students read books.

CONVERSATIONS
Teacher moves among students having two to three minute conversations with as many individuals as possible. If appropriate, discuss main parts of the plot (beginning, middle, and end), or _____.

CLIPBOARD NOTES
Teacher notes who seeks recommendations from others, or _____.

READ-ALOUD BOOK
Continue current selection or _____.

Writing

MINI-LESSON
Revision conferences: Review points for revising writings. Or _____.
   Proofreading: Clear paragraph construction with main idea and supporting details.

COMPOSING
Choose a writing to revise. Or _____.

SHARING
Read, respond, and proofread with a partner. Make corrections and additions as needed.
   Papers are dated and filed.

Word Study

CHART DEVELOPMENT
Spelling Emphasis: Three-syllable words or _____
Other Emphasis: Machines or _____
Resource: Newspapers, magazines, textbooks, or _____

WRITING
Write associations to the chart focus. Student choice

SPELLING
List words to spell in Word Study notebook. Exchange notebook with a partner for a written team test. Check and file in folder.
   Papers are dated and filed.

HOMEWORK
Team test words on spelling list.
   Notebook signed.

Lesson 125

Research

LEAD-IN
Teacher introduces the research project:
Topic and Focus: Inventions/
Presentations or _____
Resource: Student-collected informa-
tion or _____

RESEARCH PROJECT
Teams plan to "act out" what their invention does, and/or other ways to tell about
their invention. Or _____.

SHARING
Teams present their invention study to
the class. Evaluate each invention's use-
fulness to man.
  Papers are dated and filed.

Recreational Reading

For approximately 30 minutes, all students read books.

CONVERSATIONS
During the last ten minutes, the teacher
may choose to talk with some individuals
about what they have read, or
_____.

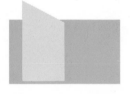

CLIPBOARD NOTES
Teacher notes titles being read by students, or _____.

READ-ALOUD BOOK
Continue current selection or _____.

Writing

MINI-LESSON
Share Day or _____
  Proofreading: Details effectively used to
support opinions.

COMPOSING
Complete revision, editing, and final
copy. Or _____.

SHARING
Read, respond in response groups. Discuss
effective use of details to support
opinions.
  Papers are dated and filed.

Word Study

CHART DEVELOPMENT
Spelling Emphasis: Three-syllable
words or Chart Review Day or
_____

Other Emphasis: Old-fashioned
things or _____
Resource: Newspapers, magazines, or
_____

WRITING
Write associations to the chart focus. Student choice

SPELLING
List words to spell in Word Study notebook. Exchange notebook with a partner
for a written team test. Check and file in
folder.
  Papers are dated and filed.

HOMEWORK
Team test words on spelling list.
  Notebook signed.

Lesson **126**

Research

LEAD-IN
Teacher introduces the research project:
Topic and Focus: World Geography/Map Reading or _____
Resource: World maps, atlases, gazetteers, or _____

RESEARCH PROJECT
With a partner, choose a foreign country to research. Locate it on a map and write clues to describe where it is. Or
_____.

SHARING
Ask another team to use the clues to locate your country on a map.
  Papers are dated and filed.

Recreational Reading

For approximately 30 minutes, all students read books.

CONVERSATIONS
During the last ten to fifteen minutes, small groups discuss books/stories members have read. Groups may be organized by topic, author, or other appropriate method. Or _____.

CLIPBOARD NOTES
Teacher notes students who call attention to illustrations or illustrators in group responses, or _____.

READ-ALOUD BOOK
Continue current selection or _____.

Writing

MINI-LESSON
Group Writing: Pictures tell stories. Or
_____. Form small groups for collaborative story writing.
  Proofreading: Stories will include a beginning, middle, and end.

COMPOSING
Group selects pictures from magazines and lists ideas for stories. Or _____.

SHARING
Students choose to write one story cooperatively or to write individual stories about the same picture.
  Papers are dated and filed.

Word Study

CHART DEVELOPMENT
Spelling Emphasis: Four-syllable words or _____
Other Emphasis: Foreign countries or _____
Resource: Newspapers, maps, or
_____

WRITING
Write associations to the chart focus. Student choice

SPELLING
List words to spell in Word Study notebook. Exchange notebook with a partner for a written team test. Check and file in folder.
  Papers are dated and filed.

HOMEWORK
Team test words on spelling list.
  Notebook signed.

Lesson 127

Research

LEAD-IN
Teacher introduces the research project:
Topic and Focus: World Geography/Map Reading or _____
Resource: Social Studies textbooks, encyclopedias, or _____

RESEARCH PROJECT
With a partner, locate a physical map and write facts based on the physical features of your country. Or _____. .

SHARING
Share statements about physical features and check on maps with another team.
  Papers are dated and filed.

Recreational Reading

For approximately 30 minutes, all students read books.

CONVERSATIONS
Teacher holds seven to ten minute conversations with three or four students individually discussing plot sequence, descriptive passages about settings and/or characters, or _____.

CLIPBOARD NOTES
Teacher notes responses of students in conversations, or _____.

READ-ALOUD BOOK
Continue current selection or _____.

Writing

MINI-LESSON
Group Writing, continued, or _____
  Proofreading: Correct use of *is, am, are, was, were.*

COMPOSING
Begin the story. Describe, name, and tell about the characters and setting in the story. Or _____.

SHARING
Group members read and proofread papers.
  Papers are dated and filed.

Word Study

CHART DEVELOPMENT
Spelling Emphasis: Four-syllable words or _____
Other Emphasis: Physical land features or _____
Resource: Maps, gazetteers, newspapers, or _____

WRITING
Write associations to the chart focus. Student choice

SPELLING
List words to spell in Word Study notebook. Exchange notebook with a partner for a written team test. Check and file in folder.
  Papers are dated and filed.

HOMEWORK
Team test words on spelling list.
  Notebook signed.

Lesson 128

Research

LEAD-IN
Teacher introduces the research project:
Topic and Focus: World Geography/Symbols (flags, landmarks, products, etc.) or _____
Resource: Encyclopedias, library books, or _____

RESEARCH PROJECT
With a partner, locate symbols which represent or give information about a country you chose. Write or draw symbols, with notes to explain. Or _____.

SHARING
Share symbols with another team or whole class, explaining their significance.
  Papers are dated and filed.

Recreational Reading

For approximately 30 minutes, all students read books.

CONVERSATIONS
Teacher holds seven to ten minute conversations with three or four students individually discussing plot sequence, descriptive passages about settings and/or characters, or _____.

CLIPBOARD NOTES
Teacher notes responses of students in conversations, or _____.

READ-ALOUD BOOK
The Midnight Fox by Betsy Byars, *My Side of the Mountain* by Jean George, or _____

Writing

MINI-LESSON
Group Writing: Opening Paragraphs. Or _____. Read opening paragraphs from several books to illustrate different techniques to begin a story.
  Proofreading: Change paragraphs to indicate action and/or time changes.

COMPOSING
Continue writing the group short story. Or _____.

SHARING
Read, respond, and proofread with a partner or all group members.
  Papers are dated and filed.

Word Study

CHART DEVELOPMENT
Spelling Emphasis: Five-syllable words or _____
Other Emphasis: Personality traits or _____
Resource: Student writings, library books, magazines, or _____

WRITING
Write associations to the chart focus. Student choice

SPELLING
List words to spell in Word Study notebook. Exchange notebook with a partner for a written team test. Check and file in folder.
  Papers are dated and filed.

HOMEWORK
Team test words on spelling list.
  Notebook signed.

Lesson **129**

Research

LEAD-IN
Teacher introduces the research project:
Topic and Focus: World Geography/Directions or _____
Resource: Local and state maps, world maps, globes, or _____

RESEARCH PROJECT
Write directions from your house to your foreign country using geographic directional words. Trace your route. Or
_____.

SHARING
Orally give directions to another team to see if they get there following your directions on a map.
   Papers are dated and filed.

Recreational Reading

For approximately 30 minutes, all students read books.

CONVERSATIONS
Teacher holds seven to ten minute conversations with three or four students individually discussing plot sequence, descriptive passages about settings and/or characters, or _____.

CLIPBOARD NOTES
Teacher notes responses of students in conversations, or _____.

READ-ALOUD BOOK
Continue current selection or _____.

Writing

MINI-LESSON
Group Writing: Story Development. Or
_____.
   Proofreading: Logical sequence of events from beginning to middle to end.

COMPOSING
Complete composing group story. Revise and edit with group members. Or
_____.

SHARING
Read, respond, and proofread to complete the group story.
   Papers are dated and filed.

Word Study

CHART DEVELOPMENT
Spelling Emphasis: Five-syllable words or _____
Other Emphasis: Current events or _____
Resource: Newspapers, magazines, or _____

WRITING
Write associations to the chart focus. Student choice

SPELLING
List words to spell in Word Study notebook. Exchange notebook with a partner for a written team test. Check and file in folder.
   Papers are dated and filed.

HOMEWORK
Team test words on spelling list.
   Notebook signed.

Lesson **130**

Research

LEAD-IN
Teacher introduces the research project:
Topic and Focus: World Geography/Summarizing or _____
Resource: Social Studies textbooks, all maps, or _____

RESEARCH PROJECT
Summarize and list facts about your country. Or _____.

SHARING
Present information to whole class, and show how to get there.
  Papers are dated and filed.

Recreational Reading

For approximately 30 minutes, all students read books.

CONVERSATIONS
Teacher holds seven to ten minute conversations with three or four students individually discussing plot sequence, descriptive passages about settings and/or characters, or _____.

CLIPBOARD NOTES
Teacher notes responses of students in conversations, and _____.

READ-ALOUD BOOK
Continue current selection or _____.

Writing

MINI-LESSON
Share Day or _____
  Proofreading: Story plot and details are consistent with the picture.

COMPOSING
Group members write final draft of story. Add a title. Or _____.

SHARING
Display picture and read group stories. Discuss group writing process and how it worked in your project.
  Papers are dated and filed.

Word Study

CHART DEVELOPMENT
Spelling Emphasis: Five- or six-syllable words or Chart Review Day or _____

Other Emphasis: Directional words or _____
Resource: Newspapers or _____

WRITING
Write associations to the chart focus. Student choice

SPELLING
List words to spell in Word Study notebook. Exchange notebook with a partner for a written team test. Check and file in folder.
  Papers are dated and filed.

HOMEWORK
Team test words on spelling list.
  Notebook signed.

Lesson **131**

Research

LEAD-IN
Teacher introduces the research project:
Topic and Focus: Archaeology/Topic selection or _____
Resource: Science texts, dictionaries, encyclopedias, or _____

RESEARCH PROJECT
In small groups, skim materials to list topic ideas for research. Or _____.

SHARING
Groups share ideas for research topics with the class. Groups select topics and locate resources.
   Papers are dated and filed.

Recreational Reading

For approximately 30 minutes, all students read books.

CONVERSATIONS
Teacher holds seven to ten minute conversations with three or four students individually discussing plot sequence, descriptive passages about settings and/or characters, or _____.

CLIPBOARD NOTES
Teacher notes responses of students in conversations, or _____.

READ-ALOUD BOOK
Mummies Made in Egypt by Aliki, *Motel of the Mysteries* by David Macaulay, or _____

Writing

MINI-LESSON
Responding to literature, or _____.
Read a short Fable aloud, asking students to list the elements.
   Proofreading: Include only one negative in a sentence.

COMPOSING
Write a story to teach a moral. Or write a story which includes talking animals. Or _____.

SHARING
Read, respond, and proofread with a partner.
   Papers are dated and filed.

Word Study

CHART DEVELOPMENT
Spelling Emphasis: _____
Other Emphasis: Archaeology (archeology) or _____
Resource: Encyclopedias, library books, or _____

WRITING
Write associations to the chart focus. Student choice

SPELLING
List words to spell in Word Study notebook. Exchange notebook with a partner for a written team test. Check and file in folder.
   Papers are dated and filed.

HOMEWORK
Team test words on spelling list.
   Notebook signed.

234

Research

LEAD-IN
Teacher introduces the research project:
Topic and Focus: Archaeology/
Notetaking or _____
Resource: Library books, encyclopedias, magazines, or _____

RESEARCH PROJECT
Students read to locate information about their topic. List facts located and form a *Why* question based on facts. Or _____.

SHARING
Group members ask questions, share answers and facts.
Papers are dated and filed.

Recreational Reading

For approximately 30 minutes, all students read books.

CONVERSATIONS
Teacher holds seven to ten minute conversations with three or four students individually discussing plot sequence, descriptive passages about settings and/or characters, or _____.

CLIPBOARD NOTES
Teacher notes responses of students in conversations, or _____.

READ-ALOUD BOOK
Selections from *Pots and Robbers* by Dora Hamblin, *Digs and Diggers: A Book of World Archeology* by Leonard Cottrell, or _____

Writing

MINI-LESSON
Responding to literature, or _____.
Share examples of interesting ABC books (*Ashanti to Zulu: African Traditions* by Margaret Musgrove, *Q Is for Duck* by Mary Elting, *Animalia* by Graeme Base, and *Alphabetics* by Sue MacDonald)
Proofreading: Set off appositive phrases with commas.

COMPOSING
Write original ABC expressions using a pattern from mini-lesson. Or write ABCs about any topic (your family, classroom, a book). Or _____.

SHARING
Read, respond, and proofread with a partner.
Papers are dated and filed.

Word Study

CHART DEVELOPMENT
Spelling Emphasis: _____
Other Emphasis: Archaeology or _____

Resource: Magazines, Science texts, newspapers, or _____

WRITING
Write associations to the chart focus. Student choice

SPELLING
List words to spell in Word Study notebook. Exchange notebook with a partner for a written team test. Check and file in folder.
Papers are dated and filed.

HOMEWORK
Team test words on spelling list.
Notebook signed.

Lesson **133**

Research

LEAD-IN
Teacher introduces the research project:
Topic and Focus: Archaeology/Collecting data or _____
Resource: Library books, Science encyclopedias, or _____

RESEARCH PROJECT
Read to locate information related to how archaeologists work or other information. Write facts and/or a *How* question to share. Or _____.

SHARING
Group members share facts and questions.
   (Homework: Bring some trash from your house to analyze as an archaeological clue.)
   Papers are dated and filed.

Recreational Reading

For approximately 30 minutes, all students read books.

CONVERSATIONS
Teacher holds seven to ten minute conversations with three or four students individually discussing plot sequence, descriptive passages about settings and/or characters, or _____.

CLIPBOARD NOTES
Teacher notes responses of students in conversations, or _____.

READ-ALOUD BOOK
Continue current selection, or *The Jolly Postman* by Janet and Allan Ahlberg, or _____.

Writing

MINI-LESSON
Responding to literature, or _____.
Read aloud *The Jolly Postman* by Janet and Allan Ahlberg, or another example of mail in books. (*Orp and the Chop Suey Burgers* by Kline)
   Proofreading: Correct letter parts and punctuation.

COMPOSING
Write a piece of mail to a fictional character. Or continue a writing in progress. Or _____.

SHARING
Read, respond, and proofread with a partner.
   Papers are dated and filed.

Word Study

CHART DEVELOPMENT
Spelling Emphasis: _____
Other Emphasis: Postal Service or _____

Resource: Newspapers, magazines, mail, or _____

WRITING
Write associations to the chart focus. Student choice

SPELLING
List words to spell in Word Study notebook. Exchange notebook with a partner for a written team test. Check and file in folder.
   Papers are dated and filed.

HOMEWORK
Team test words on spelling list.
   Notebook signed.

Lesson 134

Research

LEAD-IN
Teacher introduces the research project:
Topic and Focus: Archaeology/
Interpreting data or _____
Resource: Collected pieces of trash
(food packages, broken toys, etc.), all re-
source materials, or _____

RESEARCH PROJECT
Each group works together to examine
pieces of trash and to list conclusions
about the people based on the "find." Or
continue collecting facts. Or _____.

SHARING
Groups display their trash find and the
conclusions.
    Papers are dated and filed.

Recreational Reading

For approximately 30 minutes, all students read books.

CONVERSATIONS
Teacher moves among students having
two to three minute conversations with as
many individuals as possible. If appropriate, discuss how the book is organized,
decoding of unfamiliar words, or
_____.

CLIPBOARD NOTES
Teacher notes which students make self-
corrections of words based on sensible
meanings. Or _____.

READ-ALOUD BOOK
Jumanji by Chris Van Allsburg, or continue current selection, or _____.

Writing

MINI-LESSON
Responding to literature, or _____.
Read aloud an interesting picture book,
such as *Jumanji* by Chris Van Allsburg
or *Old Henry* by Joan W. Blos.
    Proofreading: Join sentences with con-
junctions (*and, but, or*) and a comma.

COMPOSING
Write a new part for the story, extending
it. Or write about the theme of the story.
Or _____.

SHARING
Read, respond, and proofread with a
partner.
    Papers are dated and filed.

Word Study

CHART DEVELOPMENT
Spelling Emphasis: _____
Other Emphasis: Jungle animals or
_____
Resource: Newspapers, Science texts,
library books, or _____

WRITING
Write associations to the chart focus. Student choice

SPELLING
List words to spell in Word Study notebook. Exchange notebook with a partner
for a written team test. Check and file in
folder.
    Papers are dated and filed.

HOMEWORK
Team test words on spelling list.
    Notebook signed.

237

Lesson 135

Research

LEAD-IN
Teacher introduces the research project:
Topic and Focus: Archaeology/
Summarizing or _____
Resource: Library books, encyclopedias, student notes, or _____

RESEARCH PROJECT
Group members select main ideas to summarize and put on chart paper related to archaeology. Write in list or paragraph form. Or _____.

SHARING
Read most important information to the class, or share the most unusual fact located.
  Papers are dated and filed.

Recreational Reading

For approximately 30 minutes, all students read books.

CONVERSATIONS
Teacher moves among students having two to three minute conversations with as many individuals as possible. If appropriate, discuss how the book is organized, decoding of unfamiliar words, or
_____.

CLIPBOARD NOTES
Teacher notes which students make self-corrections of words based on sensible meanings. Or _____.

READ-ALOUD BOOK
Continue current selection or _____.

Writing

MINI-LESSON
Responding to literature, or _____.
Read part of a picture book (*The Araboolies of Liberty Street* by Sam Swope or *The Garden of Abdul Gasazi* by Chris Van Allsburg).
  Proofreading: Correct use of possessive pronouns.

COMPOSING
Predict how the story will continue. Or list possible solutions for the problem in the story. Or _____.

SHARING
Read, respond, and proofread with a partner.
  Papers are dated and filed.

Word Study

CHART DEVELOPMENT
Spelling Emphasis: _____ or
Chart Review Day
Other Emphasis: Energy or
_____
Resource: Newspapers, magazines, Science texts, or _____

WRITING
Write associations to the chart focus. Student choice

SPELLING
List words to spell in Word Study notebook. Exchange notebook with a partner for a written team test. Check and file in folder.
  Papers are dated and filed.

HOMEWORK
Team test words on spelling list.
  Notebook signed.

S u c c e s **S** u c c e s **S** u c c e s **S** u c c e s **S** u c c e s **S** u c c e s **S** u c c e s **S** u c c e s **S**

Lesson **136**

Research

LEAD-IN
Teacher introduces the research project:
Topic and Focus: The Old
West/Topic Selection or _____
Resource: Social Studies textbooks,
encyclopedias, or _____

RESEARCH PROJECT
Skim resources to brainstorm topics
related to the days of the Old West (cowboys, Pony Express, Billy the Kid). Partners choose a topic. Or _____.

SHARING
Partners share topic choice and resources
with the class.
    Papers are dated and filed.

Recreational Reading

For approximately 30 minutes, all students read books.

CONVERSATIONS
Teacher moves among students having
two to three minute conversations with as
many individuals as possible. If appropriate, discuss how the book is organized,
decoding of unfamiliar words, or

_____.

CLIPBOARD NOTES
Teacher notes which students make self-
corrections of words based on sensible
meanings. Or _____.

READ-ALOUD BOOK
Cowboys of the Wild West by Russell
Freedman, *The Story of Buffalo Bill* by
Collier, or _____

Writing

MINI-LESSON
Responding to literature, or _____.
Read a Tall Tale aloud. Discuss
exaggeration.
    Proofreading: Correct use of *your* and
you're.

COMPOSING
Rewrite the story in news reporting
mode. Or list examples of exaggeration in
a tall tale. Write exaggerations. Or
_____.

SHARING
Read, respond, and proofread with a
partner.
    Papers are dated and filed.

Word Study

CHART DEVELOPMENT
Spelling Emphasis: _____
Other Emphasis: The Old West or
_____

Resource: Social Studies textbooks, library books, or _____

WRITING
Write associations to the chart focus. Student choice

SPELLING
List words to spell in Word Study notebook. Exchange notebook with a partner
for a written team test. Check and file in
folder.
    Papers are dated and filed.

HOMEWORK
Team test words on spelling list.
    Notebook signed.

Lesson 137

Research

LEAD-IN
Teacher introduces the research project:
Topic and Focus: The Old West/Collecting data or _____
Resource: Encyclopedias, library books, or _____

RESEARCH PROJECT
Partners locate, read, and take notes related to the topic. Or _____.

SHARING
Partners meet with another team to share facts located.
  Papers are dated and filed.

Recreational Reading

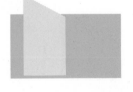

For approximately 30 minutes, all students read books.

CONVERSATIONS
For approximately 20 minutes, everyone, including the teacher, reads for pleasure. During the last ten minutes the teacher may choose to talk with some individuals about what they have read.

CLIPBOARD NOTES
Teacher notes which students are searching for meaning, or _____.

READ-ALOUD BOOK
Continue current selection or _____.

Writing

MINI-LESSON
Responding to literature or _____.
Read aloud examples of old sayings, famous quotes, and/or proverbs.
  Proofreading: Correct use of subject and/or object pronouns.

COMPOSING
Write interpretation(s) of old sayings or proverbs. Or write why you agree or disagree with a famous quote. Or _____.

SHARING
Read, respond, and proofread with a partner.
  Papers are dated and filed.

Word Study

CHART DEVELOPMENT
Spelling Emphasis: _____
Other Emphasis: Transportation or _____

Resource: Social Studies textbooks, newspapers, or _____

WRITING
Write associations to the chart focus. Student choice

SPELLING
List words to spell in Word Study notebook. Exchange notebook with a partner for a written team test. Check and file in folder.
  Papers are dated and filed.

HOMEWORK
Team test words on spelling list.
  Notebook signed.

Lesson **138**

Research

LEAD-IN
Teacher introduces the research project:
Topic and Focus: The Old West/Organizing data or _____
Resource: Library books, encyclopedias, or _____

RESEARCH PROJECT
Collect facts related to the topic with partner. Classify facts into groups and write an outline of topics for a written report. Or _____.

SHARING
Partners share outline of information with another team and respond to questions.
   Papers are dated and filed.

Recreational Reading

For approximately 30 minutes, all students read books.

CONVERSATIONS
During the last ten to fifteen minutes, small groups may form to discuss books/stories students are reading, or _____.

CLIPBOARD NOTES
Teacher notes which students are searching for meaning, or _____.

READ-ALOUD BOOK
Continue current selection or _____.

Writing

MINI-LESSON
Class Writing Project or _____. Students choose a writing project (ABC Book, Jolly Postman letters).
   Proofreading: Correctly punctuated and capitalized sentences.

COMPOSING
Choose a paper to revise for project or sharing. Or _____.

SHARING
Read, respond, and proofread with a partner.
   Papers are dated and filed.

Word Study

CHART DEVELOPMENT
Spelling Emphasis: _____
Other Emphasis: Important documents or _____
Resource: Social Studies textbooks, library books, or _____

WRITING
Write associations to the chart focus. Student choice

SPELLING
List words to spell in Word Study notebook. Exchange notebook with a partner for a written team test. Check and file in folder.
   Papers are dated and filed.

HOMEWORK
Team test words on spelling list.
   Notebook signed.

Lesson 139

Research

LEAD-IN
Teacher introduces the research project:
Topic and Focus: The Old
West/Summarizing or _____
Resource: Available resources, student
notes, or _____

RESEARCH PROJECT
Partners summarize information and
write report, following outline topics for
paragraphs. Or _____.

SHARING
Share outline and report with another
team to answer questions and add information if needed.
  Papers are dated and filed.

Recreational Reading

For approximately 30 minutes, all students read books.

CONVERSATIONS
Teacher holds seven to ten minute conversations with three or four students (individually) tape recording oral reading
selections of the student, discussing oral
reading passages, or _____.

CLIPBOARD NOTES
Teacher notes who reads aloud expressively, pausing correctly for punctuation,
or _____.

READ-ALOUD BOOK
Continue current selection or _____.

Writing

MINI-LESSON
Writing project/Final copy or _____.
Final copy checklist reviewed. Design
sharing mode for tomorrow.
  Proofreading: Use dictionaries to check
spellings, correct use of pronouns.

COMPOSING
Final editing changes before recopying.
Or _____.

SHARING
Read, respond, and proofread with a
partner.
  Papers are dated and filed.

Word Study

CHART DEVELOPMENT
Spelling Emphasis: _____
Other Emphasis: Government or
_____
Resource: Newspapers, magazines,
textbooks, or _____

WRITING
Write associations to the chart focus. Student choice

SPELLING
List words to spell in Word Study notebook. Exchange notebook with a partner
for a written team test. Check and file in
folder.
  Papers are dated and filed.

HOMEWORK
Team test words on spelling list.
  Notebook signed.

Research

LEAD-IN
Teacher introduces the research project:
Topic and Focus: The Old
West/Share Day or _____
Resource: Student reports or
_____

RESEARCH PROJECT
Class decides how to share reports (whole
class, small groups). Or _____.

SHARING
Share and discuss reports. Write evaluative comments about organization and
content, strengths, and needs.
    Papers are dated and filed.

Recreational Reading

For approximately 30 minutes, all students read books.

CONVERSATIONS
Teacher holds seven to ten minute conversations with three or four students (individually) tape recording oral reading
selections of the student, discussing oral
reading passages, or _____.

CLIPBOARD NOTES
Teacher notes who reads aloud expressively, pausing correctly for punctuation,
or _____.

READ-ALOUD BOOK
Continue current selection or _____.

Writing

MINI-LESSON
Share Day or _____. Completed
writings will be shared and collected for
evaluation.
    Proofreading: All final revision criteria.

COMPOSING
Proofread paper before sharing for final
corrections. Or _____.

SHARING
Writing groups read, write comments,
and pass papers in small groups. Discuss
comments and ideas about writings. Or
share in any way designed by the class.
    Papers are dated and filed.

Word Study

CHART DEVELOPMENT
Spelling Emphasis: _____ or
Chart Review Day
Other Emphasis: Laws or rights, or
_____
Resource: Encyclopedias, Social
Studies textbooks, or _____

WRITING
Write associations to the chart focus. Student choice

SPELLING
List words to spell in Word Study notebook. Exchange notebook with a partner
for a written team test. Check and file in
folder.
    Papers are dated and filed.

HOMEWORK
Team test words on spelling list.
    Notebook signed.

Lesson 141

Research

LEAD-IN
Teacher introduces the research project:
Topic and Focus: Flying Things/
Fluency, Classifying or _____
Resource: Any textbooks, student
choice, or _____

RESEARCH PROJECT
Groups brainstorm and list "Flying
Things." Classify lists (Living, Nonliving).
Or _____.

SHARING
Groups present lists to the class, explaining classifications. Check most interesting
items listed for research topics.
   Papers are dated and filed.

Recreational Reading

For approximately 30 minutes, all students read books.

CONVERSATIONS
Teacher holds seven to ten minute conversations with three or four students (individually) tape recording oral reading
selections of the student, discussing oral
reading passages, or _____.

CLIPBOARD NOTES
Teacher notes who reads aloud expressively, pausing correctly for punctuation,
or _____.

READ-ALOUD BOOK
Book Talk selections related to flight (*The
Wright Brothers at Kitty Hawk* by Sobol,
From Sputnik to Space Shuttle by Frank-
lyn Brantley). Or _____.

Writing

MINI-LESSON
Writing a book. Or _____. Discuss
resources for story ideas (life experiences,
new topics, previous writings).
   Proofreading: Point of view is clear in
the story.

COMPOSING
Briefly outline ideas for a book. Or
_____.

SHARING
Discuss ideas with a partner and choose a
story idea.
   Papers are dated and filed.

Word Study

CHART DEVELOPMENT
Spelling Emphasis: _____
Other Emphasis: Flight or
_____
Resource: Newspapers, any textbook,
or _____

WRITING
Write associations to the chart focus. Student choice

SPELLING
List words to spell in Word Study notebook. Exchange notebook with a partner
for a written team test. Check and file in
folder.
   Papers are dated and filed.

HOMEWORK
Team test words on spelling list.
   Notebook signed.

Research

LEAD-IN
Teacher introduces the research project: **Topic and Focus:** Flying Things (Living)/Selecting topics and resources or

_____

Resource: Class lists, encyclopedias, library books, or _____

RESEARCH PROJECT
Choose a topic (Living) from the lists of Flying Things. Collect resources and begin notetaking. Work individually or with partner. Or _____.

SHARING
Share topic and resources with partner or whole class.
   Papers are dated and filed.

Recreational Reading

For approximately 30 minutes, all students read books.

CONVERSATIONS
Teacher holds seven to ten minute conversations with three or four students (individually) tape recording oral reading selections of the student, discussing oral reading passages, or _____.

CLIPBOARD NOTES
Teacher notes who reads aloud expressively, pausing correctly for punctuation, or _____.

READ-ALOUD BOOK
The Glorious Flight: Across the Channel with Louis Bleriot by Alice and Martin Provensen, or _Dragonwings_ by Laurence Yep, or _____.

Writing

MINI-LESSON
Writing a book. Or _____. Discuss setting and main character descriptions.
   Proofreading: Use of vivid adjectives and interesting verbs.

COMPOSING
Write the beginning of story, (setting and main character). Or _____.

SHARING
Read, respond, and proofread with a partner.
   Papers are dated and filed.

Word Study

CHART DEVELOPMENT
Spelling Emphasis: _____
Other Emphasis: Circus or

_____

Resource: Newspapers, magazines, or

_____

WRITING
Write associations to the chart focus. Student choice

SPELLING
List words to spell in Word Study notebook. Exchange notebook with a partner for a written team test. Check and file in folder.
   Papers are dated and filed.

HOMEWORK
Team test words on spelling list.
   Notebook signed.

Lesson **143**

Research

LEAD-IN
Teacher introduces the research project:
Topic and Focus: Flying
Things/Notetaking or _____
Resource: Library books, encyclopedias, or _____

RESEARCH PROJECT
Students read to locate information about topic. (Include facts related to *How* it flies.) Or _____.

SHARING
Students share most interesting fact(s) with a partner.
Papers are dated and filed.

Recreational Reading

For approximately 30 minutes, all students read books.

CONVERSATIONS
Teacher holds seven to ten minute conversations with three or four students (individually) tape recording oral reading selections of the student, discussing oral reading passages, or _____.

CLIPBOARD NOTES
Teacher notes who reads aloud expressively, pausing correctly for punctuation, or _____.

READ-ALOUD BOOK
Continue current selection or _____.

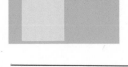

Writing

MINI-LESSON
Writing a book. Or _____. Include a main "problem" or situation in your story. Give examples in stories.
Proofreading: Change paragraphs to show action and time changes.

COMPOSING
Continue story development. Or _____.

SHARING
Read, respond, and proofread with a partner.
Papers are dated and filed.

Word Study

CHART DEVELOPMENT
Spelling Emphasis: _____
Other Emphasis: Skin or _____
Resource: Magazines, Health books, or _____

WRITING
Write associations to the chart focus. Student choice

SPELLING
List words to spell in Word Study notebook. Exchange notebook with a partner for a written team test. Check and file in folder.
Papers are dated and filed.

HOMEWORK
Team test words on spelling list.
Notebook signed.

Lesson **144**

Research

LEAD-IN
Teacher introduces the research project:
Topic and Focus: Flying
Things/Main Ideas or _____
Resource: Magazines, Science text-
books, or _____

RESEARCH PROJECT
Read to locate main ideas about the topic.
Include *When* and *Where* facts, if ap-
propriate. Or _____.

SHARING
Discuss with a partner, explaining main
ideas in your own words.
   Papers are dated and filed.

Recreational Reading

For approximately 30 minutes, all students read books.

CONVERSATIONS
Teacher holds seven to ten minute conversations with three or four students (individually) tape recording oral reading
selections of the student, discussing oral
reading passages, or _____.

CLIPBOARD NOTES
Teacher notes who reads aloud expressively, pausing correctly for punctuation,
or _____.

READ-ALOUD BOOK
Continue current selection or _____.

Writing

MINI-LESSON
Writing a book. Or _____. Use of dialogue in stories.
   Proofreading: Correct use of quotation
punctuation.

COMPOSING
Continue story development. Or
_____.

SHARING
Read, respond, and proofread with a
partner.
   Papers are dated and filed.

Word Study

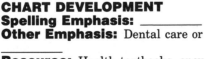

CHART DEVELOPMENT
Spelling Emphasis: _____
Other Emphasis: Dental care or
_____

Resource: Health textbooks, encyclopedias, or _____

WRITING
Write associations to the chart focus. Student choice

SPELLING
List words to spell in Word Study notebook. Exchange notebook with a partner
for a written team test. Check and file in
folder.
   Papers are dated and filed.

HOMEWORK
Team test words on spelling list.
   Notebook signed.

Lesson 145

Research

LEAD-IN
Teacher introduces the research project:
Topic and Focus: Flying
Things/Summarizing or _____
Resource: Student notes, all resources,
or _____

RESEARCH PROJECT
Summarize main ideas to write a short
report. (Graphics optional) Or _____.

SHARING
Share summaries of main ideas and most
interesting facts with a partner. Proofread for clear sentences and correct
spelling.
    Papers are dated and filed.

Recreational Reading

For approximately 30 minutes, all students read books.

CONVERSATIONS
Teacher holds seven to ten minute conversations with three or four students (individually) tape recording oral reading
selections of the student, discussing oral
reading passages, or _____.

CLIPBOARD NOTES
Teacher notes who reads aloud expressively, pausing correctly for punctuation,
or _____.

READ-ALOUD BOOK
How a Book Is Made by Aliki, or continue current selection, or _____.

Writing

MINI-LESSON
Writing a book. Or _____. Identify
the climax in fiction stories, or peak of
tension.
    Proofreading: Feelings of characters are
included; sensory words.

COMPOSING
Continue story development. Or
_____.

SHARING
Read, respond, and proofread with a
partner.
    Papers are dated and filed.

Word Study

CHART DEVELOPMENT
Spelling Emphasis: _____ or
Chart Review Day
Other Emphasis: Physical fitness or

_____
Resource: Newspapers, magazines, or

_____

WRITING
Write associations to the chart focus. Student choice

SPELLING
List words to spell in Word Study notebook. Exchange notebook with a partner
for a written team test. Check and file in
folder.
    Papers are dated and filed.

HOMEWORK
Team test words on spelling list.
    Notebook signed.

Lesson **146**

Research

LEAD-IN
Teacher introduces the research project:
Topic and Focus: Flying Things/Presentation or _____
Resource: Student reports or _____

RESEARCH PROJECT
Complete and proofread written report and graphic. Write a question for students to answer following presentation. Or _____.

SHARING
Students read and respond to projects in groups. Display projects in the classroom.
  Papers are dated and filed.

Recreational Reading

For approximately 30 minutes, all students read books.

CONVERSATIONS
Teacher moves among students having two to three minute conferences with as many students as possible. If appropriate, discuss comparisons of books students have read, or _____.

CLIPBOARD NOTES
Teacher notes who tries to discover new words and uses them in conversations, or _____.

READ-ALOUD BOOK
The Fledgling by Jane Langston, *No Flying in the House* by Betty Brock, or _____

Writing

MINI-LESSON
Writing a book. Or _____. Set up peer helping groups to respond to each other's writing, and help with any problems if needed.
  Proofreading: Use of transition words, sentences, and phrases.

COMPOSING
Work in peer groups. Make changes as needed. Or complete rough draft of story. Or _____.

SHARING
Read, respond, and proofread with a partner.
  Papers are dated and filed.

Word Study

CHART DEVELOPMENT
Spelling Emphasis: _____
Other Emphasis: Descriptive phrases or _____
Resource: Read-Aloud book, library books, or _____

WRITING
Write associations to the chart focus. Student choice

SPELLING
List words to spell in Word Study notebook. Exchange notebook with a partner for a written team test. Check and file in folder.
  Papers are dated and filed.

HOMEWORK
Team test words on spelling list.
  Notebook signed.

Lesson 147

Research

LEAD-IN
Teacher introduces the research project:
Topic and Focus: Flying Things (Nonliving)/Topic Selection or _____
Resource: Social Studies and Science texts, encyclopedias, or _____

RESEARCH PROJECT
Select a topic (Nonliving Flying Things list). Read to locate information related to topic. Or _____. Work with a partner or individually.

SHARING
Discuss topic with partner or another team.
Papers are dated and filed.

Recreational Reading

For approximately 30 minutes, all students read books.

CONVERSATIONS
Teacher moves among students having two to three minute conferences with as many students as possible. If appropriate, discuss comparisons of books students have read, or _____.

CLIPBOARD NOTES
Teacher notes who tries to discover new words and uses them in conversations, or _____.

READ-ALOUD BOOK
Continue current selection or _____.

Writing

MINI-LESSON
Writing a book. Or _____. Students volunteer sentences from stories. Expand sentences by adding adverbs and adjectives for clearer descriptions.
Proofreading: Effective use of adverbs to show *How*.

COMPOSING
Edit to complete rough draft. Or _____.

SHARING
Read, respond, and proofread with a partner.
Papers are dated and filed.

Word Study

CHART DEVELOPMENT
Spelling Emphasis: _____
Other Emphasis: Adverbs that show *How* or _____
Resource: Story collections, library books, or _____

WRITING
Write associations to the chart focus. Student choice

SPELLING
List words to spell in Word Study notebook. Exchange notebook with a partner for a written team test. Check and file in folder.
Papers are dated and filed.

HOMEWORK
Team test words on spelling list.
Notebook signed.

Lesson **148**

Research

LEAD-IN
Teacher introduces the research project:
Topic and Focus: Flying
Things/Notetaking or _____
Resource: Library books, science encyclopedias, or _____

RESEARCH PROJECT
Read to take notes about topic related to *how* it flies. Or _____.

SHARING
Share notes with a partner or another team.
Papers are dated and filed.

Recreational Reading

For approximately 30 minutes, all students read books.

CONVERSATIONS
Teacher moves among students having two to three minute conferences with as many students as possible. If appropriate, discuss comparisons of books students have read, or _____.

CLIPBOARD NOTES
Teacher notes who tries to discover new words and uses them in conversations, or _____.

READ-ALOUD BOOK
Continue current selection or _____.

Writing

MINI-LESSON
Writing a book. Or _____. Show examples of illustration placement and page divisions in books. Make a Book Plan for what will be on each sheet.
Proofreading: Use of commas in a series and to set off introductory words.

COMPOSING
Mark page breaks for final copy and final edit. Or list each page and briefly outline what will go on the page. Or _____.

SHARING
Read, respond, and proofread with a partner.
Papers are dated and filed.

Word Study

CHART DEVELOPMENT
Spelling Emphasis: _____
Other Emphasis: Similes and metaphors or _____
Resource: Read-Aloud book, library books, or _____

WRITING
Write associations to the chart focus. Student choice

SPELLING
List words to spell in Word Study notebook. Exchange notebook with a partner for a written team test. Check and file in folder.
Papers are dated and filed.

HOMEWORK
Team test words on spelling list.
Notebook signed.

Lesson **149**

Research

LEAD-IN
Teacher introduces the research project:
Topic and Focus: Flying
Things/Graphic information or
_____

Resource: Encyclopedias, research
projects or _____

RESEARCH PROJECT
Summarize main facts. Design a graphic
for presentation. Or _____.

SHARING
Proofread and share summarized informa-
tion with a partner or team.
　Papers are dated and filed.

Recreational Reading

For approximately 30 minutes, all students read books.

CONVERSATIONS
For approximately 20 minutes, everyone,
including the teacher, reads silently. During the last ten minutes the teacher may
choose to talk with some individuals
about what they have read. Or
_____.

CLIPBOARD NOTES
Teacher notes who takes books home
regularly, or _____.

READ-ALOUD BOOK
Continue current selection or _____.

Writing

MINI-LESSON
Writing a book. Or _____. Assemble
final book pages, including title page and
dedication page. Examine title pages in
books, listing what to include and printing options.
　Proofreading: Well designed, complete
title page.

COMPOSING
Create "dummy" title page. Correct and
make final copy. Or begin final copy of
page 1, text and illustration. Or
_____.

SHARING
Read, respond, and proofread with a
partner.
　Papers are dated and filed.

Word Study

CHART DEVELOPMENT
Spelling Emphasis: _____
Other Emphasis: Title pages, dedica-
tions, or _____
Resource: Library books, textbooks, or
_____

WRITING
Write associations to the chart focus. Student choice

SPELLING
List words to spell in Word Study notebook. Exchange notebook with a partner
for a written team test. Check and file in
folder.
　Papers are dated and filed.

HOMEWORK
Team test words on spelling list.
　Notebook signed.

Research

LEAD-IN
Teacher introduces the research project:
Topic and Focus: Flying
Things/Presentations or _____
Resource: Student projects or
_____

RESEARCH PROJECT
Write a question to ask after presenting
project. Or _____.

SHARING
Read and respond to reports in groups or
whole class. Display projects in classroom.
Papers are dated and filed.

Recreational Reading

For approximately 30 minutes, all students read books.

CONVERSATIONS
During the last ten to fifteen minutes
small groups discuss books/stories group
members have read. Groups may be organized by topic, author, or same book.
Or _____.

CLIPBOARD NOTES
Teacher notes who takes books home
regularly, or _____.

READ-ALOUD BOOK
Continue current selection or _____.

Writing

MINI-LESSON
Writing a book. Or _____. Continue
work on final copies of manuscript pages.
Tips for neatness, illustration decisions,
and completing plans for pages.
Proofreading: Paragraph structure and
indention, neat margins.

COMPOSING
Continue final copies of text, using a
book plan. Or _____.

SHARING
Read, respond, and proofread with a
partner.
Papers are dated and filed.

Word Study

CHART DEVELOPMENT
Spelling Emphasis: _____ or
Chart Review Day
Other Emphasis: Parts of books or
_____
Resource: Library books, textbooks,
dictionaries, or _____

WRITING
Write associations to the chart focus. Student choice

SPELLING
List words to spell in Word Study notebook. Exchange notebook with a partner
for a written team test. Check and file in
folder.
Papers are dated and filed.

HOMEWORK
Team test words on spelling list.
Notebook signed.

Lesson 151

Research

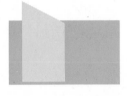

LEAD-IN
Teacher introduces the research project:
Topic and Focus: Mythology/Locating information or _____
Resource: Library books, encyclopedias, or _____

RESEARCH PROJECT
Skim resources to list different types of mythology or myths. Read about mythology. Or _____.

SHARING
Teacher compiles one main class list of types or subtopics for research. Select research topics and groups.
Papers are dated and filed.

Recreational Reading

For approximately 30 minutes, all students read books.

CONVERSATIONS
Teacher holds seven to ten minute conversations with three or four students individually, discussing sequence of events, figurative language, and/or _____.

CLIPBOARD NOTES
Teacher notes student responses during conversations, or _____.

READ-ALOUD BOOK
The Golden Fleece and the Heroes Who Lived Before Achilles by Padraic Colum, any mythology collection, or _____.

Writing

MINI-LESSON
Writing a book: About the Author or _____. Read About the Author sections from books to list suggestions.
Proofreading: Use third person point of view in About the Author section.

COMPOSING
Write an About the Author section. Or continue making final copies of text. Or _____.

SHARING
Read, respond, and proofread with a partner.
Papers are dated and filed.

Word Study

CHART DEVELOPMENT
Spelling Emphasis: _____
Other Emphasis: Mythology or _____

Resource: Encyclopedias or _____

WRITING
Write associations to the chart focus. Student choice

SPELLING
List words to spell in Word Study notebook. Exchange notebook with a partner for a written team test. Check and file in folder.
Papers are dated and filed.

HOMEWORK
Team test words on spelling list.
Notebook signed.

Lesson **152**

Research

LEAD-IN
Teacher introduces the research project:
Topic and Focus: Mythology/
Notetaking or _____
Resource: Library books, encyclope-
dias, or _____

RESEARCH PROJECT
Groups read to locate facts related to
their mythology topic. Or _____.

SHARING
Groups share facts with another group.
  Papers are dated and filed.

Recreational Reading

For approximately 30 minutes, all students read books.

CONVERSATIONS
Teacher holds seven to ten minute conversations with three or four students individually, discussing sequence of events,
figurative language, and/or _____.

CLIPBOARD NOTES
Teacher notes student responses during
conversations, or _____.

READ-ALOUD BOOK
Continue current selection or _____.

Writing

MINI-LESSON
Writing a Book: Publication. Or
_____. Plan how to share completed
books.
  Proofreading: All final draft proofread-
ing criteria.

COMPOSING
Complete final text and illustrations. Or
revise About the Author, affix photograph. Or _____.

SHARING
Read, respond, and proofread with a
partner.
  Papers are dated and filed.

Word Study

CHART DEVELOPMENT
Spelling Emphasis: _____
Other Emphasis: Mythology: Gods
and Goddesses or _____
Resource: Library books or
_____

WRITING
Write associations to the chart focus. Student choice

SPELLING
List words to spell in Word Study notebook. Exchange notebook with a partner
for a written team test. Check and file in
folder.
  Papers are dated and filed.

HOMEWORK
Team test words on spelling list.
  Notebook signed.

Lesson **153**

Research

LEAD-IN
Teacher introduces the research project:
Topic and Focus: Mythology/
Summarizing or _____
Resource: Story collections, library
books, or _____

RESEARCH PROJECT
Groups select a myth to read and summarize. Students may write summaries as a
group, with a partner, or individually. Or
_____.

SHARING
Share summary with a partner, pair, or
group. Tell the purpose of the myth.
   Papers are dated and filed.

Recreational Reading

For approximately 30 minutes, all students read books.

CONVERSATIONS
Teacher holds seven to ten minute conversations with three or four students individually, discussing sequence of events,
figurative language, and/or _____.

CLIPBOARD NOTES
Teacher notes student responses during
conversations, or _____.

READ-ALOUD BOOK
Continue current selection or _____.

Writing

MINI-LESSON
Share Day: Books or _____. Groups
of five or six students share complete
books. Discuss evaluation criteria.
   Proofreading: Clear complete sentences
and paragraph structure.

COMPOSING
Final editing of text. Or write evaluation
of your book. Or _____.

SHARING
Group members respond to presentations.
   Papers are dated and filed.

Word Study

CHART DEVELOPMENT
Spelling Emphasis: _____
Other Emphasis: Foods or

_____
Resource: Library books or
_____

WRITING
Write associations to the chart focus. Student choice

SPELLING
List words to spell in Word Study notebook. Exchange notebook with a partner
for a written team test. Check and file in
folder.
   Papers are dated and filed.

HOMEWORK
Team test words on spelling list.
   Notebook signed.

Lesson **154**

Research

LEAD-IN
Teacher introduces the research project:
Topic and Focus: Mythology/Creative thinking or _____
Resource: Mythology collections, encyclopedias, or _____

RESEARCH PROJECT
(Two-day project) Read about a main god, goddess, or hero to list his/her main qualities, symbols, and responsibilities. Create a modern god, goddess, or hero with corresponding features (God of Rock and Roll, Homework Goddess). Work with partners or group. Or _____.

SHARING
Plan how to present your creation. Collect materials needed.
  Papers are dated and filed.

Recreational Reading

For approximately 30 minutes, all students read books.

CONVERSATIONS
Teacher holds seven to ten minute conversations with three or four students individually, discussing sequence of events, figurative language, and/or _____.

CLIPBOARD NOTES
Teacher notes student responses during conversations.

READ-ALOUD BOOK
Continue current selection or _____.

Writing

MINI-LESSON
Myths or _____. Read aloud or discuss a familiar myth. List the main elements of myths.
  Proofreading: Correct use of pronouns in subjects.

COMPOSING
Write a myth to explain a natural occurrence. Or write a poem about a mythological character. Or _____.

SHARING
Read, respond, and proofread with a partner.
  Papers are dated and filed.

Word Study

CHART DEVELOPMENT
Spelling Emphasis: _____
Other Emphasis: Computers or

_____
Resource: Newspapers, magazines, or _____

WRITING
Write associations to the chart focus. Student choice

SPELLING
List words to spell in Word Study notebook. Exchange notebook with a partner for a written team test. Check and file in folder.
  Papers are dated and filed.

HOMEWORK
Team test words on spelling list.
  Notebook signed.

Lesson 155

Research

LEAD-IN
Teacher introduces the research project:
Topic and Focus: Mythology/
Presentation or _____
Resource: Student-created material or
_____

RESEARCH PROJECT
Partners or groups complete materials to
present a modern mythological character.
Or _____.

SHARING
Present projects to the class.
  Papers are dated and filed.

Recreational Reading

For approximately 30 minutes, all students read books.

CONVERSATIONS
Teacher holds seven to ten minute conversations with three or four students individually, discussing sequence of events, figurative language, and/or _____.

CLIPBOARD NOTES
Teacher notes student responses during
conversations, or _____.

READ-ALOUD BOOK
Continue current selection or _____.

Writing

MINI-LESSON
Myths/Monsters and heroes. Or
_____.

  Proofreading: Correct use of capital letters for proper nouns.

COMPOSING
Continue writing previous myth. Or describe a new hero or monster. Or
_____.

SHARING
Read, respond, and proofread with a
partner.
  Papers are dated and filed.

Word Study

CHART DEVELOPMENT
Spelling Emphasis: _____ or
Chart Review Day
Other Emphasis: Monsters or
_____
Resource: Library books, story collections, or _____

WRITING
Write associations to the chart focus. Student choice

SPELLING
List words to spell in Word Study notebook. Exchange notebook with a partner
for a written team test. Check and file in
folder.
  Papers are dated and filed.

HOMEWORK
Team test words on spelling list.
  Notebook signed.

Lesson **156**

Research

LEAD-IN
Teacher introduces the research project:
Topic and Focus: Money/Skimming
or _____
Resource: Encyclopedias, almanacs, library books, or _____

RESEARCH PROJECT
Partners skim information about money to list different forms of money or other facts. Or _____.

SHARING
Share lists with another pair or with the class. Check your most unusual fact.
   Papers are dated and filed.

Recreational Reading

For approximately 30 minutes, all students read books.

CONVERSATIONS
Teacher holds seven to ten minute conversations with three or four students individually, discussing sequence of events, figurative language, and/or _____.

CLIPBOARD NOTES
Teacher notes student responses during conversations, or _____.

READ-ALOUD BOOK
All the Money in the World by Bill Brittain, *The Family Under the Bridge* by Natalie Carlson, or _____

Writing

MINI-LESSON
"The Winning Lottery Ticket." Or
_____.
   Proofreading: Use and punctuation of interjections.

COMPOSING
Write a short story about topic suggested, or other topic. Or continue a previous writing. Or _____.

SHARING
Read, respond, and proofread with a partner.
   Papers are dated and filed.

Word Study

CHART DEVELOPMENT
Spelling Emphasis: _____
Other Emphasis: Money or
_____
Resource: Sweepstakes forms, Math textbooks, or _____

WRITING
Write associations to the chart focus. Student choice

SPELLING
List words to spell in Word Study notebook. Exchange notebook with a partner for a written team test. Check and file in folder.
   Papers are dated and filed.

HOMEWORK
Team test words on spelling list.
   Notebook signed.

Lesson 157

Research

LEAD-IN
Teacher introduces the research project:
Topic and Focus: Money/Observing
or _____
Resource: Coins and paper money, library books, or _____

RESEARCH PROJECT
With a partner, observe and list symbols and words on coins and bills. Write why you think they are used. Or _____.

SHARING
Discuss findings with another team. Select most interesting fact and share with the class.
   Papers are dated and filed.

Recreational Reading

For approximately 30 minutes, all students read books.

CONVERSATIONS
Teacher holds seven to ten minute conversations with three or four students individually, discussing sequence of events, figurative language, and/or _____.

CLIPBOARD NOTES
Teacher notes student responses during conversations, or _____.

READ-ALOUD BOOK
Book Talk selections related to money or Math theme (*How Much Is a Million* by David Schwartz or *Anno's Mysterious Multiplying Jar* by Mitsumatsu Anno), continue current selection, or _____

Writing

MINI-LESSON
Honesty or _____. Students volunteer ideas related to honesty.
   Proofreading: Correct use of pronouns as objects.

COMPOSING
Write about a true experience related to honesty. Or write an essay about the importance of honesty. Or _____.

SHARING
Read, respond, and proofread with a partner.
   Papers are dated and filed.

Word Study

CHART DEVELOPMENT
Spelling Emphasis: _____
Other Emphasis: Money or
_____
Resource: Newspapers, magazines, or _____

WRITING
Write associations to the chart focus. Student choice

SPELLING
List words to spell in Word Study notebook. Exchange notebook with a partner for a written team test. Check and file in folder.
   Papers are dated and filed.

HOMEWORK
Team test words on spelling list.
   Notebook signed.

Research

LEAD-IN
Teacher introduces the research project:
Topic and Focus: Money/Computation or _____
Resource: Menus, advertising inserts, newspapers, or _____

RESEARCH PROJECT
Using advertisements or menus, spend as close to $50.00 as possible, (including taxes, tips, and any additional charges) without going over the amount. List exact amounts and show computations. Or _____.

SHARING
Show ads or purchases and computation to another team, and check for accuracy and inclusion of all expenses.
Papers are dated and filed.

Recreational Reading

For approximately 30 minutes, all students read books.

CONVERSATIONS
Teacher moves among students having two to three minute conversations with as many students as possible. If appropriate, discuss the climax or conflict of the story they are reading, why they chose this book, and/or _____.

CLIPBOARD NOTES
Teacher notes who reads a variety of books, or _____.

READ-ALOUD BOOK
Continue current selection or _____.

Writing

MINI-LESSON
"Dining Disaster" or _____. Students volunteer ideas about dining out, at home, or at school.
Proofreading: Use commas to separate items in a series.

COMPOSING
Write about a memorable dining experience or disaster. Or write about a perfect meal, who you would have as guests, and why. Or _____.

SHARING
Read, respond, and proofread with a partner.
Papers are dated and filed.

Word Study

CHART DEVELOPMENT
Spelling Emphasis: _____
Other Emphasis: Restaurants or _____

Resource: Newspapers, telephone directories, or _____

WRITING
Write associations to the chart focus. Student choice

SPELLING
List words to spell in Word Study notebook. Exchange notebook with a partner for a written team test. Check and file in folder.
Papers are dated and filed.

HOMEWORK
Team test words on spelling list.
Notebook signed.

Lesson **159**

Research

LEAD-IN
Teacher introduces the research project:
Topic and Focus: Money/Writing problems or _____
Resource: Math texts, menus, advertisements, catalogues, or _____

RESEARCH PROJECT
Work with a partner to locate math problems related to money in textbooks. Design math problems based on menus or ads. Or _____.

SHARING
Exchange math money problems with another team. Solve the problems and compare answers. Evaluate the problems.
  Papers are dated and filed.

Recreational Reading

For approximately 30 minutes, all students read books.

CONVERSATIONS
Teacher moves among students having two to three minute conversations with as many students as possible. If appropriate, discuss the climax or conflict of the story they are reading, why they chose this book, and/or _____.

CLIPBOARD NOTES
Teacher notes who reads a variety of books, or _____.

READ-ALOUD BOOK
Continue current selection or _____.

Writing

MINI-LESSON
Revision and editing conferences. Or _____.
  Proofreading: Review proofreading foci for the last four to five lessons, if needed.

COMPOSING
Choose any writing to revise and edit for sharing. Or _____.

SHARING
Read, respond, and proofread with a partner.
  Papers are dated and filed.

Word Study

CHART DEVELOPMENT
Spelling Emphasis: _____
Other Emphasis: Decimals and fractions or _____
Resource: Math texts, library books, or _____

WRITING
Write associations to the chart focus. Student choice

SPELLING
List words to spell in Word Study notebook. Exchange notebook with a partner for a written team test. Check and file in folder.
  Papers are dated and filed.

HOMEWORK
Team test words on spelling list.
  Notebook signed.

Lesson **160**

Research

LEAD-IN
Teacher introduces the research project:
Topic and Focus: Money/Main Ideas
or _____
Resource: Encyclopedias, library
books, or _____

RESEARCH PROJECT
Locate and write main ideas about the
history of money, or other interesting
facts. Work with a partner or small
group. Or _____.

SHARING
Present main ideas located about money
to the class. Teacher lists money facts on
a chart as volunteered. Check most interesting facts located.
   Papers are dated and filed.

Recreational Reading

For approximately 30 minutes, all students read books.

CONVERSATIONS
Teacher moves among students having
two to three minute conversations with as
many students as possible. If appropriate,
discuss the climax or conflict of the story
they are reading, why they chose this
book, and/or _____.

CLIPBOARD NOTES
Teacher notes who reads a variety of
books, or _____.

READ-ALOUD BOOK
Continue current selection or _____.

Writing

MINI-LESSON
Share Day or _____. Students share
revised selections in groups of four to six.
Review procedures.
   Proofreading: Self-proofreading of final
drafts.

COMPOSING
Proofread and complete final draft. Or
_____.

SHARING
Share final drafts in groups. Read papers,
and make comments for strengths and
needs.
   Papers are dated and filed.

Word Study

CHART DEVELOPMENT
Spelling Emphasis: _____ or
Chart Review Day
Other Emphasis: Geometry words or
_____

Resource: Math texts, dictionaries, or
_____

WRITING
Write associations to the chart focus. Student choice

SPELLING
List words to spell in Word Study notebook. Exchange notebook with a partner
for a written team test. Check and file in
folder.
   Papers are dated and filed.

HOMEWORK
Team test words on spelling list.
   Notebook signed.

263

Lesson **161**

Research

LEAD-IN
Teacher introduces the research project:
Topic and Focus: Architecture/Topic Selection or _____
Resource: Library books, newspapers, Social Studies textbooks, or _____

RESEARCH PROJECT
Skim resources to brainstorm topics related to architecture. Form groups and select topics for research. Collect resources. Or _____.

SHARING
Students share topic selections with another group or whole class.
Papers are dated and filed.

Recreational Reading

For approximately 30 minutes, all students read books.

CONVERSATIONS
Everyone, including the teacher, reads for pleasure. During the last ten minutes the teacher may choose to talk with some individuals about what they have read. Or _____.

CLIPBOARD NOTES
Teacher notes who reads books previously read or introduced by the teacher, or _____.

READ-ALOUD BOOK
Book Talk selections related to architecture (*Castle, City,* and *Pyramid,* all by David Macaulay) or _____

Writing

MINI-LESSON
Writing captions or _____. Display a picture. Discuss possible captions.
Proofreading: Set off appositives with commas.

COMPOSING
Choose picture(s) from a magazine to write possible captions. Or write a conversation that is going on in the picture. Or

_____.
(Homework: Bring a photograph to write captions.)

SHARING
Read, respond, and proofread with a partner.
Papers are dated and filed.

Word Study

CHART DEVELOPMENT
Spelling Emphasis: _____
Other Emphasis: Architecture or _____

Resource: Magazines, newspapers, or _____

WRITING
Write associations to the chart focus. Student choice

SPELLING
List words to spell in Word Study notebook. Exchange notebook with a partner for a written team test. Check and file in folder.
Papers are dated and filed.

HOMEWORK
Team test words on spelling list.
Notebook signed.

Lesson **162**

Research

LEAD-IN
Teacher introduces the research project:
Topic and Focus: Architecture/
Notetaking or _____
Resource: Magazines, encyclopedias,
or _____

RESEARCH PROJECT
Read to locate information related to
topic. Take notes of main ideas. Or
_____.

SHARING
Group members share facts located.
  Papers are dated and filed.

Recreational Reading

For approximately 30 minutes, all students read books.

CONVERSATIONS
During the last ten to fifteen minutes
small groups discuss books/stories group
members are reading. Group may be organized by topic, author, same book, or
other focus. Or _____.

CLIPBOARD NOTES
Teacher notes who reads books previously
read or introduced by the teacher, or
_____.

READ-ALOUD BOOK
Abel's Island by William Steig, *Roll of
Thunder, Hear My Cry* by Mildred Tay-
lor, or _____

Writing

MINI-LESSON
Writing captions or _____. Use student photographs or newspaper photographs to discuss captions.
  Proofreading: Correct use of apostrophes
for possession and contractions.

COMPOSING
Write several captions for a photo, only
one of which is true. Or _____.

SHARING
Read, respond, and proofread with a partner. (Did they know which caption was
true?)
  Papers are dated and filed.

Word Study

CHART DEVELOPMENT
Spelling Emphasis: _____
Other Emphasis: Buildings or
_____

Resource: Encyclopedias, library
books, or _____

WRITING
Write associations to the chart focus. Student choice

SPELLING
List words to spell in Word Study notebook. Exchange notebook with a partner
for a written team test. Check and file in
folder.
  Papers are dated and filed.

HOMEWORK
Team test words on spelling list.
  Notebook signed.

Lesson **163**

Research

LEAD-IN
Teacher introduces the research project:
Topic and Focus: Architecture/
Vocabulary or _____
Resource: Dictionaries, encyclopedias,
library books, or _____

RESEARCH PROJECT
Continue notetaking. List new vocabulary
related to architecture, using words
and/or drawings. Or _____.

SHARING
Share information with another group or
whole class.
   Papers are dated and filed.

Recreational Reading

For approximately 30 minutes, all students read books.

CONVERSATIONS
Teacher holds seven to ten minute conversations with three or four students (individually) discussing the theme of their
book, describing what is happening in an
illustration, or _____.

CLIPBOARD NOTES
Teacher notes responses in conversations,
or _____.

READ-ALOUD BOOK
Continue current selection or _____.

Writing

MINI-LESSON
Writing short plays or skits. Or
_____. Students read parts of plays
to examine play form. List ideas for short
skits: The Talking Dog, Surprise Party.
   Proofreading: Correct use and punctuation of interjections.

COMPOSING
Write a skit. Or _____.

SHARING
Read, respond, and proofread by reading
play parts with partners.
   Papers are dated and filed.

Word Study

CHART DEVELOPMENT
Spelling Emphasis: _____
Other Emphasis: Furniture or
_____

Resource: Magazines, newspapers,
catalogues, or _____

WRITING
Write associations to the chart focus. Student choice

SPELLING
List words to spell in Word Study notebook. Exchange notebook with a partner
for a written team test. Check and file in
folder.
   Papers are dated and filed.

HOMEWORK
Team test words on spelling list.
   Notebook signed.

Lesson **164**

Research

LEAD-IN
Teacher introduces the research project:
Topic and Focus: Architecture/Diagrams or _____
Resource: Library books, encyclopedias, or _____

RESEARCH PROJECT
Locate and collect information to label a diagram related to topic. Or _____.

SHARING
Share diagrams with another group, or whole class.
   Papers are dated and filed.

Recreational Reading

For approximately 30 minutes, all students read books.

CONVERSATIONS
Teacher holds seven to ten minute conversations with three or four students (individually) discussing the theme of their book, describing what is happening in an illustration, or _____.

CLIPBOARD NOTES
Teacher notes responses in conversations, or _____.

READ-ALOUD BOOK
Continue current selection or _____.

Writing

MINI-LESSON
Writing plays. Or _____. Review basic play form and stage instructions.
   Proofreading: Write voice and stage directions in parentheses.

COMPOSING
Rewrite a scene from a book or a myth as a play. Or _____.

SHARING
Read, respond, and proofread with a partner.
   Papers are dated and filed.

Word Study

CHART DEVELOPMENT
Spelling Emphasis: _____
Other Emphasis: Theaters or _____

Resource: Newspapers, magazines, playbills, or _____

WRITING
Write associations to the chart focus. Student choice

SPELLING
List words to spell in Word Study notebook. Exchange notebook with a partner for a written team test. Check and file in folder.
   Papers are dated and filed.

HOMEWORK
Team test words on spelling list.
   Notebook signed.

Lesson **165**

Research

LEAD-IN
Teacher introduces the research project:
Topic and Focus: Architecture/
Summarizing or _____
Resource: All student notes, drawings,
or _____

RESEARCH PROJECT
Group summarizes main facts, and
chooses graphics to share information. Or
_____.

SHARING
Share main ideas and explain graphics to
whole class.
   Papers are dated and filed.

Recreational Reading

For approximately 30 minutes, all students read books.

CONVERSATIONS
Teacher holds seven to ten minute conversations with three or four students (individually) discussing the theme of their
book, describing what is happening in an
illustration, or _____.

CLIPBOARD NOTES
Teacher notes responses in conversations,
or _____.

READ-ALOUD BOOK
Continue current selection or _____.

Writing

MINI-LESSON
"The Magic City." Or _____. Students suggest phrases that relate to the
topic.
   Proofreading: Use vivid details and sensory words to describe the setting.

COMPOSING
Write about a magical city or place. Or
write a short play or skit about a magical
city. Or _____.

SHARING
Read, respond, and proofread with a
partner.
   Papers are dated and filed.

Word Study

CHART DEVELOPMENT
Spelling Emphasis: _____ or
Chart Review Day
Other Emphasis: City sights or
_____
Resource: Newspapers, magazines, or
_____

WRITING
Write associations to the chart focus. Student choice

SPELLING
List words to spell in Word Study notebook. Exchange notebook with a partner
for a written team test. Check and file in
folder.
   Papers are dated and filed.

HOMEWORK
Team test words on spelling list.
   Notebook signed.

Lesson **166**

Research

LEAD-IN
Teacher introduces the research project:
Topic and Focus: Vacation Planning/Topic Selection or _____
Resource: Travel brochures, newspapers, or _____

RESEARCH PROJECT
Examine travel brochures. Class brainstorms the kinds of information included. Form groups and choose a vacation destination. Collect resources. Or _____.

SHARING
Groups share: "We're going to _____, because _____."
Papers are dated and filed.

Recreational Reading

For approximately 30 minutes, all students read books.

CONVERSATIONS
Teacher holds seven to ten minute conversations with three or four students (individually) discussing the theme of their book, describing what is happening in an illustration, or _____.

CLIPBOARD NOTES
Teacher notes responses in conversations, or _____.

READ-ALOUD BOOK
Who Stole the Wizard of Oz? by Avi, *There's a Boy in the Girl's Bathroom* by Louis Sachar, or _____

Writing

MINI-LESSON
"What a Vacation!" Or _____. Students volunteer phrases about vacation experiences.
    Proofreading: Correct use of *do, did, does,* and *done.*

COMPOSING
List vacation experiences you might write about. Or write a short play about a vacation experience. Or _____.

SHARING
Read, respond, and proofread with a partner.
    Papers are dated and filed.

Word Study

CHART DEVELOPMENT
Spelling Emphasis: _____
Other Emphasis: Vacations or

Resource: Newspaper, magazines, travel brochures, or _____

WRITING
Write associations to the chart focus. Student choice

SPELLING
List words to spell in Word Study notebook. Exchange notebook with a partner for a written team test. Check and file in folder.
    Papers are dated and filed.

HOMEWORK
Team test words on spelling list.
    Notebook signed.

Lesson **167**

Research

LEAD-IN
Teacher introduces the research project:
Topic and Focus: Vacation Planning/Collecting information or _____
Resource: Travel brochures, maps, library books, or _____

RESEARCH PROJECT
Read to locate information to list travel plans (how, when, cost), and travel route. Or _____.

SHARING
Share travel arrangements with another group or whole class.
  Papers are dated and filed.

Recreational Reading

For approximately 30 minutes, all students read books.

CONVERSATIONS
Teacher holds seven to ten minute conversations with three or four students (individually) discussing the theme of their book, describing what is happening in an illustration, or _____.

CLIPBOARD NOTES
Teacher notes responses in conversations, or _____.

READ-ALOUD BOOK
Continue current selection or _____.

Writing

MINI-LESSON
Commercials or _____. Discuss favorite commercials.
  Proofreading: Use of dialect or natural dialogue for characters.

COMPOSING
Write a skit that sells a product. Or invent a product; write a radio or TV announcement to sell it. Or _____.

SHARING
Read, respond, and proofread with a partner.
  Papers are dated and filed.

Word Study

CHART DEVELOPMENT
Spelling Emphasis: _____
Other Emphasis: Household items or products or _____
Resource: Magazines, advertising inserts, or _____

WRITING
Write associations to the chart focus. Student choice

SPELLING
List words to spell in Word Study notebook. Exchange notebook with a partner for a written team test. Check and file in folder.
  Papers are dated and filed.

HOMEWORK
Team test words on spelling list.
  Notebook signed.

Lesson 168

Research

LEAD-IN
Teacher introduces the research project:
Topic and Focus: Vacation Planning/Collecting information or _____
Resource: Travel magazines, Social Studies texts, library books, or

_____

RESEARCH PROJECT
Read to locate information about sights or activities on your vacation. Choose what to see and do. Or _____.

SHARING
Group members share choices for vacation activities.
Papers are dated and filed.

Recreational Reading

For approximately 30 minutes, all students read books.

CONVERSATIONS
Teacher holds seven to ten minute conversations with three or four students (individually) discussing the theme of their book, describing what is happening in an illustration, or _____.

CLIPBOARD NOTES
Teacher notes responses in conversations, or _____.

READ-ALOUD BOOK
Continue current selection or _____.

Writing

MINI-LESSON
Collaborative writing or _____. Suggest partners collaborate on a short play to present to the class.
Proofreading: Correct play form.

COMPOSING
Choose partner(s). Review play ideas. Select one to present to the class. Or begin a new play with partner(s). Or

_____.

SHARING
Read, respond, and proofread with a partner or another pair.
Papers are dated and filed.

Word Study

CHART DEVELOPMENT
Spelling Emphasis: _____
Other Emphasis: Travel arrangements or _____
Resource: Newspaper, travel brochures, magazines, or _____

WRITING
Write associations to the chart focus. Student choice

SPELLING
List words to spell in Word Study notebook. Exchange notebook with a partner for a written team test. Check and file in folder.
Papers are dated and filed.

HOMEWORK
Team test words on spelling list.
Notebook signed.

Lesson **169**

Research

LEAD-IN
Teacher introduces the research project:
Topic and Focus: Vacation Planning/Collecting data or _____
Resource: Encyclopedias, travel books, maps, or _____

RESEARCH PROJECT
Read to locate information related to climate, foods, accommodations, or things you'll need on your vacation. Or _____.

SHARING
Groups share decisions based on information located.
   Papers are dated and filed.

Recreational Reading

For approximately 30 minutes, all students read books.

CONVERSATIONS
Teacher holds seven to ten minute conversations with three or four students (individually) discussing the theme of their book, describing what is happening in an illustration, or _____.

CLIPBOARD NOTES
Teacher notes responses in conversations, or _____.

READ-ALOUD BOOK
Continue current selection or _____.

Writing

MINI-LESSON
Final Play Form or _____. List parts of plays, including characters, scene or setting, and props.
   Proofreading: Include scene or setting information.

COMPOSING
Complete short plays. Practice dialogue and actions. Make additions and changes as needed. Or _____.

SHARING
Read, respond, and proofread with a partner.
   Papers are dated and filed.

Word Study

CHART DEVELOPMENT
Spelling Emphasis: _____
Other Emphasis: Accommodations (hotels, etc.) or _____
Resource: Newspaper, travel brochures and books, or _____

WRITING
Write associations to the chart focus. Student choice

SPELLING
List words to spell in Word Study notebook. Exchange notebook with a partner for a written team test. Check and file in folder.
   Papers are dated and filed.

HOMEWORK
Team test words on spelling list.
   Notebook signed.

Research

LEAD-IN
Teacher introduces the research project:
Topic and Focus: Vacation
Plan/Schedule/Sequence or _____
Resource: All travel plan information
or _____

RESEARCH PROJECT
Use data to make an itinerary of your vacation, or _____.

SHARING
Share vacation plan/itinerary with partner, groups, or class.
Papers are dated and filed.

Recreational Reading

For approximately 30 minutes, all students read books.

CONVERSATIONS
Teacher holds seven to ten minute conversations with three or four students (individually) discussing the theme of their book, describing what is happening in an illustration, or _____.

CLIPBOARD NOTES
Teacher notes responses in conversations, or _____.

READ-ALOUD BOOK
Continue current selection or _____.

Writing

MINI-LESSON
Play presentations. Or _____. Title cards or playbills give information about presentations.
Proofreading: Correctly written title, author, cast, setting.

COMPOSING
Design playbills on construction paper. Proofread. Display at presentation. Or
_____.

SHARING
Players present short plays. Audience comments on clarity, strengths, and needs for improvement.
Papers are dated and filed.

Word Study

CHART DEVELOPMENT
Spelling Emphasis: _____ or
Chart Review Test
Other Emphasis: Elements of plays
or _____
Resource: Plays, library books, magazines, or _____

WRITING
Write associations to the chart focus. Student choice

SPELLING
List words to spell in Word Study notebook. Exchange notebook with a partner for a written team test. Check and file in folder.
Papers are dated and filed.

HOMEWORK
Team test words on spelling list.
Notebook signed.

Lesson 171

Research

LEAD-IN
Teacher introduces the research project:
Topic and Focus: Hobbies/Interests/
Independent research or _____
Resource: Encyclopedias, magazines,
library books, or _____

RESEARCH PROJECT
Choose a personal hobby to locate background information. Write facts. Or
_____.

SHARING
Tell about your hobby or interest in small
groups, sharing facts.
   Papers are dated and filed.

Recreational Reading

For approximately 30 minutes, all students read books.

CONVERSATIONS
Teacher moves among students having
two to three minute conversations with as
many individuals as possible. If appropriate, discuss events they consider major,
character responses to the events, and/or
_____.

CLIPBOARD NOTES
Teacher notes book titles being read, or
_____.

READ-ALOUD BOOK
Miracles on Maple Hill by Virginia Soren-
sen, *From the Mixed-up Files of Mrs. Basil E. Frankenweiler* by E. L. Konigsburg,
or _____

Writing

MINI-LESSON
"Fifth Grade Memories" or _____.
Ask for suggestions for topics in a memory booklet about this year and outline a
personal data form.
   Proofreading: Use of colons and
commas.

COMPOSING
Create a personal data outline form for
booklet, page 1. Or _____.

SHARING
Read, respond, and proofread with a
partner.
   Papers are dated and filed.

Word Study

CHART DEVELOPMENT
Spelling Emphasis: _____
Other Emphasis: Hobbies or
_____
Resource: Student information,
newspapers, magazines, or _____

WRITING
Write associations to the chart focus. Student choice

SPELLING
List words to spell in Word Study notebook. Exchange notebook with a partner
for a written team test. Check and file in
folder.
   Papers are dated and filed.

HOMEWORK
Team test words on spelling list.
   Notebook signed.

Research

LEAD-IN
Teacher introduces the research project:
Topic and Focus: Hobbies/Background information or _____
Resource: Library books, personal hobby books, magazines, or _____

RESEARCH PROJECT
Read to locate and write information related to the history of your hobby or other facts of interest. Or _____.

SHARING
Share facts with partner, group, or class.
  Papers are dated and filed.

Recreational Reading

For approximately 30 minutes, all students read books.

CONVERSATIONS
Teacher moves among students having two to three minute conversations with as many individuals as possible. If appropriate, discuss events they consider major, character responses to the events, and/or _____.

CLIPBOARD NOTES
Teacher notes book titles being read, or _____.

READ-ALOUD BOOK
Continue current selection or _____.

Writing

MINI-LESSON
Memory Booklet page: Favorite Things. Or _____. Students suggest favorites list (song, color, foods, clothes, subject).
  Proofreading: Capitalize page headings.

COMPOSING
Write about or list your favorite things this year. Or _____.

SHARING
Read, respond, and proofread with a partner.
  Papers are dated and filed.

Word Study

CHART DEVELOPMENT
Spelling Emphasis: _____
Other Emphasis: Sports or _____

Resource: Newspapers, magazines, library books, or _____

WRITING
Write associations to the chart focus. Student choice

SPELLING
List words to spell in Word Study notebook. Exchange notebook with a partner for a written team test. Check and file in folder.
  Papers are dated and filed.

HOMEWORK
Team test words on spelling list.
  Notebook signed.

Lesson 173

Research

LEAD-IN
Teacher introduces the research project:
Topic and Focus: Hobbies/Personal history or _____
Resource: Student information or _____

RESEARCH PROJECT
Write the history of your involvement with the hobby. Or _____.

SHARING
Share main reasons you enjoy this, or how you got interested with a partner, group, or whole class.
Papers are dated and filed.

Recreational Reading

For approximately 30 minutes, all students read books.

CONVERSATIONS
Teacher holds seven to ten minute conversations with three or four students (individually) discussing their feelings about reading, the best books they've read this year, summer reading plans and goals, and/or _____.

CLIPBOARD NOTES
Teacher notes students' reading attitudes, or _____.

READ-ALOUD BOOK
Continue current selection or _____.

Writing

MINI-LESSON
Memory Booklet page: Field trips. Or _____.

Proofreading: Capitalize proper nouns. Correct verb use.

COMPOSING
Write about field trips this year. Illustrate. Or _____.

SHARING
Read, respond, and proofread with a partner.
Papers are dated and filed.

Word Study

CHART DEVELOPMENT
Spelling Emphasis: _____
Other Emphasis: Field trips or _____

Resource: Any appropriate material or _____

WRITING
Write associations to the chart focus. Student choice

SPELLING
List words to spell in Word Study notebook. Exchange notebook with a partner for a written team test. Check and file in folder.
Papers are dated and filed.

HOMEWORK
Team test words on spelling list.
Notebook signed.

Lesson 174

Research

LEAD-IN
Teacher introduces the research project:
Topic and Focus: Hobbies/Organizing information or _____
Resource: Student hobby materials, pictures, and information, or _____

RESEARCH PROJECT
Draw pictures, summarize facts, and plan a display in a hobby fair. Or _____.

SHARING
Share plan for hobby fair display with a partner, or group.
   Papers are dated and filed.

Recreational Reading

For approximately 30 minutes, all students read books.

CONVERSATIONS
Teacher holds seven to ten minute conversations with three or four students (individually) discussing their feelings about reading, the best books they've read this year, summer reading plans and goals, and/or _____.

CLIPBOARD NOTES
Teacher notes students' reading attitudes, or _____.

READ-ALOUD BOOK
Continue current selection or _____.

Writing

MINI-LESSON
Memory Booklet page: Fun with Friends or _____.
   Proofreading: Use of *I* and other pronouns in subjects.

COMPOSING
Write about fun times with friends this year. Illustrate or add photos of friends. Or _____.

SHARING
Read, respond, and proofread with a partner.
   Papers are dated and filed.

Word Study

CHART DEVELOPMENT
Spelling Emphasis: _____
Other Emphasis: Songs or
_____

Resource: Magazines, newspapers, library books, or _____

WRITING
Write associations to the chart focus. Student choice

SPELLING
List words to spell in Word Study notebook. Exchange notebook with a partner for a written team test. Check and file in folder.
   Papers are dated and filed.

HOMEWORK
Team test words on spelling list.
   Notebook signed.

Lesson **175**

Research

LEAD-IN
Teacher introduces the research project:
Topic and Focus: Hobby Fair/Display and Report or _____
Resource: Student projects or _____

RESEARCH PROJECT
Oral presentations of hobbies. Or _____.

SHARING
Share hobbies, ask questions, and respond to presentations.
  Papers are dated and filed.

Recreational Reading

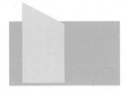

For approximately 30 minutes, all students read books.

CONVERSATIONS
Teacher holds seven to ten minute conversations with three or four students (individually) discussing their feelings about reading, the best books they've read this year, summer reading plans and goals, and/or _____.

CLIPBOARD NOTES
Teacher notes students' reading attitudes, or _____.

READ-ALOUD BOOK
Continue current selection or _____.

Writing

MINI-LESSON
Memory Booklet page: A Great Project. Or _____.
  Proofreading: Use of *were, where.*

COMPOSING
Write about memorable project(s) during the year. Or _____.

SHARING
Read, respond, and proofread with a partner.
  Papers are dated and filed.

Word Study

CHART DEVELOPMENT
Spelling Emphasis: _____
Other Emphasis: Research Projects or _____
Resource: Student Research folders or _____

WRITING
Write associations to the chart focus. Student choice

SPELLING
List words to spell in Word Study notebook. Exchange notebook with a partner for a written team test. Check and file in folder.
  Papers are dated and filed.

HOMEWORK
Team test words on spelling list.
  Notebook signed.

Research

LEAD-IN
Teacher introduces the research project:
Topic and Focus: The Future/
Predicting or _____
Resource: Newspapers, magazines, or
_____

RESEARCH PROJECT
Work with a partner or individually. Locate and read information on which you can base a prediction for the future. Write your prediction, and how the information supports your prediction. Or
_____.

SHARING
Tell your prediction and reasons to another team or whole class.
Papers are dated and filed.

Recreational Reading

For approximately 30 minutes, all students read books.

CONVERSATIONS
Teacher holds seven to ten minute conversations with three or four students (individually) discussing their feelings about reading, the best books they've read this year, summer reading plans and goals, and/or _____.

CLIPBOARD NOTES
Teacher notes students' reading attitudes, or _____.

READ-ALOUD BOOK
The Kid in the Red Jacket by Barbara Park, *Sixth Grade Secrets* by Louis Sachar, or _____

Writing

MINI-LESSON
Memory Booklet page: Best Books of the Year. Or _____.
Proofreading: No run-on sentences.

COMPOSING
Write about book favorites, and feelings about reading. Or _____.

SHARING
Read, respond, and proofread with a partner.
Papers are dated and filed.

Word Study

CHART DEVELOPMENT
Spelling Emphasis: _____
Other Emphasis: Favorite books or _____

Resource: Classroom books, library books, or _____

WRITING
Write associations to the chart focus. Student choice

SPELLING
List words to spell in Word Study notebook. Exchange notebook with a partner for a written team test. Check and file in folder.
Papers are dated and filed.

HOMEWORK
Team test words on spelling list.
Notebook signed.

Lesson 177

Research

LEAD-IN
Teacher introduces the research project:
Topic and Focus: Future/Cause and Effect or _____
Resource: Newspapers, Science textbooks, or _____

RESEARCH PROJECT
Read to locate a cause-and-effect relationship for the future. List cause, and what effect(s) it might have. Or _____.

SHARING
Share cause and effect lists with the class.
Papers are dated and filed.

Recreational Reading

For approximately 30 minutes, all students read books.

CONVERSATIONS
Teacher holds seven to ten minute conversations with three or four students (individually) discussing their feelings about reading, the best books they've read this year, summer reading plans and goals, and/or _____.

CLIPBOARD NOTES
Teacher notes students' reading attitudes, or _____.

READ-ALOUD BOOK
Continue current selection or _____.

Writing

MINI-LESSON
Memory Booklet page: The Best of Times, The Worst of Times or _____.
Proofreading: Comparative and superlative forms.

COMPOSING
Write about personal "Bests" or "Worsts" during the year. Or write a poem about fifth grade. Or _____.

SHARING
Read, respond, and proofread with a partner.
Papers are dated and filed.

Word Study

CHART DEVELOPMENT
Spelling Emphasis: _____
Other Emphasis: Summer or

_____
Resource: Newspaper, magazines, or _____

WRITING
Write associations to the chart focus. Student choice

SPELLING
List words to spell in Word Study notebook. Exchange notebook with a partner for a written team test. Check and file in folder.
Papers are dated and filed.

HOMEWORK
Team test words on spelling list.
Notebook signed.

Research

LEAD-IN
Teacher introduces the research project:
Topic and Focus: Future/Predictions
or _____
Resource: Newspapers, magazines, or
_____

RESEARCH PROJECT
Read to locate pictures of machines (or
other items), tell or draw how you predict
they might change in the future, and
why. Or _____.

SHARING
Show today and future items, and explain
changes to the class.
Papers are dated and filed.

Recreational Reading

For approximately 30 minutes, all students read books.

CONVERSATIONS
Teacher holds seven to ten minute conversations with three or four students (individually) discussing their feelings about
reading, the best books they've read this
year, summer reading plans and goals,
and/or _____.

CLIPBOARD NOTES
Teacher notes students' reading attitudes,
or _____.

READ-ALOUD BOOK
Continue current selection or _____.

Writing

MINI-LESSON
Graffiti or _____. List page topics
suggested for the memory booklet on
chart paper and tape around the room as
"grafitti stations."
Proofreading: Use of comparatives and
superlatives.

COMPOSING
Students write words or phrases at
"graffiti stations." Or continue writing
memory book pages, illustrations, or autographs. Or _____.

SHARING
Read, respond, and proofread with a
partner.
Papers are dated and filed.

Word Study

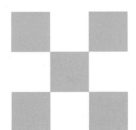

CHART DEVELOPMENT
Spelling Emphasis: _____
Other Emphasis: What's "In," What's
"Out" or _____
Resource: Newspapers, catalogues, or
student choice

WRITING
Write associations to the chart focus. Student choice

SPELLING
List words to spell in Word Study notebook. Exchange notebook with a partner
for a written team test. Check and file in
folder.
Papers are dated and filed.

HOMEWORK
Team test words on spelling list.
Notebook signed.

Lesson 179

Research

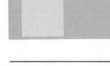

LEAD-IN
Teacher introduces the research project:
Topic and Focus: Future/Symbols or
_____
Resource: Newspapers, magazines,
food labels, advertisements, or _____

RESEARCH PROJECT
Locate pictures which symbolize today's
culture, technology, or way of life. Glue
pictures on large paper. Write how you
predict they might change in 10 to 50
years. Or each student makes a time cap-
sule in a jar to open in ten years.

SHARING
Share and explain pictures and predic-
tions of changes.
　Papers are dated and filed.

Recreational Reading

For approximately 30 minutes, all students read books.

CONVERSATIONS
Teacher holds seven to ten minute conversations with three or four students (individually) discussing their feelings about
reading, the best books they've read this
year, summer reading plans and goals,
and/or _____.

CLIPBOARD NOTES
Teacher notes students' reading attitudes,
or _____.

READ-ALOUD BOOK
Continue current selection or _____.

Writing

MINI-LESSON
"How to Survive Fifth Grade" or
_____.
　Proofreading: Correct friendly letter
form.

COMPOSING
Write a letter to a next year student to
give them tips for surviving fifth grade in
this classroom. Or continue Memory Book
pages, adding topics and illustrations. Or
_____.

SHARING
Read, respond, and proofread with a
partner.
　Papers are dated and filed.

Word Study

CHART DEVELOPMENT
Spelling Emphasis: _____
Other Emphasis: Current events or
_____
Resource: Newspapers or _____

WRITING
Write associations to the chart focus. Student choice

SPELLING
List words to spell in Word Study notebook. Exchange notebook with a partner
for a written team test. Check and file in
folder.
　Papers are dated and filed.

HOMEWORK
Team test words on spelling list.
　Notebook signed.

Research

LEAD-IN
Teacher introduces the research project:
Topic and Focus: Future/Summarizing or _____
Resource: All resources, student notes, or _____

RESEARCH PROJECT
Use collected data and predictions to summarize the future, and the main changes you predict. Or _____.

SHARING
Share summaries with the class. Classify predictions.
Research folders go home.

Recreational Reading

For approximately 30 minutes, all students read books.

CONVERSATIONS
Teacher holds seven to ten minute conversations with three or four students (individually) discussing their feelings about reading, the best books they've read this year, summer reading plans and goals, and/or _____.

CLIPBOARD NOTES
Teacher notes students' reading attitudes, or _____.

READ-ALOUD BOOK
Continue current selection or _____.
Recreational Reading folders go home.

Writing

MINI-LESSON
Complete projects. Or _____.
Proofreading: Friendly letter format. All punctuation.

COMPOSING
Revise and rewrite letter to next year's student. Or complete Memory Booklet. Compile pages, include autograph pages, and make cover. Or _____.

SHARING
Read, respond, and proofread with a partner. (Teacher collects letters to give out next year on day one.) Share completed booklets. Collect autographs of classmates and teachers.
Writing folders go home.

Word Study

CHART DEVELOPMENT
Spelling Emphasis: _____
Other Emphasis: Unfamiliar words or _____
Resource: Classroom library books or _____

WRITING
Write associations to the chart focus. Student choice

SPELLING
List words to spell in Word Study notebook. Exchange notebook with a partner for a written team test. Check and file in folder.
All work goes home.

▶ Appendix

Sources for Further Reading

Atwell, Nancie, ed. *Coming to Know: Writing to Learn in the Intermediate Grades.* Portsmouth, NH. Heinemann, 1990.

————. *In the Middle: Writing, Reading, and Learning with Adolescents.* Portsmouth, NH: Boynton/Cook, 1987.

Calkins, Lucy McCormick. *The Art of Teaching Writing.* Portsmouth, NH: Heinemann, 1986.

Hansen, Jane; Newkirk, Thomas; and Graves, Donald, eds. *Breaking Ground: Teachers Relate Reading and Writing in the Elementary School.* Portsmouth, NH: Heinemann, 1985.

Kimmel, Mary Margaret and Segel, Elizabeth. *For Reading Out Loud: A Guide to Sharing Books with Children.* New York: Delacorte Press, 1988.

Landsberg, Michele. *Reading for the Love of It: Best Books for Young Readers.* New York: Prentice Hall, 1987.

Murray, Donald M. *Expecting the Unexpected.* Portsmouth, NH: Boynton/Cook, 1989.

Olson, Carol Booth, ed. *Practical Ideas for Teaching Writing as a Process.* Sacramento, CA: California State Department of Education, 1986.

Routman, Regie. *Transitions: From Literature to Literacy.* Portsmouth, NH: Heinemann, 1988.

Smith, Frank. *Insult to Intelligence.* Portsmouth, NH: Heinemann, 1986.

Trelease, Jim. *The Read-Aloud Handbook.* New York: Penguin Books, 1982.

Research Module Sequence

Lesson	Topic/Focus	Resource
1	Kinds of information/textbooks	Social Studies texts
2	Kinds of information/textbooks	Science texts
3	Kinds of information/textbooks	Health texts
4	Kinds of information/textbooks	Mathematics texts
5	Kinds of information/textbooks	Spelling texts
6	Kinds of information/reference	dictionaries
7	Kinds of information/reference	encyclopedias
8	Kinds of information/reference	newspapers
9	Kinds of information/reference	atlases, almanacs
10	Kinds of information/reference	magazines, guides to articles
11	Kinds of information/schedules	TV Guides
12	Kinds of information/schedules	calendars, travel brochures
13	Choosing resources/Earth	globes, maps
14	Choosing resources/Earth	Social Studies, Science texts
15	Choosing resources/Earth	encyclopedias, nonfiction books
16	Taking notes/Invertebrates	encyclopedias
17	Taking notes/Invertebrates	library books
18	Taking notes/Invertebrates	Science books
19	Taking notes/Invertebrates	all resources
20	Taking notes/Invertebrates	student charts
21	Choosing resources/Automobiles	Dewey decimal system, library books
22	Choosing resources/Automobiles	encyclopedias, textbooks
23	Choosing resources/Automobiles	magazines, almanacs, nonfiction books
24	Choosing resources/Automobiles	newspapers, brochures
25	Choosing resources/Automobiles	all resources
26	Native Americans/Topic selection	Social Studies text, word study chart
27	Native Americans/Collecting Data	encyclopedias
28	Native Americans/Map data	maps
29	Native Americans/Notetaking	filmstrips
30	Native Americans/Collecting data	library books, textbooks
31	Native Americans/Organizing data	notes
32	Native Americans/Summarizing	all resources
33	Native Americans/Main ideas	all resources
34	Native Americans/Presentations	projects/reports
35	Native Americans/Presentations	projects/reports
36	Authors/Notetaking	library, class books, book covers
37	Authors/Notetaking	reference materials
38	Authors/Organizing information	library, class books
39	Authors/Organizing information	reference books
40	Authors/Locating information	library books
41	Skeleton/Bones/Locating facts	Health, Science texts
42	Skeleton/Bones/Locating facts	library books, encyclopedias
43	Skeleton/Bones/Locating facts	magazines, library books
44	Skeleton/Bones/Locating facts	all materials, notes
45	Skeleton/Bones/Reporting information	projects/reports
46	Explorers/Skimming 5 W's	maps, globes
47	Explorers/Locating information	encyclopedias, texts
48	Explorers/Locating details	library books
49	Explorers/Organizing information	student notes
50	Explorers/Presenting information	student notes
51	Fairy Tales/Headlines	newspapers
52	Fairy Tales/Survey	word study chart
53	Survey/Charts, tables, graphs	Social Studies, Science texts
54	Survey results/Charts, graphs	Math texts
55	Fairy Tales/Picture association	magazines
56	Colonies/Topic selections	Social Studies texts
57	Colonies/Main ideas	encyclopedias
58	Colonies/Main ideas	library books
59	Colonies/Picture information	filmstrips, study prints
60	Colonies/Map information	all resources
61	Colonies/Charts, graphs	all resources
62	Colonies/Classifying	all resources
63	Colonies/Planning	student notes and outline
64	Colonies/Presentations	student projects
65	Colonies/Presentations	student projects
66	Nutrition/Reading labels	food labels
67	Nutrition/Main ideas	magazines
68	Nutrition/Comparing	food labels/packages
69	Nutrition/Making charts	Health texts
70	Nutrition/Presentations	labels, projects
71	War/Forming questions	Social Studies texts
72	War/Collecting data	library books, encyclopedias
73	War/Collecting data	all resources
74	War/Collecting data	all resources
75	War/Collecting data	question/answer books
76	War/Organizing data	student notes
77	War/Organizing data	student outline
78	War/Projects	student notes
79	War/Forming conclusions	student notes
80	War/Presentations	projects
81	Summarizing/Listening skills	read-aloud materials, tapes
82	Summarizing/Fiction	library books
83	Summarizing/Nonfiction	nonfiction books
84	Summarizing/Open topic	student-chosen material

Lesson	Topic/Focus	Resource	Lesson	Topic/Focus	Resource
85	Summarizing/Visual information	videos, filmstrips, demonstrations	127	World Geography/Map reading	Social Studies texts
86	Time line/American History	Social Studies texts	128	World Geography/Map symbols	encyclopedias
87	Time line/American History	library books	129	World Geography/Directions	maps, globes
88	Time line/American History	texts, encyclopedias, class time line	130	World Geography/Summarizing	maps
			131	Archaeology/Topic selection	dictionaries
89	Time line/Your life	time line information	132	Archaeology/Notetaking	library books, encyclopedias
90	Time line/Your life	student information	133	Archaeology/Collecting data	Science books
91	Scientists/Topic, subtopics	Science, Health texts	134	Archaeology/Interpreting	collected trash
			135	Archaeology/Summarizing	project notes
92	Scientists/Notetaking	encyclopedias	136	Old West/Topic selection	Social Studies texts
93	Scientists/Notetaking	filmstrips			
94	Scientists/Cause and effect	newspapers, magazines	137	Old West/Collecting data	encyclopedia, library books
95	Scientists/presentations	student information	138	Old West/Organizing data	all resources
96	Map reading/Kinds of maps	magazines, textbooks	139	Old West/Summarizing	student notes
			140	Old West/Presentations	project reports
97	Map making/Symbols and parts	atlases	141	Flying things/Fluency, classifying	textbooks
98	Map making/Map symbols	maps	142	Flying things (living)/Topic selection	library books
99	Map making/Description	map project			
100	Map making/Presentations	map project	143	Flying things/Note-taking	encyclopedias
101	Environment/Main idea	newspapers, texts	144	Flying things/Main ideas	magazines, Science books
102	Environment/Cause and effect	magazines	145	Flying things/Summarizing	all references
103	Environment/Problem solving	newspaper, pamphlets	146	Flying things/Presentations	project reports
			147	Flying things/Topic selection (non-living)	textbooks
104	Environment/Main idea	local news, video, speakers	148	Flying things/Note-taking	library books
105	Environment/Interpreting	slogans, bumper stickers	149	Flying things/Graphic summarizing	notes
			150	Flying things/presentations	student projects
106	Superheroes/Charts	comic books, cartoons	151	Mythology/Locating information	library books
			152	Mythology/Note-taking	encyclopedias, library books
107	Superheroes/Charts	library books	153	Mythology/Summarizing	myth collections
108	Superheroes/Charts	all resources	154	Mythology/Creative thinking	myths
109	Superheroes/Charts	student charts	155	Mythology/Presentations	student projects
110	Superheroes/Charts	projects	156	Money/Skimming	almanacs, encyclopedias
111	Real heroes/Heroines/Topic selection	reference books			
112	Real heroes/Notetaking	library books, texts	157	Money/Observing	coins, paper currency
113	Real heroes/Notetaking	newspapers, magazines	158	Money/Computation	menus, ads
			159	Money/Writing problems	Math texts, menus
114	Real heroes/Organizing data	student notes	160	Money/Main ideas	library books
115	Real heroes/Written report	student reports	161	Architecture/Topic selection	newspapers, library books
116	Measurement/Classifying	Math texts, catalogues	162	Architecture/Note-taking	magazines, encyclopedias
117	Measurement/Forming Conclusions	food labels, coupons	163	Architecture/Vocabulary	dictionaries
			164	Architecture/Diagrams	library books
118	Measurement/Notetaking	encyclopedias	165	Architecture/Summarizing	student notes, drawings
119	Measurement/Interpreting	cookbooks, dictionaries	166	Vacations/Topic selection	travel brochures, newspapers
120	Measurement/Writing problems	catalogues			
121	Inventions/Topic selection	Science/Social Studies texts	167	Vacations/Collecting data	travel brochures, maps
122	Inventions/Background information	library books	168	Vacations/Collecting data	travel magazines
123	Inventions/Critical thinking	newspaper, encyclopedias	169	Vacations/Collecting data	travel books, maps
			170	Vacations/Schedule, sequence	project information
124	Inventions/Diagrams	Science books	171	Hobbies/Independent research	library books, magazines
125	Inventions/Presentations	project notes			
126	World Geography/Map reading	maps, atlases, gazeteers	172	Hobbies/Background information	student books

Lesson	Topic/Focus	Resource
173	Hobbies/Personal history	student data
174	Hobbies/Organizing information	student materials
175	Hobby Fair/Displays, oral reports	student projects
176	Future/Predicting	newspapers, magazines

Lesson	Topic/Focus	Resource
177	Future/Cause and effect	Science texts
178	Future/Predicting	newspapers
179	Future/Symbols	magazines
180	Future/Summarizing	student notes, data

Writing Sequence

Lesson	Mini-Lesson/Topic	Proofreading Focus
1	First day	capitalizing title
2	Expectations for This Year	capitalizing sentence beginnings/end punctuations
3	Who Am I?	capitalizing pronoun I
4	Choose a paper to revise	correct spelling/ punctuation
5	Share revised writing	review of proofreadings (Lessons 1–4)
6	Exciting times/Funny times	capitalizing titles
7	Rough draft/Exciting times	punctuation (use of . and !)
8	Continue exciting times	capitalizing proper nouns
9	Choose a paper to revise	reviewing of proofreading (Lessons 1–8)
10	Share/Class collection	final draft format
11	Paragraphs/Leisure	paragraph structure
12	Paragraphs/Nonfiction	paragraph structure
13	Verbs/Learning Memory	past tense verbs
14	Verbs/Working to improve	present tense verbs
15	Verbs/Pets	present, past, future tense
16	Paragraphs/Make-believe animals	paragraph changes
17	Paragraphs/Make-believe animals	paragraph changes
18	Verbs/Make-believe animals	consistency of verb tenses
19	Revise/Rewrite/Illustrate	final draft format
20	Share/Class booklet	reviewing paragraph structure
21	Complete sentences/Dream car	subject/verb identification
22	Personification/My life by A. Car	personification
23	Business letter	business letter format
24	Revising business letters	final draft/business letters

Lesson	Mini-Lesson/Topic	Proofreading Focus
25	Share revised writing	complete sentences
26	Comparison/Fruits	comparative forms (-er, -est)
27	Comparison/New school	comparative forms (-er, -est)
28	Comparison/More than two items	comparative, superlative forms
29	Comparison/Books	supporting opinion statements
30	Comparison/Character and you	and, but, and or with commas
31	Comparison/Opinions	joining sentences
32	Comparison/Life then and now	supporting opinion statements
33	Acrostic poems/Native Americans	capital letters in poems
34	Revision and editing conferences	final draft format, review
35	Share papers in response groups	responses to papers
36	Book reviews	fact and opinion statements
37	Fact and opinions/Book review	supporting opinion statements
38	Book review project/Format	underlining book titles
39	Revising and sharing book reviews	don't and doesn't
40	Friendly letter/Authors	friendly letter format
41	Letter writing/Purposes	friendly letter format
42	Letter writing/Fan letters	commas
43	Letter writing/Postcards	letter format
44	Revising a letter	address format
45	Share final drafts of letters	handwriting, spelling, final draft format
46	Descriptions/Favorite foods	sensory words
47	Descriptions/A special place	mood words, adjectives
48	Descriptions/A special someone	specific adjectives
49	Descriptive words/Revise a paper	effective adjective use
50	Share/Class booklet	effective adjective use

Lesson	Mini-Lesson/Topic	Proofreading Focus	Lesson	Mini-Lesson/Topic	Proofreading Focus
51	Fairy tales/Elements	quotation marks	85	Short story/Story leads	quotation marks
52	Fairy tales/Point of view	*I* for first person narrator	86	Story title, cover/Revision	final proofreading checklist
53	Fairy tales/Setting	quotation marks	87	Share stories/Response group tips	elements of realism
54	Revising, editing tips	capitalizing *I*, quotation marks	88	Persuasive writing/Advertisements	persuasive words
55	Share/Final drafts	final draft form, title	89	Persuasive writing/Opinions	supporting opinions
56	Class newspaper/Brainstorm	who, what, when, where, why information	90	Persuasive writing/Purpose, audience	supporting details
57	Class newspaper/Deadlines	quotation marks	91	Writer's technique/Dialogue	dialogue
58	Class newspaper/Revision	spelling, capitalizing headline	92	Writer's technique/Time	verbs to show time
			93	Writer's technique/Point of view	punctuation: complex sentences
59	Class newspaper/Final copies	all proofreading skills	94	Writer's technique/Clustering	*they're, their, there*
60	Share/Class newspaper	all proofreading skills	95	Writer's technique/Metaphors	metaphors
61	Poetry/Alliteration	alliteration and rhythm	96	Writer's technique/Similes	similes
62	Poetry/Clustering	onomatopoeia in poems	97	Writer's technique/Description	specific action, color words
63	Poetry/Haiku	haiku	98	Writer's technique/"Show, not tell"	adverbs to show how
64	Poetry/Cinquains	cinquain form	99	Writer's technique/Thesaurus	overused words
65	Free verse/Color	words of feelings or mood	100	Writer's technique/Combining sentences	combining short sentences
66	Rhyming couplet/Animals	rhyming words, punctuation	101	Story writing (8–10 days)/Fantasy	apostrophes
67	Concrete poems/Rattlesnake	rhythm or meter in poetry	102	Fantasy/Settings	mood words, adverbs to create suspense
68	Poetry project/Revision	rhythm, rhyme, mood in poems	103	Fantasy/Characters	joining sentences
69	Poetry project/Illustrations	proofreading skill: poems	104	Fantasy/Metamorphosis	point of view
70	Share poems	proofreading skill: poems	105	Science fiction/Robots, aliens	dialogue, dialect
71	Invitations, posters, cards	including necessary information	106	Fantasy/Time travel	possessive forms
			107	Fantasy/Creatures	*was, were*
			108	Fantasy/Plot sequence	logical transitions in plot
72	Writing project ideas	time and titles	109	Fantasy, science fiction/Revision	run-on sentences, *were*
73	Projects/Purpose, audience	commas	110	Share/Fantasy stories	prepositional phrases
74	Projects/Effective qualities	commas, capitals, colons	111	Factual writing/Caterpillars	compound sentences
75	Share/Response groups	spelling, final editing	112	Factual writing/Stars	plural forms
76	Writing directions	time order words	113	Factual writing/Music	plural forms
77	Writing direction/Emergencies	commas in complex sentences	114	Factual writing/Reports	indenting to change paragraphs
78	Writing directions/"How to"	time order words	115	Share/Factual writing	factual report format
79	Class project/"How to" Manual	imperative sentences	116	Interviews/Questions	question marks
80	Class project/Final copies	clear sequential order	117	Interviews/Subjects	commas in complex sentences
81	Story writing (5–7 days)/Realism	elements of realism	118	Interviews/Project ideas	nouns of direct address, commas
82	Realism/Setting	vivid adjectives	119	Interviews/Cinderella	commas, introductory words
83	Realism/Character descriptions	actions to "show" traits	120	Share/Interview projects	clear, appropriate questions
84	Short story/Story parts	adverbs			

Lesson	Mini-Lesson/Topic	Proofreading Focus	Lesson	Mini-Lesson/Topic	Proofreading Focus
121	Critique/TV program	supporting opinions	151	Writing a book/About the author	third-person point of view
122	Critique/"Good News, Bad News"	*there, they're, their*	152	Writing a book/Publication	final proofreading criteria
123	Critique/"Then and Now"	*this, that, these, those*	153	Share/Published books	clear sentences, paragraph structure
124	Revision review/Revise, edit	paragraph construction	154	Myths/Elements	pronouns as subjects
125	Share/Critique papers	details supporting opinions	155	Myths/Monsters and heroes	capitalizing proper nouns
126	Group writing/Pictures	story parts	156	"The Winning Lottery Ticket"	punctuation of interjections
127	Group writing/Story	*is, am, are, was, were*	157	Honesty	pronouns as objects
128	Group writing/Opening paragraphs	paragraph changes	158	"Dining Disaster"	commas in a series
129	Group writing/Story development	logical sequence of plot	159	Revision, editing	review proofreading
130	Share/Group stories	consistency of story with picture	160	Share revised writing in groups	final form proofreading
131	Literature/Fables	negatives in sentences	161	Writing captions	commas with appositives
132	Literature/ABC books	appositive phrases, commas	162	Writing captions/Photographs	apostrophes
133	Literature/Letters	letter parts and punctuation	163	Plays/Forms of plays	punctuation of interjections
134	Literature/Theme	conjunctions, commas	164	Plays/Stage instructions	parentheses
135	Literature/Predicting	possessive pronouns	165	Plays/"The Magic City"	setting description
136	Literature/Tall tales	*your, you're*	166	Plays/"What a Vacation!"	*do, did, does, done*
137	Literature/Sayings, proverbs	subject and object pronouns	167	Plays/Commercials	dialect, natural dialogue
138	Class writing project ideas	capitalization, punctuation	168	Plays/Collaborative writing	play format
139	Revise, edit writing project	final draft format	169	Plays/Complete short play	scene, setting information
140	Share/Final copy	final revision criteria	170	Play presentations	title card information
141	Writing a book/Story ideas	point of view	171	Memory booklet/"Fifth-Grade Memories"	colons and commas
142	Writing a book/Setting, character	vivid adjectives, verbs	172	Memory booklet/Favorite things	capitalizing page headings
143	Writing a book/Main problem	paragraph changes	173	Memory booklet/Field trips	proper nouns, verbs
144	Writing a book/Dialogue	quotation punctuation	174	Memory booklet/Friendships	subject pronouns
145	Writing a book/Climax	feelings, sensory words	175	Memory booklet/Projects	*were, where*
146	Writing a book/Helping groups	transition words, phrases	176	Memory booklet/Best books	run-on sentences
147	Writing a book/Expanding sentences	adverbs	177	Memory booklet/Best and worst	comparatives, superlatives
148	Writing a book/Book plan	commas	178	Memory booklet/Graffiti	comparatives, superlatives
149	Writing a book/Title page	title page	179	Letter/"How to Survive Fifth Grade"	friendly letter form
150	Writing a book/Revision	paragraph structure	180	Letter/Revision	friendly letter form

Word Study Sequence

Lesson	Emphasis	Resources	Lesson	Emphasis	Resources
1	*en*/school supplies	newspapers, magazines	52	*oa*/fairy tale characters	class and library books
2	*le*/school place words	school handbooks	53	*ca*/fairy tale settings	class and library books
3	*so*/school subjects	textbooks	54	*ma*/magic	poems, library books
4	*ea*/school personnel	school handbooks, rosters	55	*my*/fairy tales	magazines, newspapers
5	*ol*/lunch	newspapers, spelling texts	56	*nn*/American colonies	Social Studies texts
6	*ex*/emotions	newspapers, spelling texts	57	*la*/colonial leaders	encyclopedias
7	*er*/famous persons	newspapers, magazines	58	*ew*/newspaper	newspapers
8	*sh*/proper names (people)	Read-Aloud, library books	59	*ou*/occupations	newspapers
9	*ch*/proper names (places)	newspapers, magazines	60	*mn*/seasonal words	class newspaper
10	*lo*/writing	magazines	61	*oe*/poetry	poetry, collections, basals
11	*by*/leisure activities	newspapers, magazines	62	*oo*/sound words	newspapers, magazines
12	*ee*/calendar words	calendars, newspapers	63	*dr*/weather	newspapers, Science texts
13	*ed*/action words	newspapers, magazines	64	*ck*/poets	class and library books
14	*an*/earth	Science/Social Studies textbooks, newspapers	65	*ow*/colors	newspapers, magazines
15	*fl*/pets	newspapers, magazines	66	*ate*/nutrition	Health/Science texts
16	*al*/animals	newspapers	67	*tle*/vegetables	food labels and packages
17	*st*/animal parts/features	encyclopedias, nonfiction	68	*ter*/dairy products	newspapers, magazines
18	*sk*/invertebrates	Science texts	69	*ure*/health	magazines
19	*gr*/television	newspapers, magazines	70	*thr*/mood words	newspapers
20	*re*/proper names (things)	newspapers, magazines	71	*igh*/war	Social Studies Texts
21	*au*/automobiles	newspapers, magazines	72	*tch*/military	newspapers, magazine
22	*es*/problems (autos)	Science texts, newspapers	73	*gle*/weapons	newspapers, library books, encyclopedias
23	*ce*/businesses/careers (autos)	phone books, brochures	74	*spl*/peace	newspapers
24	*sp*/safety (autos)	safety brochures	75	*tho*/music	TV, entertainment guides
25	*ng*/auto parts and features	brochures, research projects, newspapers	76	*tion*/dance	TV guides, newspapers
26	*qu*/Native Americans	Social studies texts	77	*tious*/emergency agencies	phone books, brochures
27	*er*/homes (Native Americans)	library books, textbooks	78	*sion*/snack foods	grocery coupons, ads
28	*is*/foods (Native Americans)	encyclopedias	79	*cious*/recipe words	magazines, cookbooks
29	*ur*/customs and beliefs (Native Americans)	encyclopedias, textbooks	80	*por*/transportation	travel brochures
30	*rr*/weapons and tools (Native Americans)	newspapers, encyclopedias	81	*ent*/holidays	newspapers, magazines
31	*ss*/games (Native Americans)	dictionaries, library books	82	*ity*/settings	class and library books
32	*wa*/leaders (Native Americans)	library books	83	*ble*/character traits	newspapers, library books
33	*br*/clothing (Native Americans)	newspapers, magazines	84	*ley, ly*/"how" words	magazines, newspapers
34	*gl*/communication (Native Americans)	newspapers, textbooks	85	*bly*/movies	newspapers, magazines
35	*dl*/Americans	Word Study charts	86	*ple*/magazines	magazines, newspapers
36	*pe*/reading, books	library books	87	*dge*/computers	Science texts newspapers
37	*ar*/characters, plot	Read-Aloud books	88	*ial*/advertisements	magazines, newspapers
38	*or*/authors	library books	89	*ance*/persuasive words	ads, coupons, labels
39	*ti*/illustrators	library books, reference books	90	*tro*/time line events	Research projects
40	*ct*/genres of books	class and library books, newspapers	91	prefixes (*un, lm*)/research	Spelling Language texts
41	*te*/family titles		92	prefixes (*dis, in*)/scientists	Health, Science texts
42	*tt*/kinds of letters	magazines, newspapers	93	prefixes (*pre, re*)/diseases	newspapers, Health texts
43	*gh*/candy, Halloween	newspapers, magazines	94	prefixes (*ex, en, non*)/current events	newspapers
44	*wr*/skeleton/bones	Health textbooks	95	prefixes (*ll, lr, mis*)/ law	newspapers, magazines
45	*th*/city, state	maps	96	suffixes (*ment, sion*)/maps	Social Studies text, maps
46	*le*/foods	ad supplements	97	suffixes (*tion, ful*)/art	newspapers, magazines
47	*lc*/places	magazines, newspapers	98	suffixes (*ness, ing*)/ our town	newspapers, Chamber of Commerce information
48	*gy*/describing words	library books	99	suffixes (*ly, less*)/ land forms	maps, Social Studies texts
49	*lo*/exploration	Social Studies texts	100	suffixes (*or, er*)/ water forms	newspapers, magazines
50	*tl*/drama	newspapers, plays	101	contractions/pollution	newspapers, magazines
51	*al*/fairy tale titles	class and library books	102	contractions/air	Science texts, magazines
			103	compound words/water	Health, Science texts
			104	compound words/chemicals	newspapers, Science texts
			105	possessive nouns/fantasy	library books, newspapers

Lesson	Emphasis	Resources	Lesson	Emphasis	Resources
106	possessive nouns/ superheroes	comic books, cartoons	139	government	newspapers, magazines
107	possessive forms/cartoons	TV guides, newspapers	140	laws/rights	encyclopedias, Social Studies texts
108	past tense verbs/ancient times	Social Studies texts, encyclopedias	141	flight	newspapers, texts
109	future tense verbs/future	newspapers, library books	142	circus	newspapers, magazines
110	present tense verbs/ musicians	newspapers	143	skin	magazines, Health texts
111	plurals/crawling things	Science texts	144	dental care	Health texts
112	plurals/stars	Science texts, newspapers	145	physical fitness	newspapers, magazines
113	plurals/musical instruments	dictionaries, encyclopedias	146	descriptive phrases	library books, Read-Aloud books
114	abbreviations/addresses	telephone books, mail	147	adverbs (how)	collections, library books
115	abbreviations/measurement	catalogues, Math texts	148	similes, metaphors	Read-Aloud books
116	synonyms/slick or slimy	thesauruses, dictionaries	149	titles, dedications	library books, textbooks
117	homonyms/shiny things	newspapers, textbooks	150	parts of books	library books, textbooks, dictionaries
118	antonyms/soft things	magazines, textbooks	151	mythology	encyclopedias
119	homographs/sharp things	dictionaries, catalogues	152	mythology (deities)	library books
120	idioms/fuzzy things	magazines, library books	153	foods	library books
121	hyphenated words/inventions	Science/Social Studies texts	154	computers	newspapers, magazines
122	acronyms/organizations	telephone books	155	monsters	library books, collections
123	multiple meanings/brands	ad inserts, coupons	156	money	sweepstakes forms, Math texts
124	3-syllable words/machines	newspapers, magazines	157	money	newspapers, magazines
125	3-syllable words/ old-fashioned things	newspapers, magazines	158	restaurants	newspapers, phone books
126	4-syllable words/foreign countries	maps, newspapers	159	decimals/fractions	Math texts, library books
127	4-syllable words/land features	maps, gazetteer, newspapers	160	geometry	Math texts, dictionaries
128	5-syllable words/personal traits	student writings, library books	161	architecture	magazines, newspapers
129	5-syllable words/current events	newspapers, magazines	162	buildings	encyclopedias, library books
130	5+ syllable/direction	newspapers, textbooks	163	furniture	magazines, newspapers, catalogues
			164	theaters	newspapers, magazines, playbills
			165	city sights	newspapers, magazines
			166	vacations	travel brochures, newspapers, magazines
			167	household products	magazines, ad inserts
			168	travel arrangements	travel brochures
			169	accommodations (hotels, etc,)	travel brochures, newspapers
			170	elements of plays	plays, library books
			171	hobbies	student information
			172	sports	newspapers, magazines

Lessons 131–180 do not suggest a specific spelling emphasis. The teacher and students may choose to add a letter combination not used previously, select a letter combination for review, or complete the chart using the Other Emphasis only, and then note any special spelling focus that may appear on the chart.

Lesson	Emphasis	Resources	Lesson	Emphasis	Resources
131	archaeology	encyclopedias	173	field trips	any appropriate material
132	archaeology	magazines, Science texts	174	songs	magazines, newspapers
133	postal service	newspapers, mail	175	Research projects	student research folders
134	jungle animals	newspapers, Science texts, library books	176	favorite books	class and library books
135	energy	magazines, Science texts	177	summer	newspapers, magazines
136	Old West	Social Studies texts	178	local events/What's "In," What's "Out"	newspapers
137	transportation	Social Studies texts, newspapers	179	current events	newspapers
138	documents	Social Studies texts, library books	180	unfamiliar words	class and library books

▶ Index

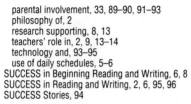